THE CONTEMPORARY WORLD

1914–Present / Revised Edition / Scott, Foresman World Civilization Series

By WILLIAM H. MCNEILL

The University of Chicago

Scott, Foresman and Company Glenview, Illinois
Dallas, Texas   Oakland, N.J.   Palo Alto, Cal.   Tucker, Ga.   Brighton, England

The photo on the cover is an aerial view of the Marine Midland Plaza in New York City with an untitled sculpture by Noguchi.
William Albert Allard, FORTUNE Magazine

Library of Congress Catalog Card Number: 74-82301
ISBN: 0-673-07908-2

Preface

The information at our disposal concerning the deeds and thoughts of men during the past fifty years is so enormous as to dwarf the efforts any single man could ever make towards cataloguing or in any way comprehending everything. What is needed, therefore, is a criterion of importance and unimportance which will tell us what *not* to pay attention to. In that way nearly everything we could find out about the recent past becomes negligible, and our minds are at liberty to fasten upon the few important events and significant changes which our criterion of relevance has defined for us. But how does one find such a simplifying principle? What *is* important? And how do we recognize it when we see it?

No single or simple answer to such questions will stand critical scrutiny. Even within the same tradition of learning, what seems important to one observer will seem trifling or "old hat" to another; and sensitivities alter radically with changes of place and across generations of time. Historians must, in other words, submit to the limitations of time and place to which all men are subject. We must think and write within boundaries defined by an intellectual style or tradition which we inherit through socially transmitted patterns of thought and language. But in a society as complex and variegated as ours, historical thought is itself complex and variegated, so that one historian may put emphasis on one thing, while another prefers something else. Presumably, personal temperament and the idiosyncrasies of one's private experience of the world generate such diversities; yet however wide they may be, we are safe in assuming that at a far enough remove in time or space we will all seem to bear the stamp of a common style of thought and sensitivity. This is because some of our most fundamental preconceptions and, therefore, the sharpest limitations upon our intellectual vision remain unconscious—even in an age as critical and self-aware as ours appears to be.

Where then lie truth and meaning? How can a historian presume to write at all?

Philosophers must concern themselves with such questions. But practicing historians ought to preserve a saving naïveté, and plunge ahead on the principle that our professional role in society is to do the best we can to make sense of the past with the concepts we happen to have personally selected from the inherited arsenal at our disposal. Because men do, always have, and always will react to their personal experience of the world largely on the basis of what they believe about the past, someone has to organize the record and put it into a form that can be comprehended by ordinary folk. If historians do not do so, other professions will arise to serve the felt need—propagandists, journalists, prophets, seers. And because historians are trained professionally to feel that the facts are themselves valuable, and that any handsome generalization ought to be thoroughly tested against a solid sampling of facts—for more distant times, indeed, against *all* the knowable facts—it is arguable that the intellectual comprehension of the past which emerges from the historian's workshop is more nearly adequate to the buzzing blooming confusion of the multifold world we actually confront than any known alternative. If this is not so, surely professional historians have small claim to exist.

Nevertheless, the organizing principle has to come first and testing against detailed information can become efficient only afterwards, when one knows what he is looking for. Accordingly, I have focused attention in this book around two great changes in human affairs which I believe to be important. These are: (1) urbanization, with the consequent emancipation of human life from the rhythms and routines of agriculture; and (2) the experience of war mobilization and peacetime defense planning. Both are aspects of a still larger change: the widening range for deliberate manipulation of human activity in order to attain consciously defined goals. If such trends continue to gather force, our age may prove to be a "take off" period when men learned how to direct their own social evolution along deliberately chosen paths. If so, the emphasis of this book may turn out to cut with the grain of things.

On the other hand, I may be radically mistaken. The really important changes of our time may lie in the experience of some still obscure group that is pioneering new forms of transrational or subrational experience. Yet human reason, even in its most inhumane and statistical manifestations, is both marvelous and beautiful. Perhaps the past as well as the future, when measured against a long enough time scale, belongs to the piercing, double-edged, and uniquely human power of reacting rationally to experience.

In such a faith this book was written during the spring of 1966.

***

I owe special thanks to Professor Paul Seaver of Stanford University for his close and careful reading of the manuscript; to Professor Franz Schulze of Lake Forest College for his essay on twentieth-century art; to James Osborn for his helpful comments on the maps and graphs; and to Nancy Abel of Scott, Foresman for her general assistance.

William H. McNeill
February 1967

PREFACE TO THE REVISED EDITION

In this Revised Edition of *The Contemporary World,* all the chapters have been updated. The maps and graphs have also been updated and redrawn for greater clarity. Two new pairs of biographical essays—Franklin Delano Roosevelt and Charles de Gaulle, Margaret Mead and Simone de Beauvoir—have been added to those of the first edition. In addition, the whole typographical design of the book has been improved.

Major alterations have been made in Chapter 4, "Postwar Perplexities," in order to take into account events since 1966, when the first edition was written. In general, however, relatively little time has passed, and too little has been learned and forgotten, at least by the undersigned, to require extensive alteration in the essential thesis of this book. Urbanization and war mobilization (and postwar armaments races) still seem to me the most important lines of development in the twentieth century, and both are aspects of the more general expansion of a deliberate manipulation of society to achieve an ever widening set of goals. The costs of success and still more of failure in such endeavors are perhaps clearer than once they were: the weakening of custom, of morals, and of traditional social patterns of cohesion that results from widening and increasingly successful deliberate manipulation has become more obvious since the 1960s. Ecological disasters have also been glimpsed, and the value of an ever increasing Gross National Product has been challenged. But so far the dawning awareness of unsuspected costs has not sufficed to check humanity's headlong pursuit of power, wealth, and glory. Instead, we are venturing still further along the path of deliberate alteration of custom and rational coordination of human effort to make possible what had been impossible before.

William H. McNeill
May 1974

Contents

MAPS AND GRAPHS

All information on which these are based was drawn from United Nations sources unless otherwise noted.

Chapter 1

World War I and Aftermath 1914–1921

PRELUDE

The Still Before the Storm. The style of life created slowly through centuries by the people of western Europe never seemed more secure than in the early summer of 1914. Nowhere on the face of the earth, except in Japan, could the heirs of different cultural traditions successfully resist the strength of Western peoples. To be sure, there were trouble spots where peace and order and the other blessings of civilization—Western style—had not yet taken firm root. But it was not absurd for Americans and Europeans to think that in time these backward parts of the earth would also enter into the circle of civilized peoples—if not of their own free will, then as subjects and wards of the great powers whose empires already circled the globe.

The recent past certainly seemed to support such an idea. In no more than a generation, the vast interior of Africa and much of southeast Asia had been partitioned among a handful of European states: Britain, France, Germany, and Italy among the great powers; and Portugal, Spain, and Belgium among the lesser. The United States had begun its own empire building in the Pacific and Caribbean, and Russia continued to expand its vast land empire in Asia with the acquisition of Outer Mongolia and effective control over northern Persia. In these and other far-flung portions of the globe a slender body of Western administrators, soldiers, traders, missionaries, and adventurers sufficed to keep a more or less effective public peace. By their mere presence and overwhelming power they disrupted older patterns of human relations among the variegated colonial peoples they governed. Simultaneously, the remaining non-Western empires of China, Turkey, and Persia were plainly falling apart. The only question seemed to be in what guise Western nations would assert their control over those regions of the earth. Japan was an anomaly. After defeating China in 1894–1895 and Russia in 1904–1905, the Japanese successfully crashed the exclusive club of imperialist nations by annexing Korea in 1910. But Japan's success was in its own way a backhanded tribute to Western civilization, for it was only after deliberately and systematically borrowing Western-style military and industrial techniques that the Japanese became so surprisingly successful.

The economic power of the Western nations was no less irresistible than their fleets and armies. Cheap goods, cheap transport, a relentlessly systematic pursuit of profit, plus easy access to large capital funds and, upon occasion, to strategic political protection gave Western businessmen enormous competitive advantages. Plantations, mines, roads, docks, and other outward signs of Western economic enterprise were spreading almost everywhere; and wherever Western goods and money penetrated into the tissues of other societies, older artisan skills and merchant traditions, together often with far more fundamental agricultural routines, were either destroyed or driven toward the margins of the economy. Few Westerners doubted that the ways of the heathen Chinee, pagan Hindoo, Moslem infidel, and African native were inferior. Abandonment of such pasts seemed no more than the proper and inevitable price of human progress.

This sort of smugness vis-à-vis the rest of mankind did not imply that all was well within the Western world itself. European society had plenty of homegrown critics and harbored its share of practicing revolutionaries. Industrialization and urbanization, along with technical change of unprecedented rapidity, upset traditional relations between social classes and groups. Countless individuals found themselves adrift in an impersonal, megalopolitan world. The result was widespread uneasiness, much revolutionary talk, and sporadic outcroppings of violence. These phenomena were especially acute toward the margins of the Western world, where peasant folkways had only recently caved in before the onrush of urbanism. Thus, for example, Mexico and Ireland were both seething with revolt in the spring and summer of 1914; and, on Europe's other flank, the Balkans and eastern Europe at large harbored numerous cliques of fanatical nationalists and/or socialists—bold speechmakers who did not always shrink from action. On June 28, 1914, one such man, Gavrilo Princep by name, a Serb by nationality, and a Bosnian by birth, triggered World War I by assassinating the heir to the Austrian throne, Archduke Francis Ferdinand of the house of Hapsburg.

A Resounding Shot. The fact that an assassin's bullet could have such far-reaching consequences pointed up a second fundamental weakness of Western society. The division of Europe between two delicately poised alliance systems meant that any disturbance anywhere in the world reverberated almost instantly through the foreign offices of all the great powers, automatically making every local crisis into a world crisis—or at least into a European crisis. Thus it had been

2

in 1905, when France and Germany jockeyed for position in Morocco; again in 1908, when Russia and Austria quarreled over influence in the Balkans; in 1911 Morocco once more; and the Balkans again in 1912–1913.

Imperial Germany, Count Otto von Bismarck's creation and Kaiser Wilhelm II's plaything, was the keystone of Europe's alliance system. Having defeated France in 1870–1871, Bismarck sought to guarantee German hegemony by friendship with Russia and alliance with Austria. He made Austria an ally in 1879. Four years later, having quarreled with France, Italy adhered to the Austro-German treaty, making it into a Triple Alliance. For a long time the French were unable to counter Bismack's policy effectively. They were embroiled with Britain in Africa and elsewhere, and the Russians preferred to cooperate with Germany rather than risk the wrath of so powerful a neighbor. But as German economic, military, and naval power increased, and as German diplomats began to press for a proportionate "place in the sun" all around the globe, France, Russia, and Great Britain eventually decided to subordinate their differences to the common fear inspired by Kaiser Wilhelm's Germany. Hence, the French and Russians signed an alliance in 1893; ten years later the French and British reached an "entente"; and then in 1907, to be better able to cooperate in Europe, the British and Russians compromised their differences in Asia. The strengthening of Germany's rivals coincided with clear signs that the Triple Alliance was in difficulty, since Italian imperial ambitions, increasingly directed toward the Adriatic coastlands and the western Balkans, found in Austria not an ally but an obstacle.

The treaties and agreements binding the two rival alliances together were defensive in character, pledging one government to come to the aid of its ally only if that ally were attacked. From this it followed that if a state openly took the offensive the various alliances would not automatically come into force. But what if effective defense required attack? By 1914 many Austrian officials felt that just such a preventive action was the only thing that could stop the little Balkan state of Serbia from stirring up trouble among the south Slavs who lived inside Austria's borders. These men felt that the murder of the Archduke in June 1914 offered a particularly good chance to punish Serbia for fomenting revolution and encouraging assassins like Gavrilo Princep. The Austrian war hawks persuaded themselves that the other European powers would be unlikely to intervene. The recent series of diplomatic crises had always halted short of general war, and what civilized government would care to risk its people's lives on behalf of a Balkan assassin? Accordingly, the Austrian government sent an ultimatum to Serbia in July, making a series of demands intended to be unacceptable. Even though the Serbs agreed to yield on nearly every point, negotiations were broken off and Austrian troops marched against Serbia on July 28, 1914. Though no one knew it yet, World War I had begun.

Mobilization Begins. Even before the first shots were fired, Austrian calculations had gone seriously awry. The Germans, indeed, backed Austria to the hilt; but the Russians and French balked at letting a small state, friendly to themselves, be crushed while they stood idly by. As for the British, they hesitated, deploring assassinations, deploring ultimatums, and deploring Germany's vast power, which could only be enhanced if the Austrians overran Serbia. No one decided for war on the grand scale. No one knew what lay in store. But each of the European great powers decided that it could not afford to back down until after the other side had made a conciliatory move. Since no one was ready to confess fear or weakness, the crisis rapidly escalated into Europe's first general war since 1815.

One after another the continental powers mobilized their armies. Mobilization took several days, and because military planning had become very exact, it was a matter of the utmost importance for rival armies to start mobilizing before, or at worst only a few hours after, their prospective enemies began the same process. Men had to be called up, uniforms and guns had to be issued, and the newly mobilized units had to be moved to the frontier—all according to a prearranged schedule. Once started, the process of mobilization could not be interrupted without risking general and potentially disastrous confusion—for what if one side kept on mobilizing according to plan while on the other side troops, supplies, and transport got bogged down in a nationwide traffic jam?

Of all the mobilization plans, the German was technically the best. Long before 1914, the German general staff had calculated that a two-front war against France and Russia could be won only by initially concentrating almost all German resources against the French. Russia's vastness and slender rail net meant slower mobilization. German strategists calculated, therefore, that they could afford merely to screen their eastern frontier with token forces until after the French had been defeated in a campaign planned to last no more than five or six weeks. This strategy required the use of Belgian soil for the full deployment of Germany's numerical superiority. (There were about 60 million Germans in 1914 against 40 million French.) To be sure, Belgium was protected by an old treaty guaranteeing that country's neutrality. But the need to bring every advantage the Germans could muster against the French at the very beginning of the war persuaded the military planners to pay no attention to such an inconvenient "scrap of paper."

Theoretically, military plans went into effect only when rulers and statesmen gave appropriate orders to the generals. But in August 1914 the technical details of preexisting mobilization plans tended to dictate political decisions. Thus, for example, the Russian government ordered general mobilization a few hours earlier than any other major power because it took the Russian high command longer to concentrate its reserves. No Russian ruler cared to negotiate from the weakness such a disadvantage created; but once the Russian order for mobilization had been given, the German and Austrian governments set their general mobilization plans into action. (Austria had previously mobilized only against Serbia.) This in turn triggered the French; and when German troops began to march across Belgium on August 3, 1914—as they *had* to do according to the German mobilization plan—the British government decided that its national interests and international obligations required war against Germany. Italy, on the other hand, broke away from the Triple Alliance by remaining neutral. The initial lineup of the war therefore pitted Germany and Austria—the Central Powers—against Russia, France, and Great Britain—the Allies.

Strategy. Until September 6, 1914, the German war plan seemed likely to succeed. To be sure, the advance of German troops across Belgium and into northern France was not quite as rapid as planned, partly because both Belgian and British troops threw their (relatively small) numerical weight into the battle against the advancing Germans. Nevertheless, matters hung in the balance for five full weeks. The Germans drove relentlessly forward, reaching toward Paris, and, as it proved, overreaching. A gap opened between adjacent columns of the German advance; a French general commandeered the taxicabs of Paris to carry French troops into that gap; and the German high command decided that the forward elements of their armies would have to withdraw behind the Marne river. The French followed close behind the retreating Germans until bad weather, supply difficulties, and the exhaustion of men and of horses stabilized a front line deep within French territory. The rival armies speedily dug themselves in. By the end of the year a series of unsuccessful efforts to outflank one position after another created a system of trenches and redoubts that extended in an unbroken line from the Swiss frontier in the south to the coast of the English Channel in the north. Stalemate ensued; undreamed, unintended, futile, bloody, and—as it seemed for three long, weary years—ineluctable.

Only the existence of an elaborate net of roads and railways in the rear made it possible to supply the millions of soldiers who manned the battle line across France. Farther east in Europe nothing similar could arise. Geographical expanses were greater, and neither manpower nor supply systems were adequate to sustain a continuously fortified front. Hence the rival Russian, Austrian, and German armies retained a degree of mobility in the field which the western front had lost. In 1914, for example, Russian armies penetrated Prussian territory, only to be driven back by German troops hastily redirected from the French to the Russian battle front. The next year, German and Austrian troops drove deep into Russian Poland; but in 1916 a great Russian offensive again penetrated Austrian territory and reached the Carpathian mountains.

Nevertheless, in the east as in the west, the rival armies failed to grapple decisively until 1917. Their vast size effectively prohibited the sort of decision on the battlefield which generals had been trained to expect. The dilemma was indeed painful. Victory required mass armies; mass armies required vast supplies; and vast supplies could not be brought up in the rear of a victorious army fast enough to keep the momentum of a massed advance going for very long. A retreating force, on the other hand, picked up strength by gathering reinforcements and supplies that had to remain strung out in the rear of every fighting front. This meant that even after the most crushing victory in the field, stalemate was rapidly and automatically restored.

The frustration on the western front in France was even greater. During the winter of 1914–1915, infantry attack against entrenched machine-gun nests proved suicidal. Both sides, therefore, set out to expand their artillery enormously, in the hope that vast preliminary bombardment would smash prepared defenses and permit successful attack and decisive breakthrough. But an increasing weight of artillery fire simply drove defenders to burrow deeper into the protective earth. Moreover, a prolonged artillery preparation forewarned of an impending assault, and allowed the defenders time to bring up sufficient reserves to check whatever local penetration the attackers might achieve. These facts could not be demonstrated all at once. It took time for the belligerents to retool their factories for the production of guns and shells on the gigantic scale required. By the spring of 1916, sufficient artillery and shells had been produced to allow the generals to try for military decision on the western front. Yet the whole vast effort proved futile. The expenditure of millions upon millions of shells in the German attack on Verdun in the spring of 1916, and in the even vaster Allied effort at the Somme in the summer of the same year, accomplished almost nothing. In each of these great battles a few square miles of devastated landscape changed hands, over a million men were killed or wounded, but the generals' strategic plans came to nought.

The warring nations responded to this totally unexpected military stalemate by both expanding and intensifying the war.

Escalation in the Old Style. The most obvious way to expand the war was to find additional allies. Certainly the belligerents spared no effort to embroil neutrals in the struggle. Noisy propaganda (often untruthful), threats, and secret promises of a share in spoils to be parceled out among the victors after the war were the means by which each side sought to gain allies. High-handed intervention in domestic political struggles did not stop short of such spectacular gestures as the bombardment of the Greek royal palace by Allied warships in 1917. Before the war ended nearly all the countries of Europe, and most of the sovereign states of the entire world, joined in the struggle, which thus earned the name by which it is commonly called today: World War I.

Some of the belligerents played only a minor part in actual military

6

operations. Japan, for example, joined the Allies almost at once, and seized a few German colonial outposts in the Far East and the Pacific area. Thereafter, the Japanese directed their attention to China, where complicated upheavals resulting from the overthrow of the Manchu dynasty in 1912 invited intervention. Turkey, on the other hand, joined the Central Powers in November 1914, and from the beginning played a critically important strategic role. The Turks' command of Constantinople and the straits between the Mediterranean and the Black Sea cut the Russians off from contact with their French and British allies, except for the distant and inadequate routes via Murmansk or Archangel in the frozen Arctic or Vladivostok in the Far East.

After Japan and Turkey had lined up on opposite sides there was a considerable pause until the initial shock had passed. But when strategic stalemate emerged on both the western and the eastern fronts, diplomats and secret agents redoubled their efforts. They met with striking success, making neutrality almost impossible. As a result, by the close of 1916 the western front in France was linked to the eastern front in Russian Poland by an almost continuous battle line that girdled even the vast bulk of the German, Austrian, and Ottoman empires. The first link in this line was the Italian front, reaching from the Swiss border to the head of the Adriatic. Operations started in this area when Italy declared war against the Central Powers in 1915, in return for a secret promise that the Allies would give the Dalmatian coast and other Austrian territories to Italy after the war. But the intervention of Italy on the Allied side in 1915 did not forestall a major success for the Central Powers in the Balkans during the winter of 1915–1916. First of all, a British attempt to seize the Turkish straits by coup de main failed when the Turks rallied to defend the Gallipoli peninsula successfully. Soon thereafter, the Bulgars aided the Austrians and Germans in overrunning all of Serbia. This provoked convulsive—and eventually successful—efforts by the Allies to bring Greece into the war on their side. The result was to create a new front that extended from the Adriatic coast of Albania along the Greek frontier and reached the Aegean east of Salonika. Across this distance Italian, Greek, French, British (withdrawn from Gallipoli), and Serbian (fleeing from their homeland) troops opposed Bulgarians and Austrians (with a few German artillerists) in a trench system essentially similar to that which had already brought stalemate to the French and Italian fronts.

Eastward, as resources got thinner, the fronts remained more mobile. In northern Arabia, for example, a British-sponsored Arab guerrilla war broke out against the Turks, and in Mesopotamia a British-Indian expeditionary force was able to push forward from Basra at the expense of the Turkish garrison of that distant outpost of the Ottoman Empire. The Russians, similarly, maintained a front east the rough terrain and by the Turks. At the other end of the Black Sea, of the Black Sea, where they operated against difficulties posed both by

Rumania joined the Allies in 1916 in return for promises of territorial acquisitions at Hungary's expense. Rumanian troops, accordingly, aided the Russians in their great offensive of that year. Then when the Central Powers began to drive the Russians back from the Carpathians, they flooded into Rumania and occupied nearly the whole of that country.

Thus by the end of 1916—save only for two gaps created in the west by neutral Holland and neutral Switzerland, and except for a somewhat larger gap in the Kurdish highlands along Turkey's eastern boundary—the entire land perimeter of the Central Powers had been turned into a battle zone several thousand miles in length, and anything from a few score yards to a few score miles in width.

German Advances. Despite this vast encirclement, and despite the failure of their initial war plans, the German cause seemed nevertheless to be prevailing, inch by inch and week by week. During 1915–1916, German counterblows had compelled the encircling Allied forces to withdraw deep into the Balkans and eastern Europe. German failures to outflank the encircling powers or to break out of the ring were real enough, yet seemed comparatively trifling when weighed against the eastern victories won by the Central Powers. The main German effort to break allied encirclement was on the high seas. The German navy tried only once to challenge the British blockade; the result was an indecisive sea fight off Jutland in May 1916. Thereafter, the German navy concentrated on submarine warfare, hoping to starve the British Isles by sinking the merchant ships upon which British food supply and industry depended. This tended to raise difficulties with the United States, for the traditional rights of neutrals were incompatible with the new German (as also with the British) strategy of naval blockade on the high seas. The Germans also made two tentative and ineffective efforts to take their enemies in the rear by means of land diversions in Ireland (vs. Britain) and Mexico (vs. the United States). But the Easter Rebellion in Ireland (1916) was quickly suppressed; and German efforts to foment a war between Mexico and the United States backfired when the British intercepted, decoded, and published (January 1917) a German diplomatic telegram that proposed, if Mexico would declare war, to return to Mexico lands the United States had annexed in 1846. Publication of this telegram fed the war fever that was already mounting in the United States. On the other hand, these failures were more than counterbalanced by the brilliant success of a simple plan for disrupting the Russian war effort: namely, arranging for the repatriation of an obscure Russian revolutionary named Lenin from his refuge in Switzerland (April 1917).

Allied resources were, of course, much greater than those available to the Central Powers. The overseas empires of Britain and France provided military manpower, raw materials, and some manufactured goods to strengthen the Allied war effort. Far more important, however, were the economic resources of the United States, which initially

Although the Central Powers were technically in possession of all territory behind the lines on this map, at no time did they exercise complete control over it, particularly in Russia. The arrows indicate the main Allied thrusts and, as can be noted from the direction of the arrow, the Gallipoli campaign was ultimately repulsed.

became available to the Allies on a business basis through a series of private loans. Since the British naval blockade was quite effective, no comparable and countervailing links were formed with the Central Powers, because, as any prudent American banker could see, the goods could not be safely delivered to a beleaguered Germany. Thus geographical facts and the practices of laissez-faire international banking tended to tie the United States to the Allied cause even before more vital national interests provoked America's formal and decisive intervention in the spring of 1917.

9

Intensification of the War Effort. Before considering the second and decisive phase of the war that began in 1917, we must look briefly at the ways in which the belligerents intensified their war effort; for in the process of doing so they inadvertently inaugurated a social revolution which gives our age its distinctive historical character.

In general, the Allies lagged in this respect. Having access to nearly all the world, they did not need to economize resources nearly so urgently as the encircled Central Powers. Great Britain, for example, did not introduce compulsory military service until 1916; and the Allies did not set up a supreme military commander for the western front, with authority over both French and British troops, until March of 1918. In both France and Britain, industrial mobilization was rather more successful. Appeals to patriotism, government war orders, paper money, fixed prices, and some compulsory reassignment of civilian labor allowed France, Britain, and the United States to produce shells and guns and a host of other military goods on a scale undreamed of before the war.

In the long run, it was their ability to mobilize industrial capacity for war production and manpower for war service that gave victory to the Allies. But in the short run, the Central Powers, or more precisely, Germany, with little help from Austria and less from Bulgaria and Turkey, counteracted the larger resources available to their enemies by mobilizing their own more limited materials and manpower far more ruthlessly than their rivals cared or dared to do. Within a few days of war's outbreak, the fact that certain key raw materials would be cut off by the British blockade forced the German general staff to recognize the need for drastic rationing and careful allocation of the stocks on hand. Nitrates, used in both fertilizers and explosives, and copper were critically short; soon nearly every other important industrial raw material also had to be rationed and controlled.

In 1914 no one clearly foresaw what had to be done. It was only after the initial German war plan had failed that the needs of longer-range war mobilization became obvious. Even much later, the men who managed the emerging war machine on the home front had no time to figure out what was happening. All they could do was make one emergency decision after another, always in haste and usually without enough information to be sure of the consequences. Circumstances and shortages dictated decisions, not theory. Nevertheless, quite without any prearranged or conscious overall plan, deliberate and drastic manipulation of the German economy soon went beyond the initial emergency allocation of raw materials. Before two years had passed officials were attempting to control all other aspects of human activity that could be made to contribute to the support of the troops at the front. Food, fuel, and clothing had to be rationed. Labor, money, and credit had to be allocated. These devices were like great hammers—beating the German economy and society on the anvil of war into a shape more or less rationally designed to maximize military striking power and to minimize any expenditure not directly related to the successful prosecution of the war.

In detail the administration of the necessary controls was enormously complex and never worked out perfectly. In principle, however, things were simple enough. War needs came first. These were defined by the strategic plans of the high command for the next campaigning season. Necessary quantities of guns, ammunition, clothing, transport, etc., could then be calculated; the supply of raw materials, fuel, food, manpower, and manufacturing capacity could also be roughly estimated. The two had then to be matched up with each other as exactly as possible, and administrative instructions had to be drawn up to tell this factory or that supplier what to do. When such calculations uncovered some bottleneck or particularly critical shortage, special efforts had to be made to find a substitute technique or source of supply. The invention of a method for using atmospheric nitrogen in the manufacture of explosives, for example, saved Germany from the danger of running out of gunpowder as soon as the stocks of Chilean nitrate that happened to be on hand in August 1914 had been used up. The theoretical problem of the fixation of nitrogen was solved by a professor of chemistry, Fritz Haber, within a few weeks of the beginning of the war; the creation of the necessary manufacturing facilities took only a bit longer. Other ersatz products and processes were less satisfactory, but taken together they sufficed to keep the German economy going, despite the blockade, through more than four years of war.

Other belligerent governments cut less deeply into ordinary civilian activity than the Germans did, but the principles behind French or British war mobilization were the same, even though less ruthlessly applied. Massive interference with the free market occurred everywhere, and this despite the fact that men of affairs all assumed that society was governed by natural and inescapable laws that required individuals to act in accord with the dictates of shifting market prices. For more than a century, economists had taught respect for the marvelous mechanisms of free markets whereby individual selfishness was transmuted into the general good. This idea in turn rested upon a view of human nature according to which individuals were believed to be both greedy and rational, so that each person would "naturally" have to maximize his income by doing whatever sort of work other people would pay him most for doing.

Armies, of course, had never been organized according to the principles of the market, and, under pressure of war, economic theory went by the boards. Administrative fiat and official allocation of resources replaced private reactions to market prices as the prime regulators of economic activity. As a result, much greater concentration of human and material resources for the attainment of a particular goal—winning the war—became possible. So long as the rank and file of the population acquiesced in bureaucratic regulation of everyday activity, most private, competing wills and demands upon the economy were quite effectively suppressed.

This sort of mass coordination of the efforts of millions of human beings burst through all previous limits upon what could be accomplished. Just as before the war the giant corporation surpassed personal partnerships and individual business enterprises, despite some losses of efficiency arising from bigness, so the nation in arms, managed as a single war-making enterprise, eclipsed any lesser integration of resources. When the daily activities of millions of men and women could be wrenched from customary routines and deliberately redirected to duties designed to contribute to a common effort, all sorts of things previously inconceivable suddenly became possible— even easy. Germany led the way, but just because every belligerent made similar innovations at roughly the same time, the heightened effort at first merely prolonged the stalemate. Thousands upon thousands of artillery pieces and millions upon millions of shells produced and deployed by the Germans canceled out similar thousands of guns and millions of shells produced and deployed by the Allies.

Despite—nay, indeed because of the failure of intensified war mobilization to bring rapid victory, the new range for conscious control of human activity arising from the war mobilization experience became the most important innovation of World War I. As the French Revolution proved beyond reasonable doubt that governments were man-made and not imposed upon a helpless humanity by God or by Nature, so World War I demonstrated that social and economic relationships, too, are man-made and can be remade by human will and intelligence—so long, that is, as agreement as to ends and means can be sustained among those whose lives are subjected to someone else's manipulation. The successes of Communist regimes since 1928 and of managed economies all round the world since 1933 have now reaffirmed, in time of peace as well as of war, what people discovered blindly and in agony during the years 1914–1917, as they sought, always in vain, to win the war with one more convulsive effort on the production lines and in the trenches.

Bureaucracy and Planned Invention. Two other aspects of World War I mobilization deserve notice. First, although the bureaucratic servants of the nation-state were the principal agents of this war-born social revolution, tentative efforts to extend the scope of planning and control beyond national boundaries were made. The financial interlocking of the American and Allied war economies, especially after 1917 when government loans superseded private credits, was one instance of effective transnational coordination. Combined commands on the eastern front, which welded German, Austrian, and even Turkish and Bulgarian troops into a single field force—at least in principle—were even more dramatic instances of cooperation across national boundaries. Fuller demonstration of this potentiality of modern bureaucratic administration waited, however, for World War II.

A second key characteristic of the war economies of World War I was sporadic resort to what we may call "planned invention." Invention had long been a rather haphazard process, the work of isolated individuals who often had to sell their idea to skeptical and indifferent men of affairs before it could be tested, much less produced in mass quantities. Under the pressure of the war, however, the process of invention came to be far better organized. Experts and engineers were systematically assembled and assigned the task of solving technical difficulties. Any resulting inventions were hurried toward the production line if substantial improvement seemed in prospect.

By the end of the war, strategic plans were even being built around military machines that had not yet been invented. The most spectacular instance of this was the British strategic plan for 1919, which called for decisive breakthrough by the use of tanks capable of traveling both faster and farther than any existing tank was able to. Because the military plan required specific performance characteristics, designers and engineers were set to work to produce the needed vehicles—and actually were in the process of doing so when the armistice interrupted the enterprise.

Applied to the whole range of industrial technology, such planned, deliberate, and directed invention obviously permitted an enormous acceleration of technical change. Conscious direction once again proved itself capable of supplementing and magnifying what had before been an almost random process. It may safely be said that this frontier of human potentiality has yet to be fully explored, despite the six decades that have elapsed since a few ruthless planners pioneered the adventure in World War I.

Russia and Its Revolution. Recognition of any of these paths toward the future was far removed from the minds of the soldiers and generals who confronted one another so uncomfortably in the trenches. Exasperation, filth, anger, and fear, lightened only by a sense of camaraderie arising from shared danger, were what the soldiers knew. Nowhere was the strain more acute than in the Russian army. Of all the major powers of Europe, the tsar's government was the least prepared to cope with the unprecedented demands of the war. Russian industry was inadequate to supply the troops after initial materiel had been expended. Distrust of authority was widespread among the peasant soldiers, as well as among the industrial workers of the cities. Small but determined cliques of revolutionaries strove systematically to foment such distrust and turn an international war into a class war. The revolutionaries got their chance when the long autumnal retreat of 1916 brought army discipline and morale to the breaking point.

During the winter of 1917, two institutions gave expression to the rising political disaffection in tsarist Russia. One was the Duma, an elected body which had initially supported the war with enthusiasm. Most Duma spokesmen criticized the government for failure to prosecute and administer the war effort with sufficient energy. The second focus of opposition was an informal council of workers, the so-called

Petrograd[1] Soviet. This council originated from meetings designed to coordinate strikes among the workers in different factories of Petrograd. Members of the Soviet wanted to bring the war to an end, and lent a sympathetic ear to various revolutionary blueprints for a radical reconstruction of Russian society.

What triggered the Russian Revolution, nevertheless, was loss of nerve on the part of the tsar and his immediate circle of ministers and advisers. In the spring of 1917, Tsar Nicholas II, Autocrat of all the Russias, ordered the Duma to disperse and the striking workers to go back to their jobs; but when this command met with defiance he tamely abdicated on March 15, 1917. A provisional government took power, but faced the same immense and insoluble problems that had brought the tsar's government down, and lacked both a united will and popular support. Quarrels soon broke out between the Duma and the Soviet, while rival parties within each body further distracted the political scene. Meanwhile, the Russian army simply crumbled, as peasant soldiers set off for home—often on foot—to take possession of the land they felt belonged to them. Frantic efforts to reorganize the army and drive the advancing Germans back merely discredited the provisional government. The radical platform—Land, Peace, Bread—proclaimed by Lenin, the strong-minded leader of the Bolshevik faction of the Social Democratic (i.e., Marxist) party, became all the more appealing. Land for the peasants, peace for the soldiers, and bread for the workers: who indeed could oppose such slogans?

Hence, when the Bolsheviks decided to seize power by a coup d'état on the night of November 6–7, 1917,[2] they met with almost no opposition. Lenin, the undisputed leader of the Bolshevik faction, emerged as ruler of Russia. He viewed himself, however, not as the tsar's successor, but as the harbinger of a proletarian and socialist revolution which he firmly expected and fondly hoped would spread rapidly through the war-ravaged nations of Europe and inaugurate the era of Communism promised by Karl Marx.

The Bolsheviks and the War. At first, Lenin and the Bolsheviks totally repudiated all "capitalist" regimes, whether at home or abroad. They published the secret treaties signed by the tsar's government before and during the war, and righteously renounced the territorial gains the Allies had promised to Russia. Such revelations were embarrassing enough to the French and British governments, but the Bolshevik effort to go over the heads of all constituted authorities and summon the workers of the world to rise against their oppressors seemed shockingly subversive to Allied and German statesmen alike.

[1]St. Petersburg was renamed Petrograd in 1914 to give a Slavic instead of a German form to the name of Russia's capital. Later the Communists renamed the city Leningrad, the name by which it is known today.

[2]In 1917 Russia still used the Julian calendar, according to which the Bolshevik seizure of power took place in October. Hence it is often called the October revolution to distinguish it from the March revolution of the same year. One of the Bolsheviks' early reforms was to change the calendar to bring Russian time reckoning into line with that of the rest of the world.

The Russian armies almost dissolved, so nothing but distance, difficulties of transportation, and a manpower shortage prevented the Central Powers from advancing towards the vitals of the Russian state. They did march along the Baltic coast as far as the outskirts of Petrograd[3] and penetrated deep into the Ukraine as well. But fortunately for the Bolsheviks, the Germans and Austrians preferred to concentrate their resources for a final push in the west, leaving Lenin and his fellows with a platform in central Russia from which to preach their revolutionary message to all who would listen.

Rival Ideologies. The Russian Revolution injected a new ideological element into the war. During the same year, after the declaration of war by the United States in April 1917, President Woodrow Wilson was elaborating an American ideology—no less revolutionary—which achieved its classical formulation on January 8, 1918, in the famous "Fourteen Points." In this and other speeches, Wilson developed the idea that, in entering World War I on the Allied side, the United States had embarked on a war to end war. The imperial, militaristic, and authoritarian governments of Germany and Austria, Wilson declared, had deliberately provoked the war. A truly democratic state, he assumed, could never be warlike, since the people would not start a war in which they themselves would have to fight. What was needed, therefore, was the removal of undemocratic militarists from power, and the substitution of regimes deriving their powers from the consent of the governed. Such just and democratic governments could then be expected to settle future international disputes through legal procedures. To assure this result a League of Nations was required, where the rights and wrongs of particular cases could be argued out in public.

How much President Wilson and his advisers themselves believed in the practicability of these simple cures for the world's ills, and how much the leaders of the United States used Wilsonian rhetoric to sell the war to the American public, can never be exactly determined. In 1917 the national interest did not seem distinguishable from the crusade to "make the world safe for democracy." People in high and low positions easily and naturally confused them, particularly since both national interest and democratic ideals more and more clearly called for American intervention on the side of the Allies.

Similar confusions between ideal aspiration and immediate self-interest prevailed elsewhere. Wilson's idealistic vision of present reality and future possibility appealed strongly to the public in all the Allied countries, for it gave them a sacred cause worthy of their sacrifices. It echoed also across the firing line, where, for example, the subject nationalities of the Hapsburg empire and the German Social Democratic party stirred at the vistas opened before their eyes by Wilson's phrases. The war had begun, more than three years before, without principles other than those of national self-interest and

---

[3]In March 1918 the Bolsheviks withdrew to Moscow, which thus became and remained the capital of the revolutionary state.

narrow self-righteousness. To be sure, the Allies had invoked the sacredness of treaties and reproached the Germans for violating Belgian neutrality, while the Germans harped upon the danger to German culture and European civilization presented by the armed barbarism of Russia. By 1917, however, these appeals had worn very thin. How could Belgian neutrality or the dissolving Russian threat possibly justify the daily loss of life in the trenches? How indeed?

In 1917–1918 the question was not quite so acute for the Germans, since, having defeated the Russians, they seemed to have a real chance of defending German culture and winning the war more or less on the terms originally proclaimed by their political leaders. All that was needed was one final effort in the west, before American troops could be brought into the balance in decisive numbers. The question of war aims was far more critical for the Allies, since Italian, French, and British soldiers needed something worth dying for. Minor territorial readjustments in Europe and the partition of the Ottoman Empire, as projected by the secret treaties Lenin had just published, were definitely inadequate.

Thus the Bolshevik vision of revolution as the passport to a classless society of peace and plenty, and Wilson's no less naive vision of a world made safe for democracy, competed for the allegiance of a war-weary Europe. Ideas and ideals became almost as important as guns and soldiers in determining the war's upshot. As it turned out, Wilsonianism prevailed everywhere outside Russia, not least because the military and economic strength of the United States was thrown unreservedly into the struggle. The Bolsheviks, meanwhile, barely survived a squalid civil war which disrupted the Russian economy and paralyzed Russian state power just at the time when the wealth and strength of the United States came fully into play on the international scene.

Thus it happened that a war generated by Austrian efforts to check Balkan revolutionaries ended with revolutionary slogans in the mouths of even the most conservative of the victorious statesmen. Nothing less sufficed to relieve the strains in Europe's body politic created by the almost intolerable prolongation of the struggle. In this fashion deliberate manipulation of social energies achieved another and very treacherous victory. Propaganda and high-sounding ideology might indeed help hold a people together and make the sacrifices of war seem more bearable. But extravagant hopes for the future ("A home fit for heroes") and promises that could not be realized (Marx's "From each according to his ability; to each according to his needs" and Wilson's "Open covenants openly arrived at") had a nasty way of coming back to haunt even the sincerest of political prophets.

Nevertheless, whatever difficulties Leninism and Wilsonianism created for the future, in the crisis year November 1917 to November 1918, the two rival blueprints for peace through justice, even at the cost of revolution, gave a profoundly new character to the war.

Russia Under Lenin. Once in power, the Bolsheviks found it difficult to live up to their revolutionary promises. To be sure, a vast, unregulated transfer of land took place in the Russian countryside, as peasants and returning soldiers took possession of the plots they and their fathers before them had tilled. This put the great majority of the population on the side of the revolution. In the months that followed, even though the peasants violently disliked some of the things the government did, they still felt safer with Lenin's followers in control than with any conceivable alternative. The "dark and deaf" peasantry of Russia chose what seemed the lesser of two evils by opting for the Bolsheviks. Thereby they assured the ultimate victory of the revolution, though not until after three years of brutal civil war.

"Peace" and "Bread," the other two promises of Lenin's revolution, were harder to achieve. In the face of general economic breakdown, bread could only be supplied to those who did not cultivate the soil by directly confiscating grain from the peasants. High-handed requisitioning therefore replaced ordinary taxation. All sorts of drastic shortages and difficulties of distribution developed. "War Communism," as this period came to be called, was catastrophic for all groups in the Russian population. Yet forcible requisitioning from the peasants did bring in enough grain to feed the workers, soldiers, and other city folk whom the Bolsheviks needed to enforce their authority over most of the old Russian empire.

Peace also proved elusive. At first Lenin refused either to make peace or to continue the war, hoping that revolution in the rear would break up the armies of the Central Powers just as the Russian armies had been broken up. When this expectation failed, the Bolsheviks reluctantly signed a peace treaty at Brest-Litovsk (March 3, 1918) by which they surrendered Russian Poland, the Ukraine, and the Baltic provinces. But this did not suffice to bring peace. Instead, counter-revolutionary movements, with Allied assistance, set out to overthrow the Bolsheviks. The result was full-scale war.

The "Whites," those who were trying to overthrow the Bolsheviks, were led by ex-tsarist army officers and other members of the upper classes of prewar Russia. Most peasants feared that they would take back the land if they could; and when substantial foreign aid began to reach the Whites, Russian patriotism also turned against commanders who looked more and more like cat's-paws for foreign capitalists, as the Bolsheviks declared them to be. In the fringe areas of the Russian empire, however, nationalist, anti-Russian sentiments penetrated the ranks of the peasantry. Accordingly, in the western borderlands—Poland, Lithuania, Latvia, Estonia, and Finland—local politicians mobilized popular support. Eventually, after three years of doubtful battle, these countries won political independence. Simultaneously, of course, the rest of the Russian empire accepted a Bolshevik—or as we should now call it, Communist—regime, shaped and tempered by the harsh necessities of the civil war years.

WILSON AND LENIN

Wilson: Culver Pictures

Thomas Woodrow Wilson (1856–1924) and Vladimir Ilich Ulyanov (1870–1924), better known by his revolutionary alias of Lenin, were both outsiders who mobilized the discontent of other outsiders to win power for themselves, and thus to transform the world.

Wilson, the son of a Presbyterian minister in the Virginia piedmont, attended Princeton University. When he found himself snubbed by the sons of the new rich of industrial America, he deeply resented it. After a flirtation with the law, he became a professor of political science and wrote books advocating a strong executive to push through reforms.

Wilson soon had a chance to act on his principles, first as president of Princeton University (1902–1910), then as governor of New Jersey (1910–1912), and finally as President of the United States (1912–1921). In each of these offices, Wilson sought to check privilege. At Princeton, for instance, he tried to break up the fraternity system; as President of the United States he set out to fight monopolies and make America more genuinely democratic.

Like Wilson, Lenin was born into a professional family of modest means but high local social status. His father was a school inspector in a remote provincial town on the Volga. The key event of Lenin's youth was the execution of his elder brother in 1887 for plotting against the life of the tsar. From that time on, Lenin was an impassioned revolutionary. He soon convinced himself that political assassination of the kind his brother had planned was futile. The thing to do was to change the whole system. But how?

Lenin found an answer in the doctrines of Karl Marx. Although, according to Marx, a backward agricultural country like Russia was not ready for socialist revolution, Lenin simply refused to wait.

He advocated the formation of a party of professional revolutionaries who could function in spite of the tsar's secret police and without mass support. In 1903 the Russian Marxists split on the issue. A majority, the Bolsheviks, accepted Lenin's leadership; the Mensheviks rejected his policies.

At the time, the quarrel seemed like a tempest in a teapot. Lenin had to live in Switzerland to be safe from the tsar's police, and his followers inside Russia were very few indeed. When the March Revolution of 1917 broke out, however, Lenin suddenly became influential. The Germans let him return to Russia in hopes of weakening the Russian war effort. Upon his arrival in the Russian capital, Lenin took complete command of the Bolshevik party, and he soon made its slogan—Peace, Land, Bread—resound throughout the world.

In November 1917, as soon as Lenin and his Bolshevik followers had seized control of the government, they invited the workers of the world to follow the example they had set in Russia—that is, to end the war by refusing to fight and to inaugurate socialism by revolutionary action. Wilson's famous Fourteen Points, defining his vision of a democratic peace, were meant as an answer to Lenin's propaganda. They, too, were revolutionary and resounded throughout the world. Between them, therefore, Lenin and Wilson made a return to prewar social and political patterns utterly impossible.

Lenin: Culver Pictures

The parallel between the two men's lives extended to the circumstances of their deaths, which came lingeringly, and after repeated strokes, in 1924. Wilson lived to see the United States repudiate his policies at home and abroad, including the League of Nations upon which he believed the peace of the world depended. Lenin was forced to approve a New Economic Policy in 1921 which looked as though it would permit the return of capitalism in Russia. Thus the two great political prophets of the twentieth century died in the same year, each with the bitter taste of failure in his mouth.

Enter America. Russia's withdrawal from the war against the Central Powers in 1917 precisely coincided with America's entry into the struggle. When the United States Congress declared war against Germany on April 4, 1917, it did so on the ground that the German government had violated America's rights as a neutral by sending out submarines to sink American ships on the high seas without warning. As a matter of fact, Germany's decision to begin unrestricted submarine warfare, announced January 31, 1917, was taken with the knowledge that the American government might declare war. But the Germans calculated that, if allowed to shoot on sight, their submarines could sufficiently diminish the flow of war supplies across the Atlantic to give their armies a chance to push ahead to victory on the western front before the United States could effectively mobilize its military potential.

The fact that they were willing to take such a risk reflected a crisis of hope and desperation among German statesmen and strategists. Despite all the ingenuity with which chemists and engineers created substitutes for the raw materials that could no longer be imported, the British naval blockade was slowly but surely throttling the German economy. Food, in particular, was running short, and a time when the imperial armies could be neither properly fed nor adequately supplied loomed unmistakably ahead.

Rights and wrongs in international law were publicly argued on both sides of the Atlantic. But the real issue between the United States and Germany was not whether a neutral flag should protect a ship from submarine attack, or whether preliminary warning should permit crewmen to escape from a vessel before it was torpedoed. Such debaters' points merely obscured the fundamental fact that more and more Americans had come to feel that German victory would endanger the United States by creating on the continent of Europe a single militaristic empire powerful enough to dominate the world single-handedly. Banking interests that had made vast loans to the Allies, traditional sympathies among English-speaking peoples, and lopsided exposure to Allied propaganda all came into play as well; but at bottom the American decision to enter the fight turned upon the belief that German victory would be contrary to the national interest and democratic principles of the United States.

Having once declared war, the United States put enormous energy and unstinted resources into the struggle. A host of civilians were hurried into uniform and sent off to France, where by war's end more than two million U.S. troops had debarked, and about half that number had actually seen combat. These massive reinforcements arrived at a very crucial time. Between March 21 and July 18, 1917, the German armies were once again in motion, pressing towards Paris with what seemed irresistible force. By midsummer the Germans had reached the Marne river for the second time, but halted there as more and more American troops, fresh and eager to prove themselves in battle, reached the front.

The War's End. As their great spring and summer offensive of 1918 ground fruitlessly to a halt, the German will to win crumbled. Soon the front was again in motion, this time in reverse, recoiling toward the French and Belgian frontiers. Nowhere could the Germans hold for more than a short time. Before this retreat turned into a rout, however, and while the discipline of their troops remained intact, the German high command decided to ask for an armistice. Allied conditions were so severe as to make any resumption of the war impossible; but despite this Germany submitted on November 11, 1918. Thus the war came finally to an end, after more than four years of unprecedentedly heavy bloodletting, and after a consumption of armaments and a series of social revolutions and near-revolutions that dwarfed anything the world had previously known.

Statistics are unreliable, but provide some indication of the magnitude of social upheaval brought about by the war. Some 65 million men were mobilized into the armed services of the combatant nations; nearly ten million died in action; and about 20 million were wounded. Civilian deaths attributable to the war probably equalled or exceeded military casualties. Almost no one emerged unchanged from his war experiences, which, of course, varied infinitely in detail. The central transformation was well expressed in the words of a popular song:

> *How can we keep them down on the farm*
> *Now that they've seen Paree?*

The prewar structure of society everywhere in the world had been anchored upon the immemorial routines of agriculture. In every major country, except Great Britain, agriculturalists constituted a majority of the population in 1914. After 1918, even when the peasants did, as in Russia, go back to the farm, they went with new ideas, new habits, new expectations. Nowhere in the Western world was automatic resumption of the prewar patterns of society possible. Too many men and women had done too many new things—too many had seen Paree or its equivalent—to slide back smoothly into their prewar groove, especially since in many parts of Europe there was no familiar groove awaiting their return. In Asia and Africa, to be sure, the patterns of village life and the routines of the agricultural year remained essentially intact. But, as we shall see, World War II was to have a similarly disruptive impact upon the traditional rural communities of the non-Western world only a generation afterwards.

Armistice and Negotiations. Two points about the armistice of November 11, 1918, deserve emphasis. First, when the war ended German troops were still on French and Belgian soil. No foreign victor penetrated the German frontier until after the fighting had ended. Hence the German patriots' idea that they had not really been defeated in battle, but had been betrayed from within, could—and did—gain wide credence. This "stab in the back" theory was all the more persuasive because until almost the very end, Germany so clearly seemed to be winning.

Secondly, the armistice on the western front came into effect only after Bulgaria (on September 30), Turkey (on October 31), and Austria (on November 3) had come to terms with the Allied powers. The surrender of Turkey and of Austria became the signal for disruption of the imperial governments of those two states. Arabs, Armenians, Greeks, and other subject nationalities of the Ottoman Empire, and Czechs, Slovaks, Serbs, Croats, Slovenes, Rumanians, Poles, and still other nationalities of the Austrian empire, repudiated their old subjections and demanded political independence and a place among the ranks of the Allies. The result was to throw the entire area from the Baltic to the Persian Gulf into profound confusion. Throughout this vast region political legitimacy vanished. Suddenly succession to the Russian, Austrian, and Ottoman empires was up for grabs. New states sprang up like mushrooms: Czechoslovakia, Yugoslavia, Poland, Lithuania, Latvia, Estonia, Finland, Armenia, and Georgia, Syria, and Iraq were among the more successful new growths. Others, like the Ukraine, Macedonia, or the great Turkish state of central Asia of which pan-Turks dreamed, guttered out into hopeless guerrilla warfare.

Amidst this maelstrom, Wilson's principle of democratic self-determination reverberated loudly, but could seldom find genuine application. How could the popular will be tested amid war's alarms? Was there in fact a real popular will that could direct political reconstruction? Or did the peasant majority of eastern Europe and the Middle East entertain only negative aspirations, i.e., relief from taxes and rents?

Finally, what if a popular will did unmistakably exist, but ran counter to the interests of the victors, as, for example, when the Austrians opted in 1919 for incorporation into Germany? How, in other words, could self-determination be reconciled with an international political order that would keep Germany weak, make the Allies strong, and banish forever the possibility of recurrence of a war so disastrous as that of 1914–1918?

In the flush of victory, such questions were not asked—at least not publicly. Instead, the Allied statesmen pandered to naive hopes and vengeful hatreds that war propaganda had implanted in their elec-

TERRITORIAL CHANGES IN EUROPE RESULTING FROM WORLD WAR I

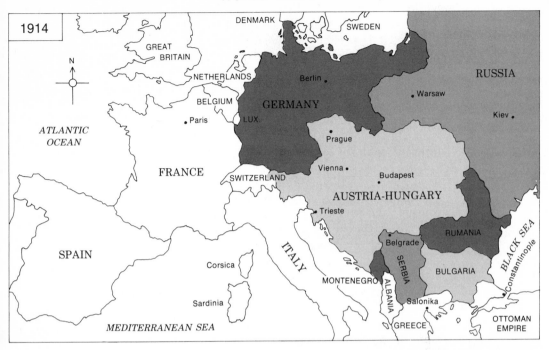

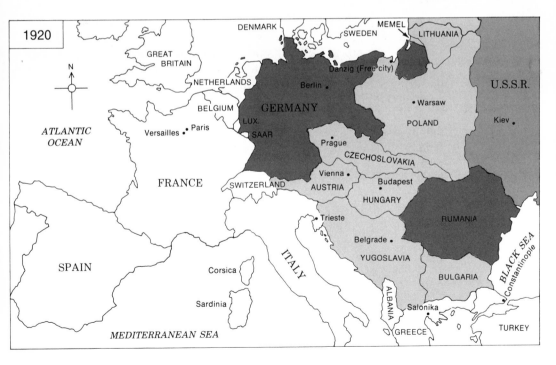

A glance at the maps will show how extensive were the territorial changes in Europe which resulted from World War I. Poland, Lithuania, Czechoslovakia, and Yugoslavia all sprang new from the ashes of old Europe, while Germany was sundered by the Polish Corridor, a wound which rankled until World War II.

torates back home. "Hang the Kaiser," "A World Safe for Democracy," "The Boche must pay"—these were the slogans of the day in the west; while far to the east, in Russia, Lenin's voice summoned the workers of the world to rise against their capitalist oppressors. Under the circumstances, it is perhaps surprising that the peace settlement of 1919–1920 was as workable as turned out to be the case. One reason was that the statesmen who assembled in Paris in January 1919 to draw up peace treaties with each of the defeated Central Powers operated on the basis of a series of faits accomplis, and more often than not simply gave legal sanction to a state of affairs already existing. When—as with the Treaty of Sèvres (1920), which partitioned Turkey—facts failed to conform to the provisions of the treaties, it was the treaties, not the facts, that gave way.

Looked at in this light, day-to-day decisions made before and during the peace conference, sometimes by single nations, sometimes in concert, and sometimes in defiance of the victors, were more significant than the haggling in Paris over details of the treaties. The haggling, nevertheless, was heartfelt. In many details the decisions of the Allied and Associated Powers (to use the official nomenclature) accorded ill with Wilson's principles of national self-determination. But the President comforted himself with the thought that all such injustices could sooner or later be set right if only the League of Nations, upon which he pinned his hope for the future pacific settlement of international disputes, were properly set up.

The Conference at Paris. The peace conference assembled at Paris on January 18, 1919, and brought its formal sessions to a close a year later on January 21, 1920. Its procedures guaranteed that the treaties it drafted would be a very lopsided expression of the will of the great powers, for both Germany and Russia were excluded from any formal part in the negotiation. Instead, the plan was to reach Allied agreement—a difficult undertaking in itself—and then to require the defeated enemy governments to accept the texts submitted to them. As for the Bolsheviks and the Russian land they controlled, their own principles, as well as those of the Allied statesmen in Paris, excluded them from any sort of regular diplomatic relations with other powers.

When, therefore, the German, Austrian, Hungarian, Bulgarian, and Turkish governments were presented with the treaties prepared by the Allied diplomats for each of them,[4] the choice lay between hopeless and impossible renewal of the war and acceptance of terms that seemed radically unjust to each of the defeated peoples. The Turks chose revolt instead of acquiescence; the other nations submitted angrily, with a sense of having been cheated by their foes, who, in the person of Wilson, had promised a just peace and democratic self-determination.

[4]Each treaty had a distinguishing name assigned according to the place where it was signed. Thus the Germans signed the Versailles Treaty, the Austrians the Treaty of St. Germain, the Hungarians the Treaty of Trianon, the Bulgarians the Treaty of Neuilly, and the Turks revolted against the Treaty of Sèvres.

Each of the peace treaties contained clauses establishing a League of Nations; each of the treaties prescribed new boundaries with substantial losses of territory for the defeated states; and each also contained clauses requiring the defeated governments to pay reparations to the victors. In addition, the German government was required to accept blame for causing the war. The war-guilt clause, in turn, provided the legal and moral basis for reparations, on the simple theory that those who had been responsible for the war ought to be made to pay for it. The victors refused to face the fact that any conceivable trade pattern between the victorious and defeated nations would not permit the Germans to pay France and England for the astronomic costs of war damages. They also overlooked the equally obvious fact that a system of treaties imposed upon a bitterly resentful Germany, and without the support of revolutionary Russia, could scarcely hope to endure for very long. Or perhaps it would be fairer to say that both these gross defects in the peace settlement were accepted because the Allied statesmen saw no other way in which to satisfy their home electorates and at the same time agree among themselves.

As a matter of fact, cooperation among the victors began to wear thin even while the peace conference remained in session. The Italians withdrew in anger when their claims to the Dalmatian coast were disallowed. The British found cooperation with the French in the Middle East to be quite impossible. As for the United States, during 1919 and 1920 a great revulsion of popular feeling set in. Instead of supporting Wilson's crusade for peace and democracy all over the earth, the U.S. Senate repudiated the peace treaties because, among other things, they accorded the British Commonwealth multiple votes in the new League of Nations.

The breakup of a wartime alliance after the defeat of the common enemy is a familiar phenomenon of history. Any other upshot of the Paris Peace Conference would have been surprising. That the conference failed to solve or even to give a stable definition to some of the world's crying problems was no less to be expected, despite the millennial hopes with which Wilson and others had approached the task of peacemaking. Here we need merely note three major unsolved questions that emerged out of the year of peacemaking.

Problems in Europe. First, and in a sense most critical of all, was the political condition of central and eastern Europe. The provisions of the peace treaties drawn up in Paris made no attempt to deal with Russia, and accepted the premise that the internal regime, even of so powerful a nation as Germany, ought to be decided without outside interference. The victors insisted that the German government submit to the terms of the Treaty of Versailles; otherwise what happened inside Germany was, at least in principle, none of their business. In fact, however, fear of revolutionary contagion from Russia was very lively among the Allied statesmen. At the same time Wilson pinned high hopes on the contagious force of American democratic and republican ideas. After a precarious passage, democratic and republican government did come to prevail in Germany. But farther east in Europe elections were mainly used to ratify regimes forged by war and coup d'état. Democracy could not flourish amid the ruins of the Austrian, Russian, German, and Ottoman empires because consensus on public issues was usually lacking. Factions, parties, nationalities, and social classes were satisfied with the verdict of the polls only when they won; losers charged (often with good reason) that elections had been rigged.

The main political issue in east central Europe between 1918 and 1920 was where the frontier between Leninist and Wilsonian forms of government would fall. In practice the question turned upon the fate of Poland and the Ukraine, although there were subordinate theaters of action in Hungary-Rumania and even in Bavaria and Saxony, where Communist governments came briefly to power. But the decisive region ran the length of the Vistula and Dnieper rivers, where in the sixteenth and seventeenth centuries a great Polish-Lithuanian state had extended almost all the way from the Baltic to the Black Sea. Polish nationalists sought to reestablish this state, perhaps through some sort of federal arrangement with Ukrainians and Lithuanians. The Russian Bolsheviks, on the other hand, dreamed of revolution in Germany, and knew that they would have to control Poland in order to link up with the German proletariat.

The upshot was disappointment for both revolutionary plans. After several dramatic and sudden shifts, by December 1920 most of the Ukraine had fallen securely into Bolshevik hands. A federal connection between the Ukrainian Soviet Socialist Republic and the Russian Socialist Soviet Republic was then forged, to which a White Russian, a Transcaucasian, and, eventually, a central Asian Socialist Soviet republic were subsequently added. In 1922 the new relationship was formalized by a constitution which established the Union of Soviet Socialist Republics. Each republic was in theory independent and was in practice accorded wide scope for the expression of the linguistic and cultural individuality of local nationalities. In this way the Russians accommodated the nationalistic sentiments that had plainly manifested themselves in the Ukraine and elsewhere, and yet were able to assure effective centralization through the hierarchical structure of the Communist party, which settled all really important issues before the government could act. The Poles lost both Lithuania and part of the Ukraine by their settlement with Russia, formalized in March 1921 by the Treaty of Riga. Yet Poland's new eastern frontier brought a considerable number of White Russians and some Ukrainians under Polish dominion.

Severe internal weakness and direst poverty compelled both Poles and Russians to agree to peace in 1920. The further fact that the German proletariat seemed incapable of organizing revolution along Leninist lines confirmed the Russians in the decision to give up their efforts to export the revolution by armed force. In fact, Russian agents who tried to stimulate a Communist revolution in Germany simply split the Social Democratic party of Germany into bitterly hostile factions and compelled the anti-Communist majority Socialists to follow a more conservative policy than they might otherwise have done.

The German Socialists had already had their revolution. On November 9, 1918, when Kaiser Wilhelm II abdicated, the leaders of the Social Democratic party in the Reichstag took power and proclaimed a republic. Once in office, the Socialists' Marxism had an unhappy way of becoming irrelevant to the situation. Instead of transforming property relations in some sweeping and dramatic fashion, the new government found itself allied with leaders of the German army in an attempt to keep back Communist disorder. In ensuing months, as a quid pro quo, the army authorities helped suppress rightist risings. The Allies maintained the blockade against Germany until June 1919, when the Socialist guardians of the infant republic (by then in collaboration with the Catholic Center party) reluctantly signed the Versailles Treaty. This meant continued and serious food shortages and other economic dislocations. It also nourished among all Germans a deep sense of grievance against their conquerors, who quite literally starved Germany into submission.

In spite of these difficulties, the majority Socialists, with support from other moderate parties, summoned a constituent assembly to meet at Weimar in February 1919. The assembly drew up a democratic, parliamentary constitution which was adopted in July 1919. The first elections in mid-1920 brought a coalition government to office from which the Socialists were excluded. In order faithfully to register the opinion of all, the Weimar constitution prescribed proportional representation. This assured the separate existence of numerous political parties, so that the Socialists soon found themselves sharing power again. No single party ever had a majority, with the result that the ideological programs upon which party divisions were based could never be acted on. In the Weimar Republic, consequently, political rhetoric and practical politics diverged more than usual—a fact that tended to discredit parliamentary government in the eyes of many Germans.

Farther east, only Czechoslovakia and Austria were able to create viable and more or less democratic regimes. Poland and all of the Balkan countries experienced upheavals and coups d'etat in which revolutionary nationalists, revolutionary socialists, and revolutionary peasant parties all played a role, along with cliques of army officers, palace intriguers, and hired gunmen. Elections, when they were held, were often farcical and seldom did more than ratify the power of those already in office.

Upheaval in the Ottoman Lands. The second major issue left unsolved by the peace conference was how to impose terms on a revolutionary Turkish nationalism which, under the leadership of

Mustapha Kemal, boldly defied both the Sultan in Constantinople and the Allied diplomats in Paris. The Allies' first impulse was to let the Greeks do it. Greek troops landed in Asia Minor in 1919 to take possession of a stretch of Aegean coastland which the peace conference had promised to award to the Greek government. The next year the Greeks decided to advance into the interior, hoping to gain more territory for "Great Greece" and to crush the Turkish resistance. Instead, Mustapha Kemal, with the aid of vital supplies from the Russians, was soon able to drive the Greeks all the way back to the sea. As they advanced, the victorious Turks uprooted all Christians from their path. Greeks and Armenians were the main sufferers; but when, in 1923, a new treaty (Lausanne) brought peace to the Aegean area, republican Turkey and defeated Greece had both become ethnically almost homogeneous.

However brutal (more than a million and a half Greeks were driven from Asia Minor and lesser numbers of Turks and Bulgars were harried out of Greece), this sort of mass social surgery eased national frictions afterwards. An opposite process occurred in the Arab lands. The New League of Nations mandates in Syria, Iraq, and Palestine brought the French and British into the Middle East. More significant, however, was the arrival of an increasing number of Jews who, in response to the Zionist form of nationalism, sought to create a national home for themselves in Palestine.

Tremors in East Asia. The third major problem area was in the Far East. In that part of the world the overthrow of the Manchu imperial regime in China (1912) inaugurated a prolonged period of political instability. Inside China tradition-minded warlords contended with revolutionary enthusiasts who, for the most part, grouped themselves around the figure of Sun Yat-sen (d. 1925) and the Kuomintang party. The intrigues and calculations of foreign diplomats and businessmen added a very important complicating factor. This was dramatically manifested in 1915 when the Japanese government took advantage of the war to make twenty-one demands for privileges and guarantees which, if granted, would have almost made China into a Japanese protectorate. The Chinese stalled, then made concessions in Manchuria and Mongolia, but staved off real commitments affecting China proper. In 1917, the Bolshevik revolution opened a new field to the Japanese, who promptly dispatched an expeditionary force into eastern Siberia. The Americans followed suit, as much to keep on eye on the Japanese as to oppose the Bolsheviks.

With the end of the war in Europe, the Allies—and more particularly the United States—began to assert their interests in the Far East more emphatically. Prompted also by domestic political changes, the Japanese government moderated its ambitions accordingly. The new situation achieved definition at the Washington Conference (November 1921—February 1922) which was summoned to settle the outstanding issues of the Pacific and east Asia in the same way that the

Paris Peace Conference had dealt with European problems. The upshot was compromise. Japan and all the principal European imperial powers affirmed China's territorial integrity and the "Open Door"— i.e., equal trade opportunities in China for all. This represented a concession to American wishes. On the other side, the naval limits agreed to at the conference assured the Japanese of supremacy in their home waters and along the China coast. This was a concession both to geographical fact and to Japanese self-esteem. Russia was not represented at the Washington Conference, yet was one of the main gainers, for the withdrawal of Japanese forces from Manchuria and Mongolia—agreed to at Washington—involved also retreat from Siberia. Bolshevik power advanced as the Japanese drew back, so that by 1922 the boundaries of 1914 were again established in east Asia, save for the erasure of German concessions along the China coast.

Despite the formal diplomatic quarantine which the victors maintained against the Bolsheviks, the geographical vastness of the new Soviet Union involved it in each of these three disturbed areas. In another and more important sense also the Russians were involved, for in central and eastern Europe, in Turkey and the Middle East, and in China and its fringe lands (Mongolia, Sinkiang) the ultimate issue behind all the political confusion was whether socialist or nationalist revolution would prevail. The Russians claimed to have found out how to reconcile nationalism and socialism through the federal structure of the Soviet Union. The Americans were usually sympathetic with nationalist movements ("self-determination"), but tended to fear or distrust socialists—at least when they called themselves by that name. France and Britain were in a more ambiguous position, for as great imperial powers they could not really sympathize with either form of revolutionary aspiration. Nor could the two victorious European powers welcome Japan as a new recruit to the circle of imperial nations. That would have meant diminution of their position in China and, most important of all, alienation of the United States, upon whose good will the stability of the entire peace settlement, so painfully and precariously worked out, depended.

Hence, in a modified and muted fashion, the clash between Leninism and Wilsonianism which had appeared so clear and compelling in 1917 survived all the compromises and half-measures of the peace settlements. Neither the democratic nor the socialist revolution had been completed. Whether and in what fashion they would continue to flourish and interact with one another became the central political problem of the postwar world.

MODERN ART AND THE SEARCH FOR REALITY

Franz Schulze

In their scrupulous study of the effects which light and air can have on seen objects, the impressionists were the last painters to work within the great Renaissance tradition of physical realism. That tradition had been founded on the conviction that the most important reality was the visible, material world, and the painting of the old masters was consequently undertaken in accordance with the principles governing that world. Hence the development of rational perspective and space; hence naturalistic art.

Already by the 1880's, however, this centuries-old trust in the preëminence of material reality was breaking down. The postimpressionists, Cézanne, Seurat, Van Gogh, and

Old St. Lazare Station, Paris by Claude Monet, 1877. The Art Institute of Chicago, Mr. and Mrs. Martin A. Ryerson Collection.

Less concerned with the immutable or "absolute" look of things and more with the appearance of the seen world as affected by the momentary play of light and atmosphere, the impressionists moved their easels out-of-doors so that they could study the "motif," as they called it, first-hand. In the work of an artist as sensitive as Monet, the commonest scenes not only take on a new and heightened reality, but are frequently conveyed with an exquisite poetry of color and tone as well.

Gauguin, were united in no point of view except the urgent belief that reality is too large to be encompassed by naturalism alone; that the artist's own interpretation of the world is a crucial part of total reality. For Van Gogh and Gauguin this grand subjectivity took the form of a search for pictorial means through which the strongest and most elemental emotional reaction to the world could be conveyed in painting. For Cézanne the problem was one of form rather than feeling: it was to remake the physical world in terms of substantial plastic form, a process which could be governed only by the refining and reconstructive sensibilities of the artist. The postimpressionist generation, then, saw the painting as a vehicle either of emotion or of form, and it was these ends, plus the artist's primacy over them, which superseded nature. Wherever abstract means were needed to advance them at the cost of naturalism, these means were taken.

The Basket of Apples by Paul Cézanne, 1890-1894. The Art Institute of Chicago, Helen Birch Bartlett Memorial Collection.

Cézanne learned much from the impressionists' notions about color and brushwork, but he was less favorably disposed toward the casualness of their composition and their frequent tendency to dissolve form in a mist of air. In his own painstaking still lifes he sought to organize the component parts of the painting into a firm and logical relation of plastic forms, even occasionally distorting the shapes of objects and bending perspective to suit his will. Thus the composition is welded tightly together, and the purely formal integrity of its elements affirmed.

The Starry Night by Vincent van Gogh, 1889. Collection, The Museum of Modern Art, New York. Acquired through the Lillie P. Bliss Bequest.

Van Gogh was almost constitutionally incapable of the cool dispassion which Monet brought to landscape painting. The fierce ardor of this young Dutchman's temperament is nearly always evident in his painting, sometimes reaching—as here—an intense and brilliant exuberance. It is Van Gogh's passionate personal response to a given scene, rather than the scene itself, which remains most indelibly with the viewer.

"Ma Jolie" (Woman with a Zither or Guitar) by Pablo Picasso, 1911-1912.
Collection, The Museum of Modern Art, New York. Acquired through the Lillie P. Bliss Bequest.

If impressionism qualified Renaissance realism, cubism completely shattered Renaissance space. In Picasso's complex interpenetration of geometrically fragmented solids and voids, the placement and scale of things are dictated by the artist's concept of an abstract whole rather than by the look of objective nature.

Virtually all of twentieth-century painting has grown out of this profound redefinition of the artist's role which occurred at the end of the nineteenth century. Led by the youthful innovators Picasso and Braque, the cubists around 1910 pushed the constructive ideas of Cézanne to such a point that rational space was ignored altogether. Cubism presumes a conceptual or purely pictorial space in which abstract forms are free to assume a size and shape and architectonic relationship that accord with only one standard—that of the artist's judgments.

The followers of Van Gogh and Gauguin were just as radical in their assault on tradition. Seeking expressive, rather than constructive, meaning in their work, the fauves in France—Matisse, Derain, Vlaminck—and the expressionists in Germany—Kirchner, Nolde, Heckel—produced an art of spontaneous feeling articulated through bold contour, broad pattern, and vigorous

Dance by Henri Matisse, 1909. Collection, The Museum of Modern Art, New York. Gift of Gov. Nelson A. Rockefeller in honor of Alfred H. Barry, Jr.

In their attempt to bring a new strength and vivacity to painting, the fauves reduced their subjects to a simplicity of bold, calligraphic line, broad pattern, and bright, powerful color. Matisse, the outstanding member of the fauve group, here reveals the vibrancy of mood and authority of handling that have gained him one of the several most respected reputations among painters of this century.

Russian Peasants by Emil Nolde, 1915. Collection, The Museum of Modern Art, New York, Matthew T. Mellon Foundation Fund.

German expressionism arose about the same time as fauvism did in France, and out of the same strong desire for a simpler, more direct kind of expressive emotion in painting. But the northern European nervous energy, a temper which goes back to the restless dynamism of the Gothic period, was an added factor. In their raw, primitive vigor, Nolde's images are an example of the psychic force which marks the best German expressionism.

Suprematist Composition (Airplane Flying) by Kazimir Malevich, 1914.
Collection, The Museum of Modern Art, New York.

Shortly before the onset of World War I, painters in widely separated parts of Europe (France, Germany, Holland, Russia) were pushing their work to the point of utter nonrepresentationalism, in an attempt to find what they felt to be the essences and absolutes of painterly form. Malevich's stark geometry is an instance of this quest for the distillation of pure pictorial elements.

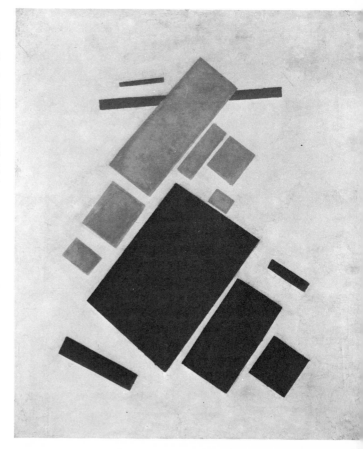

color. The fauves tended to confine their emotional expressiveness to the effects straightforwardly achieved by formal means alone—line, plane, and hue, whereas the Germans communicated powerful, sometimes even anguished, psychological states. The difference between these two germinal groups in France and Germany can be traced through much of the art which has appeared subsequently in both countries.

Art in the second decade of the twentieth century did not surrender the momentum gained in the first. An uncompromisingly purist, nonrepresentational idiom of painting, conceived at opposite ends of Europe by the Russian Malevich and the Dutchman Mondrian, drove cubist abstraction to its logical conclusion. The futurists in Italy rejected all aspects of the past, which they associated with a "dead" humanist tradition; in turn they glorified the machine and anything which was aggressively modern and technological—even warfare. Dada, a movement which spanned the Atlantic, assumed a still more extreme position. The dadaists attacked art itself, mocking all things aesthetic while singing the praises of chaos and relying on irrational motives together with the operation of sheer chance in arriving at their antiart works. Dada was clearly a symptom of the perplexity and despair which gripped the Western psyche during the decade of the First World War. This is suggested further by the fact that surrealism, a more earnestly programmatic movement, was an outgrowth of Dada which took identifiable shape during the 1920's. But neither surrealism nor the 1920's was all that stable, and Dada can hardly be considered over and done with today. Both developments are indicative of the anxious groping of twentieth-century Western man for some grip on the slippery, fluid, and complex reality of modern life—a search which is one of the hallmarks of the century.

Hence dada and surrealism—along with a persistent yearning for the refinements and wide experimental possibilities of abstraction—have continued in one

Diagonal Composition by Piet Mondrian, 1921.
The Art Institute of Chicago. Gift of Mr. Edgar Kaufmann, Jr.

Like Malevich, Mondrian, too, occupied himself with the basic stuff of form, which he came to regard as straight lines in rectilinear relationships, together with the primary colors and black and white. From these austere fundamentals, he constructed a body of paintings whose clean rhythms have influenced much of the subsequent design and architecture of the twentieth century.

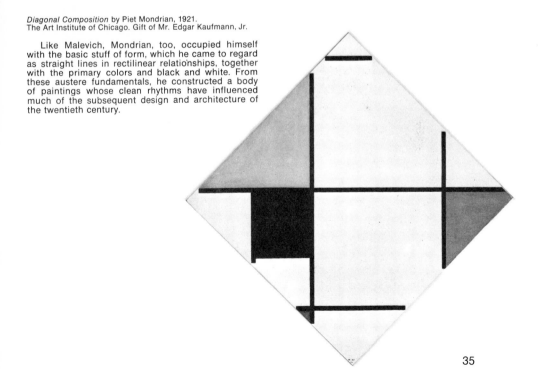

"Ready-Made," *Why not Sneeze Rose Sélavy?* by Marcel Duchamp, 1921.
Philadelphia Museum of Art, Louise and Walter Arensberg Collection.

Duchamp's singular contribution to the rebellious art of our time—the found object, or "ready-made"—has raised a whole army of doubts as to what an art work is and what the art experience amounts to. Such fetching but enigmatic forms as the whimsical dadaist construction "Why Not Sneeze?" with its literary overtones and mutely machine-like quality, leave one uneasy about questions of merit and significance, which is pretty much what the irony-loving Duchamp was striving for in putting it together.

Dog Barking at the Moon by Joan Miró, 1926. Philadelphia Museum of Art, A. E. Gallatin Collection.

If Duchamp's antirational attitudes were important to the development of dada, Miró's role in the surrealist movement which followed was no less vital. The spontaneous invention of visual ideas and shapes, resulting from a free play of subconscious impulses in the artist, is a basic doctrine of surrealism. The charming fantasies of Miró were among the first and most influential articulations of this point of view.

form or another down to the present day. Abstract expressionism, the dominant mode of painting at the mid-century, was largely based on the automatic expression of inner impulses that is part of the surrealist doctrine. And the ruthless irony of pop art is unmistakably a manifestation of a neo-dada sentiment.

There is such a variety of approaches in the experimental art of the twentieth century that its common characteristics seem almost impossible to isolate. Yet that fact in itself points to certain shared attributes. The restless, unremitting pursuit of new and often revolutionary ways of seeing, thinking, and feeling has produced, paradoxically, a rather consistent, multifaceted modern style which is practiced not only in established art centers like New York, Paris, and London, but in places once remote from the mainstream: South America, India, Japan, and Africa.

The part of the world which has most intransigently refused to accept these Western attitudes has been the Communist bloc of nations. There, especially in Stalin's Russia and Mao Tse-tung's China, a Marxist aesthetic has demanded a literally illustrated social message in painting, particularly of the kind which exalts the ideals of socialism and the state. The importance which the West has put on the formal sovereignty of the painting and the subjective authority of the artist has customarily been condemned by Communist critics as symptomatic of bourgeois decadence.

Grayed Rainbow by Jackson Pollock, 1953.
The Art Institute of Chicago. Gift of the Society for Contemporary American Art.

Jackson Pollock's generation responded to the extremity of the World War II years by developing a painting style in the late 1940's which stressed full freedom of action and called for a painting format large enough to contain such unbridled action. Pollock was one of the most rhapsodically powerful—and one of the most original—of the abstract expressionists, as this generation was known in the United States.

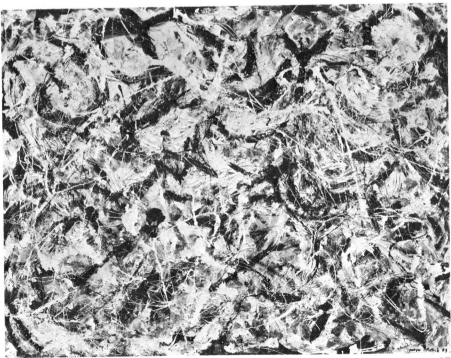

Live Ammo by Roy Lichtenstein, 1962. Private collection.

Pop art is in no small way a latter-day revival of Duchamp's assault on historic standards of judgment. Roy Lichtenstein's enormous comic strip, like Duchamp's ready-mades, draws attention to a type of subject matter traditionally considered of low artistic value or of none at all. Yet by his magnification of it, the subject takes on a different quality from the original; a curious, detached elegance which puts it at far remove from the comic strip that inspired it.

White Relief #11 by Henryk Stazewski, 1963. Kazimir Gallery.

Meanwhile, artists in the more sophisticated iron-curtain countries—usually those countries closest to the West—have for more than a decade been using the kind of modernist idioms which Communist critics once unanimously branded anathema. Indeed, some recent Polish abstraction, like that illustrated here, is pretty much undistinguishable from the purist kind of art which by now has a long tradition in Western Europe.

Yet evidence has been increasing in the past decade that this rigid Marxist posture is relaxing somewhat. In Poland and Yugoslavia, and to a lesser extent in several other iron-curtain countries, Western modernist manners have been openly adopted by individual artists and exported with unblushing enthusiasm by official government agencies. Chinese art, at this writing, remains unswerving in its allegiance to old Marxist dogma, and the course of contemporary Soviet art is itself still uncertain. But the international tide currently seems to be flowing in the direction taken by Western forms and concepts. These forms are often still problematical, even among many bewildered onlookers in the West, and there is no sure prediction to be made about the final destiny of what we call modern art. But its comparatively long life—it is already about three quarters of a century old—is persuasive evidence that modern art is no mere momentary diversion of an aberrant or extremist minority. Rather, it appears to be the authentic expression of an age in spiritual ferment, a period in which violent change alone seems unchanging. In giving visual form to the energy that results from the clash of old values and new motives, modern art has provided us with one of the most eloquent symbolic summaries of our time.

Race Against Time by Tien Ling, 1950's. East Foto.

Since a brief early flirtation and subsequent disenchantment with modern art, Marxist societies have been contemptuous of what they have called "Western formalism." They have relied instead upon an aesthetic of social realism, insisting that painting restrict itself to themes and narratives which clearly forward or clearly accord with socialist doctrine. Many of these Communist cultures have lately softened their official demands for art of this sort, but the Chinese, in their current arch-conservatism, have sternly reasserted the older Marxist criteria. Here the Chinese painter Tien Ling works in a sober, illustrative manner that totally ignores the revolution of abstraction that has altered twentieth-century art in the West.

SUGGESTED READING

On the general background of World War I, Laurence Lafore, *The Long Fuse: An Interpretation of the Origins of World War I** is brief, recent, and readable. The three standard treatments in English are Sidney B. Fay, *The Origins of the World War,** 2 vols., Bernadotte E. Schmitt, *The Coming of the War, 1914,* 2 vols., and Luigi Albertini, *The Origins of the War of 1914,* 3 vols. Of these, Fay is revisionist; that is to say, he exonerates the Germans from any special war guilt, whereas Schmitt tends to reaffirm the Allied case, and Albertini comes closer than his predecessors to exhausting the evidence and maintaining an aloof nonpartisan stance. For the events that triggered the war, Vladimir Dedijer, *The Road to Sarajevo* is best.

Standard accounts of the war itself include Hanson Baldwin, *World War I,** C. R. M. F. Cruttwell, *A History of the Great War, 1914–1918,* Cyril Falls, *The Great War, 1914–1918,** and B. H. L. Hart, *A History of the World War, 1914–1918.* Two eminently readable recent books about special phases of the war are Barbara Tuchman, *The Guns of August,** which describes the initial German thrust into France and its failure, and Alan Moorehead, *Gallipoli,** which treats of the British campaign on that peninsula. J. F. C. Fuller, *Tanks in the Great War, 1914–1918* offers a contemporary voice appraising the most pregnant innovation in military technique that emerged from the war. Jack L. Roth, ed., *World War I: A Turning Point in Modern History** is a collection of essays seeking to assess the longer range significance of the conflict. For the war's diplomacy, Z. A. B. Zeman, *Gentlemen Negotiators: A Diplomatic History of World War I* emphasizes the old-fashioned bargaining behind the scenes; Arno J. Mayer, *Political Origins of the New Diplomacy, 1917–1918** analyzes the breakup of this tradition.

The Russian Revolution is still too close to us and too controversial to have generated a "standard" history. A good place to start is with Theodore H. Von Laue, *Why Lenin? Why Stalin? A Reappraisal of the Russian Revolution, 1900–1930.** Longer works include Edward Hallett Carr, *The Bolshevik Revolution, 1917–23,** the first three volumes of a projected *History of Soviet Russia* which is detailed and authoritative, and distinctly more sympathetic to the Bolsheviks than William H. Chamberlain, *The Russian Revolution,** 2 vols. John Reed, *Ten Days That Shook the World** is an account by a participant and sympathizer that captures some of the excitement and emotion of the revolution itself. Leon Trotsky, *A History of the Russian Revolution,* 3 vols., is a doctrinaire but interesting effort at analyzing the social structures that directed the revolution. Isaac Deutscher, *The Prophet Armed: Trotsky, 1879–1921,** Louis Fischer, *Lenin,** and Bertram D. Wolfe, *Three Who Made a Revolution: A Biographical History** are all interesting biographies of the leaders of the Russian Revolution. J. W. Wheeler Bennett, *Brest-Litovsk, the Forgotten Peace,** and Louis Fischer, *The Soviet in World Affairs,* 2 vols., cast interesting light on revolutionary foreign policy. Richard Pipes, *The Formation of the Soviet Union: Communism and Nationalism, 1917–1923* attains the level of a "standard" work on the internal relations between the nationalities of the Soviet Union in the revolutionary era.

*Available in a paperback edition.

On the peace settlement at Versailles, *History of the Peace Conference,* 6 vols., ed. by Harold Temperly, is a good place to look up details. Paul Birdsall, *Versailles Twenty Years After* is the best short account of what happened, and Harold Nicholson, *Peacemaking, 1919** offers sidelights from a participant's diary. But for devastating analysis of persons, motives, and folly, John Maynard Keynes, *The Economic Consequence of the Peace* is a classic, which proved so persuasive as to affect British public opinion in the years after its publication. A French rebuttal, Etienne Mantoux, *The Carthaginian Peace, or the Economic Consequences of Mr. Keynes** was both belated and a good deal less powerful than the little volume it tried to rebut.

Chapter 2

The World Between the Wars 1921–1939

NORMALCY VS. THE RIVAL REVOLUTIONS

The Two Camps. The rival programs for the world, enunciated by President Woodrow Wilson of the United States and by Lenin of Russia in 1917, continued to compete for the assent of all the world—or at least for the politically responsive portion of the world—during the immediate postwar years; and, in a sense, with appropriate changes in both ideals, the same contest continues even to the present day. Other movements—fascism and Chinese Communism in particular—altered and complicated the scene; and human life does not revolve entirely around politics. But the enduring polarity between Russian Communism and American "pluralism" serves usefully to organize the confusing rush of much recent history.

Between 1921 and 1929 both ideals, which had gleamed so brightly in 1917, were badly tarnished by exposure to the world's political weather. Wilsonianism suffered its most dramatic setback in the United States itself, where in March 1920 the Senate finally and formally repudiated the Versailles Treaty and thereby published to the world the unwillingness of the United States to carry forward the crusade for international peace and order Wilson had proclaimed so eloquently only two and a half years earlier. "Normalcy" was coined to express the spirit of President Warren G. Harding's campaign, which brought him to the White House in 1921. And more than anything else, normalcy meant return to the prewar simplicities and securities of American life, when foreign difficulties and complexities had scarcely mattered.

"Normalcy" might also describe the aspiration of the British public that put a Conservative government into office in 1922, in succession to the coalition ministry (also predominantly Conservative) which had supervised peacemaking and demobilization. Americans and Britons assumed that there was a normal peacetime ordering of society to go back to; the only problem was to remove wartime restrictions upon that order so as to allow it spontaneously to emerge from its temporary hiding.

42

Facts never very closely conformed to this vision of reality. Society was never stable; return to a preexisting state was inherently impossible. Indeed, the pace of technological and social change in both America and Britain continued to accelerate as it had during the whole of the nineteenth century. Yet the prewar framework of society survived, and the English-speaking nations acted on the assumption that the continual emergencies arising from foreigners' unaccountable foibles could be met somehow without any fundamental change at home. A minority disagreed, and in Britain the minority was at times important. But even radical Labourites and professed Socialists in Britain preferred to work within the parliamentary system, both fearing and disdaining violent revolution.

France faced a far more difficult problem after the American withdrawal from Europe. Extraordinary efforts were required to restore the areas of northern France that had been devastated by the war. No automatic resumption of prewar life was possible in those parts of the country until systematic government investment had cleared the rubble, filled the trenches, rebuilt the towns and factories, and restored communications. By the terms of the treaty, the Germans would pay; and the French government, having authorized enormous expenditures for reconstruction of the devastated areas, fully intended to make the Germans pay whether they wished to or not.

The treaty itself left details of the reparations settlement for future negotiation, and almost at once the French ran into trouble in realizing their hopes. British statesmen soon began to doubt whether it was practicable to extort compensation from the Germans for the full costs of the war; Americans contented themselves with dickering for repayment of the debts France and Britain owed to the United States on the principle enunciated by Harding's successor, President Calvin Coolidge: "They hired the money, didn't they?" Repayment was difficult, especially in the face of American tariffs which were raised in 1922 and again in 1930; and German reparations never equalled the French government's expenditures for reconstruction. Rather drastic inflation, with hardship for all on fixed incomes, resulted. Indignant Frenchmen blamed it all on faithless allies and the unregenerate "Boche." A defensive military alliance with Poland, concluded in 1921 and directed against both Germany and Russia, was a poor substitute for the guarantees of British and American support which had been written into the Treaty of Versailles only to be repudiated.

While Wilsonianism failed to solve the world's problems for the principal allies of the war, Leninism, too, encountered a series of disappointments and setbacks. The Russian economy suffered drastic disruption during the civil war. The expected revolution in Germany somehow failed to arrive, in spite of all the help and advice Russian Communists showered upon their German comrades. Not unnaturally, the Russians tended to attribute such failures to a lack of true Bolshevik discipline among the Marxists of Germany and other foreign countries. Accordingly, in 1920 at the second meeting of the

Comintern (the international organization of Communist parties founded in 1919), the Russians insisted on a very hard-nosed list of prerequisites for membership in the organization. Only dedicated, professional revolutionaries—people of the sort Lenin had recruited into the Bolshevik faction of the Russian Social Democratic party before 1917—could subscribe to the twenty-one conditions thus laid down. Most European Marxists were quite unwilling to accept such terms; but some conformed, founding new Communist parties in every country of Europe and, before long, in most of the other parts of the world as well. In the short run, the result was to divide the forces of the left, and, by all ordinary calculation, to reduce the likelihood of successful revolution.

The Comintern's doctrinaire line abroad accorded ill with the New Economic Policy (NEP) which Lenin reluctantly announced in March 1921 to encourage the peasants to resume sending their crops to market. According to this policy, arbitrary requisitioning would cease, and individual peasants would be permitted to sell, at any price they could get, whatever surplus remained after they had paid their taxes in kind. Small-scale trading and manufacture were also authorized, although the state retained control of what Lenin referred to as the "commanding heights" of the economy—banks, railroads, and all large industrial plants. Nevertheless, the return to limited free enterprise and private profit-making seemed to many dedicated Communists, both in Russia and beyond Russian borders, to be a gross betrayal of revolutionary principle. Conservatives, on the other hand, greeted the NEP as irrefragable evidence of the unworkability of socialism.

Marx's materialist dialectic of history, as interpreted by Lenin, could of course, be stretched to accommodate even the NEP. This was by no means Lenin's first transgression against Marxian orthodoxy. After all, according to Marx, Russia was not ready for Communist revolution, since the industrial proletariat was no more than an island in the peasant sea. The real revolution must come where the proletariat was strong, in Germany and England.

Accordingly, Communist hopes revived abruptly in 1923 when the prospect of revolution in Germany suddenly improved. This, in turn, resulted from French efforts to enforce the full rigor of the Versailles Treaty against the defeated foe—if necessary even without British and American support. When German reparations deliveries fell into arrears, the exasperated French decided in January 1923 to march into the Ruhr valley in order to seize at the pithead coal the Germans had failed to deliver to the French border. The Germans reacted to this move by refusing to dig coal or do any other sort of work for the French. A paralyzing general strike spread wherever French soldiers appeared. The result soon became catastrophic, for the Ruhr was Germany's principal center of heavy industry. Runaway inflation—incontinently aided by the policy of the German government—rapidly reduced the currency to complete worthlessness. All ordinary economic activity stopped.

But once again Leninist hopes were disappointed, for Communist revolution failed to come even to a humiliated, impoverished, and paralyzed Germany. Instead, the Ruhr crisis provoked a new American intervention in European affairs—not political this time but financial. Charles G. Dawes, a Chicago banker, was invited to chair an international committee to settle the reparations issue. Even the French were now convinced that they could not seize by force what the Germans were unwilling to dig from the earth on their behalf; and important groups in Germany, too, felt that cooperation with the allies was the only way to escape violent revolution and become once more a great power. Hence, the so-called Dawes Plan was duly ratified in 1924, and the French pulled their troops back to the Rhine, as prescribed by the treaty.

German Recovery. The Dawes Plan reduced the total sum of reparations Germany would have to pay and provided for a massive international loan to stabilize the German currency. It seemed to work like magic, providing the basis for an abrupt industrial recovery in Germany. Until 1930, relatively large sums of American capital were loaned to Germany. This allowed the Germans to pay reparations to France and Britain; and these nations in turn paid installments on their war debts to the United States, whereupon American banks shipped off more money to Germany to keep the circle of payments going. But in the course of this financial legerdemain, important sums were spun off for industrial capital investment in Germany. Hence, for a few short years full-blown prosperity came to the Weimar Republic.

As prosperity flowed in, Germany's revolutionary tides receded. The German Communists were soon torn by bitter factional fights and recriminations; and as their leaders' slavish subordination to Moscow became more and more evident, the party became vulnerable to the charge of lack of patriotism. At the other end of the political spectrum, the National Socialists, or Nazis, also suffered a crippling setback. This party of war veterans and other malcontents had come to the fore briefly in 1923, when the party's new leader, Corporal Adolf Hitler, tried to organize a putsch in Munich, but discovered to his dismay that the army preferred to obey the government instead of letting him take power. Hitler was imprisoned for this infraction of the public peace. When he emerged in 1925, his cause was discredited and most of his party dispersed.

As the revolutionary threat thus dramatically receded, the German government, under the leadership of Gustav Stresemann, publicly proclaimed its intention of fulfilling the terms of the Treaty of Versailles. A change of government in France made it easier for the French to accept these German protestations more or less at face value. Their failure in the Ruhr convinced most Frenchmen that they could not act alone against Germany with any hope of success, but must have British and, possibly, also American support to counterbalance Germany's inherently greater strength. Under American and

British leadership, therefore, a policy of reconciliation came into its own. In 1925 a series of treaties signed at Locarno guaranteed Germany's western frontier and prepared the way for Germany to enter the League of Nations in 1926. The new amity found further expression in the Kellogg-Briand Pact of 1928 (named after an American secretary of state and the French foreign minister), whereby almost all the nations of the world formally renounced resort to war as an instrument of national policy. A year later the Young Plan, named for another American banker, substantially scaled down the amount of German reparations and established a Bank of International Settlements to facilitate large-scale international transfers of funds. A corollary of the Young Plan was the withdrawal of Allied troops from the Rhinelands, where they had been stationed since 1919 in accordance with the Versailles Treaty.

Much had been accomplished toward smoothing over the scars left by World War I—or so it seemed. The renewal of American initiative in international affairs, even if still mainly on an informal and financial rather than political and military level, had borne good fruit. The Wilsonian prescription for settlement of the world's problems had certainly not worked in all particulars—the United States itself was still unready to take part in the League of Nations upon which Wilson had set such store—but the pragmatic pluralism of the American and British tradition seemed to have met the challenges of the immediate postwar years in a generally successful fashion. Russian Communism, on the other hand, had little more than its own survival to boast of. A brief survey of domestic conditions on the eve of the great crash of 1929 will show how plausible American optimism then seemed.

The Return to Normalcy. In the United States return to normalcy paid off in a boom that far eclipsed anything known before. New technologies—automobiles, radios, movies, advertising, industrial assembly lines, and innumerable less dramatic innovations—bit deeply into the texture of everyday life and sustained a massive retooling of the nation's industrial plant. Farmers failed to prosper, but this merely accelerated the migration from country to city which maintained the necessary supply of industrial manpower[1] and made the United States for the first time a predominantly urban nation.

A constitutional amendment prohibiting the sale or manufacture of alcoholic beverages came into effect in 1919; but the readiness of a substantial proportion of the population to flout the law of the land gave a peculiar tone to the ensuing decade, and made the bootlegger into a figure of folklore. Extravagant speculation in the stock market, especially toward the end of the period, became, at least in retrospect, a second distinguishing characteristic of the "roaring twenties."

[1]In 1921 a quota system reduced immigration into the United States to a trickle compared to the flood tide that had brought millions of peasants from European villages to American cities in the decade before World War I. In the 1920s therefore, American farms rather than European villages supplied industrial recruits.

In Britain, normalcy turned out to be far less attractive. Bankers and industrialists lagged behind both the United States and Germany in introducing new techniques; and dreary mass unemployment settled upon the land, particularly after 1925 when the pound was again made exchangeable for gold at the prewar rate. This benefited creditors, penalized borrowers, and acted generally to discourage exports by raising British prices in terms of other, less well-backed currencies. The industrial working force of Great Britain was both pained and angered by persistent unemployment, and made the Labour Party the vehicle of its displeasure. Yet when elected to office—first in 1924 and for a second time in 1929—the leader of the Labour Party, Ramsay MacDonald, was as baffled by the problem of unemployment as the Conservatives. In between, the failure of a half-hearted general strike in 1926 discredited syndicalist notions of solving the nation's social and economic troubles by going outside the parliamentary process. World depression, radiating out from Germany and the United States, made the British industrial scene even more dismal in the early 1930s, but no one cared or dared to embark on radical new paths like those German Nazis, Russian Communists, and American New Dealers were exploring.

After 1923 the French did all they could to avoid risks. The petty bourgeoisie, who had seen a decade of inflation deprive them of a large part of their savings, were determined to prevent any recurrence. Investment was very cautious, while new technology lagged far behind the pace set by German and American entrepreneurs. Consequently, both the boom and the subsequent bust, which assumed such dramatic proportions in the United States and in Germany, were cushioned in France by the fiscal caution of the population.

In Germany the inflation of 1923 broke up the petty bourgeoisie at a time when their counterparts were coming to dominate French life. The war had discredited and decimated the aristocracy. Socialists had become ministers striving to maintain a social order their Marxism deplored. German society, in short, was profoundly upset. Old patterns of deference and social hierarchy were broken, save in remote and rural regions like East Prussia. But the hold of new leaders—whether businessmen and captains of industry, or union leaders and politicians—was insecure. So was the existence of a democratic consensus, despite the fact that moderate parties continued, until after 1930, to win solid majorities in elections to the Reichstag. Nor was any German reconciled to the boundaries which had been drawn in the east, giving Poland a corridor to the Baltic through mainly German lands and cutting East Prussia off from the rest of Germany.

The Wilsonian Ideal. Yet despite these shortcomings and fragilities, ten years after the end of the war the world picture as a whole seemed reasonably encouraging for those who had subscribed even partially to the Wilsonian ideal. In eastern Europe the new nations which had been called into existence by the peace treaties all had governments which paid at least lip service to democratic principles by professing to derive their powers from popular support. Rigged elections and tyrannous officials were the rule rather than the exception, and the best efforts of the national governments of the region had not been able to bring anything like prosperity to the peasant mass over which they ruled. But poverty and oppression were not new in eastern Europe, and an optimist could hope that in time the practices of liberal self-government might take root and flourish.

The League of Nations, even without the participation of the United States, had also made some progress. To be sure, the general disarmament promised in the Treaty of Versailles had not proved practicable, though important limitations on naval building had been agreed to at the Washington Conference of 1921–1922. Nevertheless, the League successfully adjudicated a few disputes between small nations, though its main practical importance lay in the administration of a variety of international services—postal conventions and the like—and in publicly auditing European colonial administration over each of the new "mandates" which had been formed from the Arab lands of the Ottoman Empire and from the former German colonies of Africa and Oceania.

Even in distant Japan, a liberal and parliamentary regime came to power in the 1920s; and, with the establishment of universal male suffrage in 1925, democratic control of the Imperial government seemed assured. The militaristic and authoritarian aspects of Japanese society appeared to be fading away as the country became more and more industrialized. China, too, seemed to be on the verge of emerging from the prolonged disorders that had afflicted that land since 1912, when the Manchu dynasty had been overthrown. In 1928 the revolutionary Kuomintang party, under the leadership of Chiang Kai-shek, established its authority in northern China through alliances with some of the local warlords and a limited resort to direct military action. All of China thus became, at least in theory, united under a single government; and in 1931 a provisional constitution gave legal definition to Chiang's new power. Guided democracy was the official term used to describe the party dictatorship of the Kuomintang. It was a dictatorship tempered in reality by innumerable local autonomies and vested interests, as well as by a nest of Communist insurgency in the far south. But these aspects of Chinese government could be viewed as vestiges of the past, destined to wither as pacification brought prosperity and as a strengthened central government channeled the popular will more effectively to its support.

The Colonial World. India and the entire Moslem world were certainly restive during the 1920s. A glaring defect of the British liberal tradition was particularly apparent in India, for that vast land, seat of an ancient civilization, was governed by a powerful civil service controlled ultimately from London. In 1920 Mohandas Gandhi organized his first civil disobedience campaign, demanding a share in

Indian government for his followers. Gandhi was imprisoned, and the agitation died down for a while, partly at least because the British government did give Indians limited but real responsibility in local and state governments and in nationwide matters not affecting defense or foreign policy.

This halfway house soon ceased to satisfy a majority of the politically active Indians. In 1930 the Indian National Congress for the first time demanded full independence, and Gandhi organized a second and more widespread civil disobedience campaign that demonstrated how a busy decade of political organization and agitation had penetrated all levels of the Indian social fabric. This very success, however, had the effect of alarming many Indian Moslems, who feared the prospect of being ruled by Hindus, who were the immense majority. The obvious response was to try to counterbalance the political organization of the Congress through a Moslem League, whose principal leader, Mohammed Ali Jinnah, demanded a separate Moslem state for his followers.

Elsewhere in the Islamic world the profound discontent almost all Moslems felt at their political subjugation to European imperial powers seldom found effective expression. The French suppressed old-fashioned revolts in Morocco and Syria by equally old-fashioned, brief colonial wars. In Egypt a more or less popular party, the Wafd, mobilized sentiment against the British, and induced them to grant Egypt a nominal sovereignty in 1922, while retaining the right to garrison the country with British troops. In Turkey and in Iran upstart military leaders carried through successful revolutions between 1921 and 1925. In Arabia, too, the puritanical Wahhabi sect found an effective champion in Abdul-Aziz ibn-Saud, who united most of the peninsula under his rule by 1926. But whether these movements enthusiastically espoused Western ways, as in Turkey and (less emphatically) in Iran, or spurned and detested them, as in Saudi Arabia, the result always remained disappointing to Moslem pride and aspiration. Turkey, indeed, under the relentless goad of Mustapha Kemal's leadership, ceased to be a Moslem state. Outward signs of piety were suppressed as energetically as the Communists in Russia were simultaneously attacking Christianity. But repudiation of Islam meant repudiation also of an age-old cultural identity, and the new Turks of the republic found it difficult to discover a satisfactory new pattern of life for themselves. No other Moslem people tried the radical Turkish solution. No other portion of the Moslem world advanced as far as the Turks toward respected independent nationhood, either. The stumbling block was that Islam's universalism simply did not accord with national particularism; yet efforts at pan-Islamic renewal, whether intellectual, moral, economic, or political, could not—or at least did not—achieve practical significance.

In most of the rest of the world, multifarious social variety was masked by European colonial administration, as in Africa and Oceania, or by the dominance of men of European descent and culture, as in Latin America and the British dominions. Changes were certainly occurring that became evident only after 1945; but in the 1920s and 1930s, the faiths and aspirations of the handful of students from Asia and Africa who attended European, American, or Japanese universities seemed remote indeed from the concerns of statesmen and men of affairs. Mexico was an exception. There a revolution beginning in 1911 broke the power of the church and shook, though in the end it did not destroy, the dominant power of the Spanish-descended (as against the Amerindian) element in the population. A more genuinely popular government had emerged by the end of the 1920s, which proudly asserted its sovereign rights against the United States by expropriating oil concessions and other privileges granted to foreign companies by former regimes.

International trade, tourism, investment, news services, postal systems, electrical and presently radio communications knit this great wide world into a whole, and did so more effectually and intimately than in any previous time. Year by year telephone nets expanded, newspaper circulation increased, movement of goods and of persons became easier. Efforts to withdraw from the system of international business and politics were never entirely successful, even in the case of Communist Russia; and legal barriers to trade and migration which tended to multiply throughout the postwar period did not prevent the movement of ideas and techniques across political frontiers. Indeed, a leading purpose of tariff laws was to facilitate the spread of industrial techniques by protecting new industries from the rigors of foreign competition.

Economic planning along the lines explored during the war years (1914–1918) was associated in everyone's mind with shortages, hardship, bloodshed. No one wished to prolong such conditions, and the obvious cure was to return as quickly as possible to the prewar system of private control of business. In particular cases, to be sure, businessmen and farmers of the Western world sought and secured help from government—tariff protection, cheaper credit, regulated (i.e., diminished) competition. But the idea that some overall planning or deliberate general policy should direct the economic process seemed ridiculous and, in fact, subversive, hampering individual initiative and requiring of the planner more knowledge and wisdom than any human being could actually possess. A laissez-faire philosophy, honored in the breach by its most ardent exponents when their own interests were at stake, may not have been very logical, but in 1929 it certainly seemed to work, and who needed better validation than that?

Social and Political Experiments: Russia and Italy. By comparison, the two professedly revolutionary regimes of Russia and Italy, where liberal ideas and practices were scorned and derided, had no very impressive accomplishments to their credit. In Communist Russia, to be sure, the ticklish nationalities issue seemed to have been satisfactorily settled by the federal structure of the Union of Soviet Socialist Republics. But in economics the Bolsheviks met with difficulties. The NEP certainly helped some of the richer or more energetic peasants, who began to prosper in a small way. But the restoration of industrial production was more difficult. Persistent shortages of consumer goods induced the peasants to consume more of their crops since there was so little to buy with the money they received for what they did sell. As a result, the cities continued to be short of food. This in turn hindered industrial recovery and prevented expansion beyond the production levels of 1913.

These economic difficulties coincided with a period of political uncertainty. Lenin suffered a stroke in 1922 from which he never entirely recovered, but he did not die until 1924. During this period, and for three years after his death, the question of succession to leadership in the state and party could not be resolved. In theory, the Communist party was run by a series of committees—each responsible to the one above it, until, at the pinnacle itself, the Central Committee submitted itself periodically to the will of all the members of the party. The will of the party rank and file expressed itself at periodic congresses to which delegates were elected by all the local party units. The delegates listened to reports from the Central Committee and elected (or reelected) members of that body. In this way, Lenin claimed to combine intraparty democracy with the centralization of command he felt necessary for real revolutionary action. As long as Lenin lived, intraparty democracy had a limited reality. Lenin was always ready to listen to debate, but expected to prevail, mainly through the force of his own personality. He also expected those who had disagreed before party policy had been defined on a particular issue to abandon their former "opposition" views for the sake of united action.

These practices had deep roots in Russian life. The informal village councils which traditionally took care of local issues also demanded unanimity after decision had been reached, no matter what the initial disagreement may have been. An unyielding minority, much less the concept of a loyal opposition ready at some future time to take over leadership, was completely alien to Russian experience. Most Russians viewed dissidents as stubborn traitors, who had to be cut off from the community if they persisted in preferring their own private will to that of the nation as a whole, which, by analogy with village custom, was assumed to require unanimity on all important issues.

The man who best succeeded in exploiting these traits of the Russian populace and in manipulating the rules of the Communist party to suit his own interests was Joseph Dzhugashvili, a Georgian best known by his revolutionary pseudonym, Stalin. He skillfully outmaneuvered men far more clever and more popular than he—the brilliant commissar for war, Leon Trotsky in particular—until at the Tenth Party Congress in 1927, Trotsky and several other of Lenin's former companions were read out of the party. Stalin emerged as unquestioned master of Russia. He had lived as an outlaw inside Russian borders before the revolution and, unlike Lenin, neither knew nor cared much about the world of the West. "Socialism in one country" rather than world revolution became his slogan; and once securely in power he addressed himself to the elemental question of how the revolution could be made to prosper in a predominantly peasant land.

Stalin's answer was the first Five-Year Plan, promulgated in 1928. The plan projected massive investment in electric power plants and heavy industry. The tasks were grandiose and verged upon the impossible; yet the very magnitude of the undertaking helped fire the imagination of thousands of young Russians who set to work, sometimes under the direction of foreign engineers and technicians, to realize the plan.

Soviet Agriculture. The real pinch came in the countryside. To feed the construction laborers required for the new projects, and to pay for essential imports of machinery and items that could not be produced inside Russia, the government needed vast amounts of grain and other foodstuffs. The peasantry was entirely unready to supply such quantities of its own free will. Stalin's planners took this fact into account by setting out to collectivize the countryside.

From the government's point of view, collective farms had the great advantage of being easy to tax, since before any distribution of the year's harvest to the peasants was allowed, the government took its share. At the same time, the new collectives were intended to benefit the peasants. Tractors and other farm machinery would—in time—be made available to lighten the tasks of cultivation and harvesting. More efficient use of land, aided by technical advice from competent agronomists, would raise productivity, thereby increasing both tax yield and peasant income. And, the planners hoped, collective labor on land redeemed from the taint of private ownership would advance the socialist mentality among Russia's peasantry, which had always before remained cut off and alienated from the world of cities, civilization, knowledge, and power.

Efforts to persuade the Russian peasants to accept this view of their future met with stubborn resistance. Many richer peasants—the "kulaks"—suffered exile and death. On the other hand, in many villages a considerable proportion of the poorest saw no objection to sharing in their richer neighbors' land and livestock, so there was some support for collectivization in the countryside. But when agents of the party commanded collectivization, innumerable angry peasants reacted by slaughtering their livestock—frequently even draught animals—and reducing the acreage under cultivation to just enough to feed themselves and their families. Agricultural production therefore took a spectacular nosedive in 1930–1931, when collectivization was at its height. Stalin decided to seize the prescribed amounts of grain

52

anyway. He had the choice of allowing either the industrial work force or the mutinous peasantry to starve, and in such a situation a party and policy based on the industrial proletariat had to favor the cities. As a result, grain was requisitioned by naked force from hungry villages. Millions suffered and many died of hunger, but thereafter the peasants' will was effectually broken. They did not again deliberately fail to plant enough ground to meet the assessed grain deliveries and to feed themselves as well. However, nothing like the adventurous spirit that informed the industrial sector of the Soviet economy established itself in the countryside. The peasants retained a sense of grievance and did as little as they dared to improve or increase the collective farms' agricultural production, even when tractors, harvesters, and other machinery did begin to arrive in the countryside in significant numbers, as happened in the later 1930s.

Nevertheless, the first Five-Year Plan, in its grand outlines and central thrust, worked. Russia's industrial plant began to expand at a very rapid rate, and a wide range of new careers opened up for anyone with even rudimentary training. Millions migrated from the countryside to face all the hardships and discomforts of working in bleak factories or at construction sites while living in intensely overcrowded, often jerry-built, housing. Yet for most the effort seemed worthwhile. They were building for the future, and responded to party appeals for still greater effort and more resolute self-discipline in a generally positive way. For the ambitious and talented, when every sort of skill was in such short supply, an exciting, variegated career lay easily within reach.

Stalin's success in Russia depended in good part on the fact that comparatively vast resources in manpower, minerals, and food production capacity needed only the catalyst of technical skill and an entrepreneurial will to react on one another in massive and dramatic fashion. The Russians were able, initially, to borrow Western technology wholesale, and, like the United States on the other flank of Europe, also enjoyed some economies of scale from operating within so vast a geographical unit as the Soviet Union.

Italy Under Mussolini. Italy enjoyed none of these advantages. Despite the bravura of Benito Mussolini's rhetoric, the Fascist regime that came to power in 1922 made only modest changes in Italian society. Economic power continued to rest with private industrialists and landlords as before. A modus vivendi was arranged with the papacy in 1929, according to which the pope became temporal sovereign of a miniscule Vatican City, and the Church was guaranteed certain authority over Italian marriage law and education. This concordat healed a breach between the papacy and the government of Italy which had begun in 1870.

All this was essentially conservative. Mussolini's radical rhetoric—his belligerence and his exhortation to serve nation instead of self, to find true freedom in obedience and fulfillment in work—met with only a quizzical acquiescence from most Italians. Fascist experiments with occupational instead of geographical representation in the legislative chamber failed to alter relationships between capital and labor, landlord and tenant in any very palpable sense; and the economic undertakings of the government—rearmament, land reclamation, the colonization of Libya, and making the trains run on time—never attained such a scale as to alter the main lines of the Italian economy. On the other hand, political dissent was silenced after 1925, strikes were forbidden, and the doctrine of elitist rule in the interest of all, but emancipated from crippling dependence on popular opinion, parliamentary votes, and the other trappings of liberal democracy, was flamboyantly proclaimed. These traits distinguished Italy from the other countries of Europe.

CULTURAL VISTAS

The crash of 1929 and the Great Depression that followed abruptly changed the climate of opinion and marked a definite watershed between the post-World War I and pre-World War II periods. Before we consider the course of events that led to the second war, however, it seems well to remind ourselves that politics do not embrace all human life, and to survey the social, cultural, and intellectual achievements and limitations of the interwar period as a whole.

In matters cultural, the avant-garde camped in Paris between the wars, whereas the major innovations in mass culture tended to find their most uninhibited expression in the United States. The cultural eminence of Paris was enhanced by colonies of American and Russian émigrés—persons like Ernest Hemingway and Igor Stravinsky—who found their native societies inhospitable. For the same reason, Irishmen like James Joyce and Spaniards like Pablo Picasso spent much of their time in the French capital. This strong tendency to cluster together in one center reflected a prevailing alienation of artists from society as a whole. Creative spirits, seeking new modes of expression, found scant sympathy or comprehension from devotees of normalcy, and tended therefore to seek out the handful of like-minded persons who could provide the alert, sensitive, and critical audience they needed to be able to work well and with a sense of inner satisfaction. Run-down sections of Paris played host, therefore, to an amazing proportion of the Western world's greatest artists and writers in the 1920s. In the next decade, however, these coteries tended to break up, partly because a few, like Hemingway, attained popular recognition, and partly because those who did not began to feel, under the pressure of both fascism and communism, a need to make their art meaningful to a wider public than any provided by the artistic ingroups of Paris.

Without a longer time perspective than is yet available, it is difficult to know which of the innovations so energetically pursued in Paris during the 1920s will prove fertile and influential, and which will be discarded as mere froth and frenzy of the postwar era. Obviously, when a relentless search for revolutionary novelty was the only path to artistic respectability—as tended to be the case in the 1920s—only a few of the innovations can ever attract more than passing attention. Gertrude Stein's experiments with automatic writing, for example, do not seem likely to enrich literature; James Joyce's *Ulysses* (published in 1922), on the other hand, has done so. The great figures of twentieth-century painting—Pablo Picasso, Georges Braque, Henri Matisse, Georges Roualt, Wassily Kandinsky, and others—certainly enlarged the world's sensibility and broke away from older traditions of European painting with a ruthlessness and vigor unequaled by any of the other arts. The genesis of modern painting, however, is to be found at least a decade before World War I began; the 1920s can only claim a widened variety of styles and continued intense creativity.

It seems still uncertain whether experimentation with new scales and sounds, which also found exponents in the 1920s, will prove to be the entering wedge for new and viable musical forms. On the other hand, the so-called international style of architecture, which was defined in Germany in the 1920s, seems certain to rank with nonrepresentational painting as one of the major cultural achievements of the twentieth century. The geometrical simplicity of shapes, and the free use of new materials and technical advances in construction methods, gave this style one enormous advantage: many buildings could be built more cheaply of glass, metal, and concrete than by using conventional stone or brick; and this, together with the real aesthetic success of some of the new buildings, assured the rapid spread and genuinely "international" character of the style.

Equally radical, and in the long run probably just as significant as new avant-garde styles, was the rise of mass entertainment, attuned to the tastes of a very wide segment of the population and propagated principally by the new mass media of radio and motion pictures. Here the United States took the lead, summoning jazz from the black underworld and cheerful banality from the morals of the middle class in order to fill the radio waves with soap opera and music, and the movies with sentiment, sex, and adventure. Only occasionally, as with the music of George Gershwin, or in movies like *The Cabinet of Dr. Caligari,* in which the use of special camera lenses to distort visual reality created images reminiscent of cubism and dadaism, did high art and the mass media recognize each other's existence, and then, usually, with imperfect artistic success.

T. S. ELIOT AND PICASSO

Eliot: Blau/Blau-Publix

In youth, the Spanish painter Pablo Ruiz y Picasso (1881–1973) and the American poet Thomas Stearns Eliot (1888–1965) departed from their native lands, and from congenial vantage points in Paris and London set out to explore the rebellious fringes of the human spirit. In middle age, each surrendered to external authority. Picasso pinned his faith on Communism; Eliot preferred Anglo-Catholic Christianity.

Throughout his prolific career, Picasso remained protean. His first stylistic shift came between 1906 and 1910 when he helped invent "cubism," an effort to reduce visual forms to geometry, and to suggest movement by painting successive positions of an object on the same canvas. Picasso soon cut loose from representational art completely, putting forms on canvas that had no reference to anything beyond themselves. But art totally freed from dependence on things sacrificed the natural human response of recognition of visual experience as transformed by the artist. Perhaps for this reason, Picasso returned to figure art after World War I. But he continued to dissect and jumble ordinary visual experience in startling new ways.

In the 1930s, the Spanish Civil War brought politics home to him as never before. He responded with his brush, by expressing his horror, in a famous and powerful painting, at the way Nazi planes had bombed Guernica. Oddly enough, the Nazis left Picasso undisturbed during World War II. When it ended, he announced he had become a Communist. All the same, his politics did not make him conform to "socialist realism." On the contrary, he experimented with new media in his old age—mainly pottery and sculpture—and even wrote a play.

T. S. Eliot was far more intellectual than Picasso. Born in St. Louis of middle-class parents, he attended Harvard, the Sorbonne, and Oxford before settling down in London (1914). He took no active part in either world war, working instead as a teacher, bank clerk, and editor. These jobs were avocations, offering respectability and needed income. His real career was poet and literary critic.

In the 1920s Eliot expressed disillusionment with everything cultured Europeans had valued before the war. *The Waste Land* (1922) was his most ambitious statement of this mood. Here and in other early poems he stretched familiar verse forms and grammar to the breaking point, studding his poems with verbal fragments torn from their normal contexts, but familiar from liturgical or other common usage.

In these years, Eliot's techniques resembled Picasso's strikingly. Both were breaking with convention, yet wished to retain immediately recognizable meaning. Words, obviously, are easier to tear loose from their moorings than visual shapes. Even minor changes destroy verbal meaning, whereas Picasso could distort familiar images drastically and still expect (perhaps puzzled) recognition. Accordingly, Picasso continued to stretch visual recognition to fit novel stylizations, but Eliot soon abandoned such experimentation and instead reaffirmed the high tradition of English literature through a series of critical essays.

Eliot's reappraisal restored poets who had long been out of fashion—particularly the "metaphysical" poets of the late seventeenth century—to a place of high esteem. These poets had wrestled with the problem of reconciling Christian belief with the new Newtonian science. Eliot found his own posture very much like theirs, and in the late 1920s announced his conversion to Anglicanism. Thereafter, his poems and plays—*Ash Wednesday* (1930), *Murder in the Cathedral* (1935), *The Cocktail Party* (1950)—explored the necessity for belief and tradition as guides to personal conduct.

We cannot know whether the works of Picasso and Eliot will continue to command admiration far into the future. From close up, they both look like giants whose breaks with tradition and deliberate return to faith—Communist and Christian—poignantly expressed the anguish of the age in which they lived.

Picasso: York-Publix

Science, Pure and Applied. A similar dichotomy between the pursuits of recondite scientific research and the practical application of new knowledge to engineering was very pronounced in the 1920s and 1930s. One reason for this was that physics changed fundamentally during these two decades, and, in a sense, left engineering behind. What happened in physics was partly philosophical. The Newtonian vision of physical nature was radically modified by the discovery that the laws of motion and such basic principles as the conservation of mass did not necessarily apply either to the very small or to the very large. Albert Einstein, in two famous papers, one published in 1905 and the second in 1915, rejected the absolutes of space and time within which the entire Newtonian system had been thought to exist. Instead, Einstein said that the results of measurement, both in space and in time, depended on the relative motion of the measurer and the thing measured. As a corollary of his new assumptions, Einstein derived a formula $E = mc^2$ (as elegantly simple as those Newton had published two and a quarter centuries before) to define the equivalence of energy with matter. Observations confirmed Einstein's theories by detecting, for example, the deflection of light passing close to the sun. Thus the four basic terms of Newtonian physics—space, time, matter, and energy—each acquired a new meaning, much to the distress of many physicists and to the confusion of most ordinary people.

While Einstein was thus transforming the basic assumptions of physics, a group of ingenious experimentalists penetrated inside the atom, once believed to be the ultimate building block of the universe. They discovered a confusing variety of subatomic particles, which sometimes behaved like waves. At first, Niels Bohr seemed able to explain these results by constructing a physical model of the atom which depicted it as similar to a miniature solar system. But by about 1925, Bohr's model of a dense nucleus surrounded by planetary electrons arranged at different distances from the nucleus according to definite geometrical patternings had to be abandoned. Physicists simply gave up trying to make geometrical models of subatomic reality. They contented themselves with mathematical formulae that described probabilities, and merged particles and waves, space and time, matter and energy into one another in a way completely incomprehensible to anyone who did not understand the complicated mathematical symbolism involved.

While theoretical scientists were energetically straining against the bounds of common sense in this fashion, practical engineers paid very little attention to what the physicists were doing. Innumerable, often very complicated, engineering improvements were made in detail; but the general thrust was simple. Individuals began to analyze systematically the acts involved in manufacturing a particular product, and then figured out ways in which each step could be simplified, standardized, and accelerated. Results were sometimes startling. When Henry Ford arranged his automobile assembly lines so that every worker had a simple task to perform that took just long enough

58

TRANSPORT

Motor Vehicles

Number of Vehicles per 10,000 People

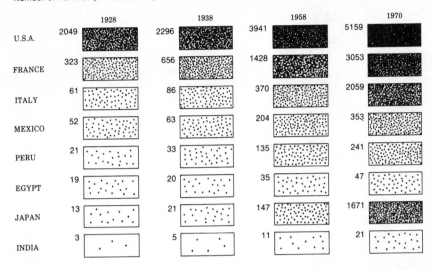

	1928	1938	1958	1970
U.S.A.	2049	2296	3941	5159
FRANCE	323	656	1428	3053
ITALY	61	86	370	2059
MEXICO	52	63	204	353
PERU	21	33	135	241
EGYPT	19	20	35	47
JAPAN	13	21	147	1671
INDIA	3	5	11	21

to keep him busy while a moving belt carried the car past the place where he was stationed, and when each such task had been arranged sequentially to bring thousands of separate parts together to constitute a finished car, it proved possible to complete the whole process in less than two hours from start to finish. Thousands of substantially identical vehicles could come off the assembly lines in a single day.

Artisan skills and craftsmanship went by the boards in such a system; but mass production of cheap cars became possible as could never otherwise have occurred. Just as the United States tended to take the lead in popular culture and the development of mass media, so also in the field of mass production American entrepreneurs led the world. Europe remained supreme in theoretical physics and science generally until the later 1930s, when scientists and other intellectuals fleeing Hitler enriched the work done in American universities, and put them for the first time in the front rank of world science.

In other fields of science, the gap between theory and practice was not nearly so wide. Chemistry, for example, continued, as before World War I, to find ready and extremely varied application in industry. Plastics and synthetics of many sorts became commonplace. Rayon, nylon, and detergents were perhaps the most obvious novelties, but they were only a small sample of the range of new materials that enriched the world in the interwar decades. Biology provided a second example of a close linkage between scientific theory and practice, for physiological research, probing the chemical exchanges that constituted life processes, found almost immediate entry into medical practice as new drugs (sulfanilamides, penicillin), vaccines, vitamins, hormones, and the like were first discovered and then made available for clinical or general use.

59

FREUD AND EINSTEIN

Freud: Brown Brothers

German Jews played a very distinguished part in the intellectual life of Europe in the early twentieth century. Chief among those who shared this background were the psychologist Sigmund Freud (1856–1939) and the physicist Albert Einstein (1879–1955).

Of course, both built on the work of others. In Freud's case, a Viennese doctor, Josef Breuer, hypnotized mental patients and made them "relive" past experiences. On waking, they often left their symptoms behind, at least temporarily. Freud worked with Breuer for a while, but soon developed an easier technique. He simply asked his patients to lie down on a couch and relax, and then, by "free association," to tell what they remembered about their dreams, as well as infantile and other emotion-charged experiences. In this way, Freud believed, he could lead his patients to understand their subconscious wishes and fears, often with beneficial psychological results.

Initially Freud's method and ideas aroused sharp criticism. Many people were shocked by his assertion that sex was of great subconscious psychological importance, even for small children. But after World War I his doctrines began to catch on widely and provoked far-reaching innovations in conduct, child-rearing, literature, and art, especially in the English-speaking world.

Albert Einstein lived an outwardly more varied and far less controversial life than Freud, who spent all his active years in Vienna and fled to London from the Nazis only shortly before he died. Born at Ulm in south Germany, Einstein grew up in Italy and Switzerland, and took his first job in the Swiss patent office. Later he held professorships in Prague, Zurich, and Berlin.

In 1905 he published a paper on relativity, but his speculations attracted little attention. Einstein's early fame rested instead on his discovery of photons (he got a Nobel prize for this in 1921) and an analysis of atomic vibration. During World War I he expanded his initial leap in the dark into a general theory of relativity. Unlike his paper of 1905, the new theory was capable of experimental verification. In effect, Einstein redefined the relationships between the four basic terms of Newtonian physics—space, time, matter, and energy. Tests at once suggested themselves: notably measurement of the deflection of starlight passing through the sun's gravitational field. The predicted effect was found during a total eclipse in 1919. Einstein's theory at once commanded world attention, and a long series of experiments further demonstrated its validity.

For the rest of his life Einstein tried to surpass himself by finding a still more general theory that could explain magnetism and subatomic forces, as well as those phenomena already encompassed by the theory of relativity. But the formulas he published in 1950, like his first paper on relativity, were not capable of experimental verification. His last great effort therefore remained unfruitful.

Einstein: UPI-Compix

Before this anticlimax, Einstein had to flee from Nazi Germany to the United States. There he helped persuade President Franklin Roosevelt to start work on the atom bomb. Despite his fears that German scientists might be about to give this weapon to Hitler, Einstein took no personal part in achieving the controlled conversion of matter to energy first carried out in Chicago in 1942. His political views made weapons work distasteful, for he was a pacifist and an advocate of world government and disarmament.

Both Freud and Einstein had the ability to jettison familiar assumptions and explore the consequences of radically new presuppositions. The social circumstances in which they grew up as Jews, in yet not entirely of German society, may have made it easier for them to examine things freshly with the quizzical eyes of supremely intelligent outsiders who could not afford to take anything for granted. But many thousands shared this ambiguous status: only Freud and Einstein responded, thanks to their individual genius, with world-shaking new ideas.

Human Behavior—Individual and Collective. To understand the vogue for psychoanalysis according to the school of Sigmund Freud, we must leave the world of medicine for that of social science. There was, of course, an important kernel of truth in Freud's doctrines. More than any other individual, he drew attention to the fact that people often behave in response to subconscious motives and in accordance with elemental drives that can only be partially channeled and controlled by custom and habit. Freud's use of dreams as a key to unconscious levels of our mental processes, and his recognition of sexuality as a pervasive element in our psychology, enlarged scientific awareness. Yet Freud's anatomy of the unconscious—id, ego, superego, and the rest—seems unlikely to endure, for it lacked any base in the physiology of the brain, and rested purely on his own intuition.

Freud's popularity, therefore, depended not on definite and demonstrable theory like Newton's, but on a doctrine that appealed to people who wished to rebel against the customs and habits of their ancestors, and who found justification for their new manners in Freud's phrases. The vulgarization of Freud which equated inhibition with psychological deformity, and imagined that a noble savage lurked in every human breast if only parental repression had not interferred with spontaneous self-expression, restated in suitably new and shocking language a theme which was at least two hundred years old in European thought.

Other social sciences were affected by similar romanticisms. Cultural anthropology, for example, in the hands of persons like Bronislaw Malinowski or Ruth Benedict, discovered in primitive communities a wholeness and completeness of life which was conspicuously lacking in the tumultuous, varied, and discordant world of the twentieth century. Detachment from any particular set of values, especially those of one's parents, and sweeping cultural relativism could thus be combined with sympathy for real savages whose inhibitions, unlike those of civilized people, seemed to make sense because they fit a pattern of culture that was self-consistent and complete.

Detachment from any particular system of values was, indeed, a leading trait of many social theorists. Among the most influential was the German sociologist Max Weber, who made explicit the divorce between values and observed reality, and tried to discern amid all the variety of historical mankind a series of "ideal types." These were abstractions, analogous to the anthropologists' culture patternings of primitive societies, which would permit systematic comparison and intellectual comprehension of the structure and functioning of complex civilizations.

Not all the social sciences were detached, however. In the United States a flourishing school of empirical sociology, whose surveys of the social landscape were saturated with democratic idealism, derived directly from Christian missionary enthusiasm. Economics, too, stubbornly took the rational values of eighteenth- and nineteenth-century theorists for granted. In many ways economics played the central role among the social sciences that physics played among the natural sciences. Like physics, economics started the twentieth century with a classical definition of its subject matter, derived fundamentally from Adam Smith, and perfected by such theorists as Alfred Marshall, who introduced the concept of marginal utility to explain more perfectly the behavior of individuals in the marketplace. A clear moral commitment to the economic virtues of rationality and hard work informed economic thought; and the bankers and industrialists, who made the principal decisions upon which the day-to-day economy of the world depended, shared these ideals and rejoiced, through most of the 1920s, that theory and practice, virtue and wealth, rationality and pecuniary reward had come to be so closely congruent.

Keynes and the New Economics. The Wall Street crash of October 1929 and the worldwide depression that developed from it came as a brutal shock to economic theorists and businessmen alike. Clearly something had been wrong with classical economic theory, but to begin with, no persuasive alternative analysis could be found, save for old-fashioned Marxism, which in details (e.g., the labor theory of value) was demonstrably wrong. Nevertheless, many bright and angry young people of Europe and America found the practical achievements of the first and second Russian Five-Year Plans, coming as they did at a time when economic retrogression was everywhere paralyzing Western societies, persuasive enough. As with Freudianism, the appeal of Marxism in the 1930s was not so much intellectual as emotional. Violent revolution, resolute action, purposeful and grandiose behavior: all the excitement of the Five-Year Plans without the brutality and hardship, this was what rebellious Westerners wanted; and because they wanted it, they tended to project their ideal uncritically upon Soviet realities. Unfortunately for such "fellow travelers" with communism, their time of greatest need coincided with brutal purges in Stalin's Russia, where between 1936 and 1938 thousands of innocent people were executed, while falsified evidence, lying confessions, police terror, and all the other instruments of tyranny were paraded before the world.

At this juncture, the British economist John Maynard Keynes stepped into the breach by publishing *The General Theory of Employment, Interest and Money,* in 1936. This book provided a new and generally persuasive theoretical analysis of what had gone wrong with the world of the 1920s, and offered a simple remedy for the Depression: massive deficit spending by national governments to raise purchasing power and set the wheels of industry again in motion. It took about a decade for professional economists to absorb and react to Keynes' arguments, and universal agreement was not achieved at any time. Nevertheless, the idea that governments could and should manipulate the level of economic activity by deliberately adjusting money supply and interest rates spread relatively rapidly.

This was revolutionary on at least two counts. Traditional liberals had assumed that the economic system ran itself according to natural laws. Government's proper role was, through the law courts, to keep the rules of the game constant, but to take no initiative. Socialists, on the other hand, had long believed that only expropriation of private capital could solve the problem of poverty and social injustice. Hence, when Keynes recommended manipulation of such determinants of business activity as the central bank discount rate, and a policy of deliberately launching programs of public investment in times of depression to compensate for shrinking private demands on the economy, his ideas challenged old ideas of both the left and the right. In effect, Keynes opened a new middle way by inquiring into the theoretical consequences of creating a mixed private-public economy. This provided eager doctors, who (particularly in the United States) had already begun to prescribe all sorts of economic remedies for the Depression, with a powerful theoretical justification for governmental intervention aimed at indirect control of economic activity.

It would be wrong to suggest that Keynes or anyone else achieved the knowledge needed to foresee all the consequences of deliberate manipulation of economic controls. But the helplessness with which people contemplated the onset of the Depression of 1930, their sense of dismay at witnessing such a betrayal of their expectations, can never again paralyze public action. Fiscal devices for palliating the effect and reversing the decay of economic activity are sufficiently well understood that, even if belatedly, too little, or too much, adjustments can be made. The long bitter years of suffering, unemployment, and waste the world experienced in the 1930s can never recur, in large part because of the better understanding of monetary and fiscal policy which John Maynard Keynes pioneered.

Generally, then, the years between the wars must be described as extraordinarily fertile. In physics and in economics fundamental breakthroughs occurred of a sort that can happen only rarely in human history. New styles of art and widened ranges of sensibility were ushered in, and the venture toward a mass culture was brashly begun on a scale far surpassing earlier attempts in the same direction. Sharp alternation between excessive optimism and equally excessive despair stimulated a continued relentless striving after truth, beauty, and power, regardless of costs, and with scant respect for ancestral wisdom and example.

The limitations of the age were also real. One glaring inconsistency was the incompatibility between democratic political belief and the practice of colonial government, which excluded the governed from more than occasional, marginal participation in or control over public policy. The excluded peoples of Africa and Asia had their counterparts in the West among the numerous lost souls who withered in the anonymity of urban life. Many such persons felt the need to project their frustrations upon some tangible foe and to fix their affections upon some sort of community greater than themselves. Totalitarianism fed upon the discontents of such lost souls; and totalitarianism got its chance in Europe when the Depression discredited moderate policies and democratic leadership—leadership which had always been insecure in Germany even when prosperity briefly blossomed there (1925–1929).

THE GREAT DEPRESSION AND RESPONSES TO IT

The New York stock market panic began, as many similar panics had begun, when enough investors decided that stock prices had outrun prospective returns—a situation which had prevailed for well over a year before October 1929. But the ramifications of the New York panic were entirely unprecedented, and reflected the new financial predominance the United States had won during and after World War I. New York banks began recalling credits they had advanced to Germany; this precipitated financial collapse there, and the effect of Germany's paralysis spread to other European countries and rebounded upon the United States. Within two years, nearly half the German industrial labor force was either unemployed or working only part-time; elsewhere the Depression, though not so drastic, was crippling enough. About 15 million Americans were out of work at the end of 1932—and no one knew what to do about it.

Traditional liberal response to fluctuations in the business cycle was to wait until good times returned. Bankruptcies, lowered wages and prices, unemployment, and reduced government expenditures commensurate with the lessened tax income would in due course find their "natural" levels until a new equilibrium, propitious for fresh investment and new expansion, established itself. As long as industrial employment had occupied a relatively small proportion of the population, so that many workers had rural homes to return to in time of need and could count on help from farm relatives for short periods of unusual emergency, this sort of laissez-faire reaction to depression was tolerable, and, indeed, worked quite well.

Prior to 1914 even in the most industrialized nations (with the important exception of Great Britain) most of the population continued to pursue basic rhythms of life built around the tasks of cultivation, and did so more or less independently—at least in the short run—of booms or busts. By 1932, however, urbanization had advanced beyond the point that allowed the traditional rural refuge and balance wheel to cushion a depression effectively. In all the leading nations of the Western world, where exchanges among the urbanized population had come to constitute the bulk of business, a wait-and-see response to bad times on the money market no longer sufficed.

Theory there was none. Keynes came along only afterwards. People acted in the absence of theory, and in the United States and Germany, the two countries where the Depression hit hardest and where the responses were most effective, people naturally and inevitably fell back upon patterns of economic mobilization which had first been tried during World War I.

Dramatic changes of government in both the United States and Germany in 1933 symbolized and permitted this return to wartime patterns of economic management. The Democrats, who had last governed the United States during World War I, returned to national office in the elections of 1932. Under the leadership of Franklin D. Roosevelt, they proceeded to inaugurate the "New Deal" in March 1933. Three months previously a fanatical ex-corporal, Adolf Hitler, had become chancellor of Germany and proceeded to fasten his dictatorship on the nation. A little earlier Japan and Russia had launched their own versions of economic mobilization, with Stalin's Five-Year Plans and the Japanese invasion of, followed by massive investment in, Manchuria. Each of these movements deserves a little scrutiny before we consider how a fresh series of international clashes led to the outbreak of World War II.

Soviet Five-Year Plans. Beginning in 1928, the first Five-Year Plan gave the Russians a chronological head start in coping with economic crisis. The ruthlessness with which Stalin and his subordinates were able to command the human and natural resources of the Soviet Union also gave the Russians a certain advantage. But the scant industrial base and lack of skills with which the Russians started was a tremendous handicap. Two points seem worth making here. First, the conception and methods of Russian economic planning were closely related to military planning as practiced during World War I. Calculations rested on command decisions: to erect a dam here, a factory there, a new railroad or some other major installation somewhere else. Then the necessary material supplies and labor resources were marshaled, much as a general marshaled his troops and supplies for a campaign. Shortages, when they appeared, were overcome by command, prescription, emergency decree—as in a military campaign. Even Communist rhetoric was military—the campaign of the grain, the industrial front, the struggle against saboteurs, etc.

Secondly, the goals of the first two Five-Year Plans were primarily industrial. In the course of the second Five-Year Plan, 1932–1937, the military threat from Hitler's Germany began to look serious. In response, Stalin, quietly and without publicity, shifted industrial priorities from civilian to military production, and began to build up and reequip the Russian armies on a massive scale. Consumer goods, housing, and other amenities steadily fell short, whereas basic industry and armaments increased very rapidly.

Despite fatigue and strain, the Russian peoples as a whole acquiesced in what the planners demanded of them. The need for armaments in a world where Hitler was loudly demanding *lebensraum* in the Ukrainian plains did not need elaborate proof. Even the purges of 1936–1938, which removed almost all the surviving old Bolsheviks and sacrificed many skilled people to Stalin's paranoiac fears, had no effect upon the traditional submissiveness of the Russian masses. The Five-Year Plans thus made Soviet Russia an enormously greater military power in 1939 than Czar Nicholas II's empire had been in 1914. But this fact was not evident from abroad. The purges had resulted in the execution of most of the senior officers of the army. This left most observers wondering what was left of Russian military morale.

Japan's Rising Sun. The Japanese were, in a sense, the most conventional of the four great innovative powers in their methods of economic mobilization. The others transformed their economies in time of peace; Japan first went to war, and then bit by bit, under the pressures of long-drawn-out military operations, expanded and reorganized the imperial economy. Fighting started in 1931 when Japanese troops invaded Manchuria. Reaction of the European powers and of the League of Nations to this open infraction of the peace was muffled and ineffective: when Japan angrily withdrew from the League in 1933, the only Western riposte was to refuse to recognize the new puppet state of Manchukuo which the Japanese military had erected in the former Chinese province of Manchuria.

From the beginning, the civilian government of Japan had only imperfect control over what the Japanese army undertook on the mainland. Even reluctant ministers had to yield to demands for money and equipment needed by the troops. Anything else would have been unpatriotic as well as dangerous, for on several occasions fanatical young army officers assassinated political leaders who fell short of the army's definition of patriotism. Financiers similarly were compelled to cooperate, whether they wished to or not, in developing the mineral and other resources of the Manchurian plains. A semi-independent power thus developed within the ranks of the Japanese army. This shadow government held the Japanese home authorities to ransom more than once, and developed Manchuria and Korea almost as a separate military fief.

No theory and very little system emerged from this sort of arrangement. The decision to invade China proper in 1937, and subsequent expansion of the theater of operations deeper and deeper into that vast land, complicated matters. Nothing like the systematic and successful development of Manchurian coal and iron came to China in the wake of the Japanese invasion. This was partly because of persistent Chinese resentment and unwillingness to cooperate even in regions where neither Chiang Kai-shek's Kuomintang nor the Chinese Communist party had any hope of challenging the Japanese occupation. Another reason was that the Japanese began to confront critical shortages within their economy. Little could be spared for investment in the relatively exposed regions of China proper when the home islands and Manchuria were already clamoring for more funds and resources than could easily be found.

The Japanese militarized economy differed from the Russian planned economy in two significant respects. The Japanese clung to the idea of prowess: most soldiers believed that if one were sufficiently brave and determined, success would come. Their record between 1931 and 1943 certainly seemed to support such a view. But this meant that the risk of military overcommitment was built into the very marrow of the entire imperial venture. Secondly, there was no really unified command and control from the top in Japan, analogous to the control Stalin and the Communist party exercised in Russia. Emperor Hirohito had a sacrosanct authority which was largely ineffective in practice. Constitutionally, the civilian ministers did not control the military representatives who sat in the cabinet. Much less could mere civilians control commanders in the field. Even the ministers of war and of the navy—who were always high-ranking officers of the respective services—could not always control junior officers, whose ideal of prowess sporadically found expression in suicidal public assassinations of "unpatriotic" ministers.

Such a diffused pattern of authority may have had advantages at times. Local flexibility and improvization often made much of little. Local commanders and factory managers sometimes accomplished more than a really centralized system could have done. On the other hand, Japan as a whole was liable for commitments made by relatively quite subordinate commanders who acted in ignorance of the real limits of national resources. In the long run this feature of the system proved fatal. By emphasizing will and minimizing calculation, the Japanese pattern of mobilization tended also to underestimate the power of human intelligence to direct action successfully. This deficiency they shared with their fascist allies—Germany above all— who sacrificed intelligence deliberately in the name of racial purity and the power of the will.

Hitler and the Nazis. Hitler came to power in January 1933, after two years of depression. As was to be expected, the immediate response to the onset of the depression in Germany was the rise of revolutionary political movements: Hitler's National Socialists, or Nazis, on the one hand, and Communists on the other. At no time did either of these parties win a majority in a free election, and it was only after the Nazi tide seemed to be waning, when Hitler had suffered a considerable setback at the polls in November 1932, that he was made chancellor. He got his chance because conservative nationalists believed they could use the Nazis to provide a wider popular support for their policies. Instead, Hitler used them, and within three months of his accession to office had acquired—through legal forms—dictatorial power. He used his authority to suppress other political parties, to persecute the Jews, whom he had made a scapegoat for most of

Germany's woes, and to launch a program of public works and secret rearmament that in a comparatively short time relieved the unemployment problem.

Hitler's ideas were partly the result of miscellaneous reading of nineteenth-century racialists who had argued the inherent superiority of a (largely mythical) Aryan race. These and related doctrines found expression in *Mein Kampf,* a strange, incoherent book that Hitler wrote while imprisoned after his attempted putsch of 1923. A second element shaping Nazi doctrine and practice was the comradeship of the trenches remembered from World War I. The Nazis tried to recapture the wartime sense of purpose and comradeship by making their party a simulacrum of the army they had known. They wore uniforms and saluted one another on every possible occasion. They staged vast ceremonial marches and rallies, and started street fights with Communists and other political rivals. They cultivated the habits of command and obedience according to rank, and thereby found a welcome surcease from the moral ambiguities of normal civilian life.

All this, together with an enemy to hate—the Jews—and the German *Volk* to love, proved to be a heady brew. Few Germans resisted it entirely, though few subscribed to all the absurdities of Nazi doctrine. Organized resistance faded rapidly after the first months of Nazi rule, and a watchful and unscrupulous secret police made sure that no undercover opposition could organize itself. Only the churches and the officer corps of the army retained independent corporate existence. Relations between these bodies and the Nazi party were always difficult, since, in the eyes of fanatical Nazis, anything less than total dedication to the national goals as defined by Hitler verged on treason.

Hitler aimed at restoring German greatness. This meant purging the German race from mixture with Jews, Slavs, or other "inferior" peoples. To realize this illusory ideal—since racially the Germans were as mixed as any other people of Europe—Hitler was ready to drive thousands of the most talented and highly trained German citizens to foreign lands, where they enormously enriched the cultural and intellectual life of the receiving nations. Hitler also, of course, set out to restore and reequip the German army and navy, and intended to use the nation's restored military strength to unite all Germans into a single great empire that would extend from Flanders and Lorraine on the west to somewhere in the Ukraine on the east, thus making the German people the greatest power on earth.

The Nazis positively distrusted and disliked intelligence. Will and emotion, blood and soil were what mattered. Hitler certainly had the will, and proposed to get possession of the soil of most of Europe by the same combination of bluff and brutality that served him so well between 1933 and 1936 in mastering Germany itself. The ultimate consequence was World War II and the utter defeat and destruction of the Nazi movement. In the short run, however, the ready availability within Germany of idle men and machines lent to Hitler's mystique of the will an almost magical success—or so it seemed in years when other European nations were limping along under the burden of massive unemployment amid drab depression such as Germany, too, had suffered before Hitler's advent to power.

Lesser European states tried in various ways to imitate the Nazi example, or, dreading attack, searched nervously for refuge. Until almost the eve of war, Britain and France, each preoccupied with a difficult internal situation, found little energy to spare for mustering their strength against resurgent Germany. Their memories of World War I were too dismal to contemplate the possibility of another war. Politicians and the public alike refused to think seriously of resorting again, voluntarily, to the sort of paramilitary economic mobilization which lay at the root of both Russian and German success. To arm again and prepare for war seemed a confession of failure which the people of both France and England hesitated to make. Appeasement, aimed at repairing some of the injustices of Versailles, seemed a better policy. Hitler was therefore able to undo the Versailles settlement very quickly, by ruthlessly and skillfully exploiting both the reasonableness and the fears of the French and British public.

F.D.R. and the New Deal. In the United States, World War I had left behind no such ineradicable distaste as in France and Britain. When Franklin D. Roosevelt became president in 1933 and set out to cope with the economic crisis, he therefore summoned veterans of the war years who drew upon their recollections of how they had mobilized the nation's resources in 1917–1918. Emergency agencies like General Hugh Johnson's National Recovery Administration and the Civilian Conservation Corps clearly showed their World War I paternity. Other important New Deal measures like the devaluation of the dollar and the Agriculture Adjustment Act had no direct wartime parallel. But the overarching general idea of deliberately adjusting supply to demand, fixing prices, and using government funds to make the civilian economy behave in a way public policy prescribed all stemmed directly from the wartime years. In practice, however, the scale of governmental intervention in the American economy never reached a level that could absorb all the manpower and productive capacity of the nation until after World War II broke out in Europe.

Despite the moderation and half measures which characterized the American New Deal when compared to Nazi, Russian, or Japanese policies, it nevertheless brought such a spirit of adventure and derring-do into the halls of government as to persuade most Americans and some Europeans that liberal parliamentary institutions were not incapable of coping with the crisis of the Depression. Communism and other political extremes found little scope in the United States. Instead of joining such movements, citizens of good will could hope to accomplish something practical by finding a job in the government and helping to administer some new program for social betterment. Conservative critics denounced the New Deal as socialistic, but most

Americans approved, as the unprecedented reelections of Franklin D. Roosevelt in 1936, 1940, and 1944 amply proved.

The Rumble of Approaching War. The New Deal, though in many ways harking back to Wilsonianism in matters domestic, did not resume Wilson's crusade for democracy abroad. American sentiment was strongly anti-Nazi, but Europe's affairs seemed far away, and it was easier to blame the Western powers and the League of Nations for failing to stop aggression than to do anything really serious about it. As the drift toward war became more and more apparent, the U.S. Congress took steps to prevent any second involvement of the New World in the quarrels of the Old. The Neutrality Act of 1936, for example, prohibited American ships from traveling in war zones and forbade extension of credit for war purchases. The theory behind this legislation was that munitions makers and international bankers had been mainly responsible for involving the United States in World War I, and should not be given the opportunity to do so again.

The Americans, therefore, left the French and British very much to their own devices. With serious domestic crisis always threatening, and with fear of Communist Russia almost as vivid as fear of Nazi Germany in the minds of many French and British statesmen, the two victors of World War I made a sorry showing. In 1935, for example, the French concluded a military alliance with Soviet Russia, while the British concluded a naval agreement with Germany. Each of these treaties shocked and frightened the excluded partner, without being really worth it, since neither treaty ever became truly effective.

In this nervous situation, Italy seemed to have a crucial importance. Mussolini used his advantage to the full. At first he opposed Hitler, and with French support prevented the Nazis from annexing Austria in 1934. The next year the Italian dictator attacked Ethiopia, and conquered that country in a single campaign. This put the French and British in a quandary, for if they followed their principles and called upon the machinery of the League to penalize aggression, they would antagonize Mussolini. But they both wanted him badly as an ally against Hitler. In the face of this dilemma, French and British hesitation and double-talk had the unfortunate consequence of alienating Mussolini and discrediting the League at the same time.

The critical turning point came in 1936. In March of that year, when the Ethiopian crisis was at its height, the Germans marched into the demilitarized zone of the Rhineland and began fortifying the frontier. The French did nothing but protest at this unilateral infraction of the Versailles Treaty. When Hitler had thus secured his vulnerable western flank, the last of the restraints upon German power, so carefully devised at Versailles in 1919, was gone. The nations along Germany's eastern frontiers, allied with France, realized that their treaties with that nation were now all but worthless, since the French neither could nor would invade Germany from the west if war broke out in the east. Mussolini, too, decided that it was better to cooperate with Hitler than to try to rival him.

MUSSOLINI AND HITLER

Mussolini: Wide World Photos

Benito Mussolini's (1883–1945) father was a black-smith who preached atheism and socialism. His mother was a pious Catholic who taught school. His parents thus embodied the extreme poles of Italian opinion, and their son's Fascism sought to reconcile the opposites.

Like his mother, Mussolini qualified as a school-teacher. He was, however, fiercely rebellious, and like his father became a socialist. Once out of school, Mussolini faced the draft, but his socialism forbade military service. He fled to Switzerland and became a journalist. In 1904, however, he abruptly returned to Italy, did his military service enthusiastically, and then took up socialist agitation again. When World War I broke out, Mussolini reversed himself once more, volunteering for the army, where he served until wounded. Discharged, he resumed political agitation, but no longer as a socialist. He had become something new—a Fascist.

Fascism combined nationalism and socialism. Military life provided the pattern, and uniforms, marching, and street violence became Fascist hallmarks. Naturally enough, Mussolini's first supporters were mostly veterans. Fascist ideology or *myth,* as Mussolini sometimes called it, emphasized the identity between individual and nation. Strict obedience toward those above and resolute control of those below in the chain of command was what Italy needed, not endless, divisive parliamentary debates.

Fascist authority, hierarchy, and myth paralleled the Catholicism professed by Mussolini's mother and most Italians; the vision of a radically revitalized nation resembled his father's socialist ideal. Combining such antithetical elements, Fascism had wide appeal and met with almost no resistance when Mussolini ordered a "March on Rome" in 1922.

He remained in power until 1943, and "made the

trains run on time" all right, but failed to make Italians live up to his militarist ideal. By threat and bluster he made Italy important internationally until Hitler took over as Europe's chief troublemaker after 1936.

Adolf Hitler (1889–1945) was the son of a petty Austrian customs official. The young Adolf ran off to Vienna hoping to become an artist. Instead he became a solitary drifter, living by doing odd jobs, and a virulent anti-Semite, blaming the Jews for all that was wrong with his own life and the lives of the German people.

World War I found Hitler in Munich. He volunteered for the German army and experienced a profound emotional release in the comradeship of shared danger in the trenches. When the war ended he had no place to go—a fate he shared with millions of other veterans. In 1919 he drifted into a beer hall in Munich to listen to a small group of political extremists. Hitler hesitated, then decided to enroll in what later became the National Socialist German Workers' Party—Nazi for short. When invited to speak, he discovered a gift for impassioned oratory that quickly made him a prime drawing card. The movement grew until Hitler tried to imitate Mussolini's March on Rome by staging a coup d'état in Munich. It failed miserably.

Hitler: Blau/IWN-Publix

Condemned to prison, Hitler used his time to dictate *Mein Kampf* (My Battle), a hodgepodge of autobiography and political diatribe that combined hatred of Jews, socialists, and other "traitors" to Germany with brutal cynicism about how to win and use power. Unlike Mussolini, who talked more boldly than he acted, Hitler really believed what he said. Accordingly, when the depression of the early 1930s raised him to power in Germany, Hitler set out to win *lebensraum* (living space) for the German people by force. World War II was the result.

As the fighting drew to a close, Mussolini met an ugly death at the hands of Italian partisans in April 1945. A few days later, Hitler committed suicide in his Berlin bunker, which had begun to quake with the noise of approaching Russian guns. The dictators' squalid deaths aptly reflected the blind alley into which fascism had pushed the German and Italian nations.

The Russians, meanwhile, sought to counter the Nazi danger by operating on the level of formal diplomacy—the alliance with France of 1935—and by directing the world's Communist parties to cooperate with socialists and liberals of any stripe in "popular fronts" against the fascists. Russia's effort to operate on two distinct levels in this fashion proved self-defeating. Patriots tended to be conservative and refused to trust Communists; leftists, who were more ready to collaborate with Communists, were also pacifists and found it hard to support rearmament and the other measures that effective resistance to Nazi threats required.

The ironies of this situation came into sharp focus in Spain. Elections in that country put a popular front government in power in February 1936, whereupon military revolt in July of the same year started a bitter civil war. Italy aided the rebels from the start; Germany also soon sent military help on a limited scale. On the other side, the French intervened halfheartedly in support of the Loyalists, and so did the Russians. The thought that the Spanish Civil War might escalate into a full-scale European war appalled French and British statesmen. They therefore organized a nonintervention committee, whose purpose was to prevent aid from reaching either side. But their professed policy of neutrality was effectively nullified by the fact that France and Britain felt obliged to avoid offending Hitler and Mussolini. Italian support, therefore, continued to flow in defiance of the nonintervention agreements until General Francisco Franco's armies finally won the war in May 1939. With Spain friendly to the new Rome-Berlin Axis, the French strategic position was again seriously weakened. The Russian alliance of 1935 had also become worthless, since Stalin no longer believed that the French would fight for anything.

British statesmen still hoped that if Hitler were allowed to unite all Germans into one great nation—a program that seemed in accordance with the Wilsonian principle of self-determination—then perhaps he would quiet down. If worst came to worst, they hoped that the Nazis would attack to the east, where *lebensraum* and their anti-Communist crusade both seemed to beckon. As for the French, they had come to the conclusion that they could do nothing without the British. Hitler was thus enabled to annex Austria in the spring of 1938 and the German-inhabited regions of Czechoslovakia in the fall of the same year. Russia took no active part in the Munich conference of September 1938 that sealed these German victories. The popular front was dead; so was any serious effort on the part of either the Russians or the Western nations to collaborate against the Germans.

In the spring of 1939, however, British policy changed abruptly. On March 15 of that year Hitler coolly annexed the rump of Bohemia which the Munich agreements of the preceding fall had left independent. Neville Chamberlain, prime minister of Great Britain and the leading spirit of the whole appeasement effort, felt personally betrayed by this callous disregard for a solemn undertaking—a disregard which could not be justified by claiming that oppressed fellow Germans required liberation as in previous cases of Nazi territorial expansion. Chamberlain promptly abandoned appeasement, urged on a program of rearmament, and directed British policy toward the containment of German power.

But it was too late. The Russians, distrusting British and French intentions, decided to come to terms with Hitler. During the summer of 1939, as Hitler unleashed a propaganda war against the Poles, Stalin secretly negotiated a pact dividing Poland and the Baltic states between Russian and German spheres of influence. The signing of an innocuous nonaggression treaty between the two states was announced to a stunned world on the eve of a German ultimatum to Poland. Britain had guaranteed Polish frontiers only a few months before, and the French also had a military alliance of long standing with the Poles. Accordingly, when German troops crossed the Polish frontier on September 1, 1939, the British and French, much against their will and despite all their efforts to escape the risks of another war, on September 3 declared war against Hitler's Germany. What started as a European war soon spread like its predecessor of 1914–1918 to become World War II, marking another momentous chapter in the troubled history of the twentieth century.

SUGGESTED READING

G. M. Gathorne-Hardy, *A Short History of International Affairs, 1920–1939* covers its subject admirably. *The Diplomats, 1919–1939,** ed. by Gordon A. Craig and Felix Gilbert, treats the same themes episodically through a series of essays about leading figures of the period.

Among the histories of the various European nations, the following may be especially recommended: **Great Britain:** Charles Lach Mowat, *Britain Between the Wars, 1918–1940,* F. S. Northedge, *The Troubled Giant: Britain Among the Great Powers, 1916–1939,* David Thomson, *England in the Twentieth Century, 1914–1963,** A. J. P. Taylor, *English History, 1914–1945,* and Nicholas Mansergh, *The Commonwealth and the Nations.* **France:** David Thomson, *Democracy in France,** and E. J. Knapton, *France Since Versailles.* **Germany:** S. W. Halperin, *Germany Tried Democracy: A Political History of the Reich from 1918 to 1933,** and Arthur Rosenberg, *A History of the German Republic, 1918–1930* treat the Weimar period. On Nazi origins and rise to power, Adolph Hitler, *Mein Kampf** is a document of first importance. Alan Bullock, *Hitler: A Study in Tyranny** is a standard biography. Franz Neumann, *Behemoth: The Structure and Practice of National Socialism,** and William L. Shirer, *The Rise and Fall of the Third Reich** are among the best general accounts of the Nazi period. George L. Mosse, *Crisis of German Ideology: Intellectual Origins of the Third Reich,** and John W. Wheeler-Bennett, *The Nemesis of Power: The German Army in Politics, 1918–1945** illumine special aspects of the Nazi period, but no really satisfactory book on

Hitler's economic policies seems to exist. **Italy:** A. Rossi, *The Rise of Italian Fascism, 1918–1922,* and Ivone A. Kirkpatrick, *Mussolini: Study in Power* deal with the life and career of Mussolini. Christopher Seton-Watson, *Italy from Liberalism to Fascism* supplies a bit more of Fascism's background. D. A. Binchy, *Church and State in Fascist Italy* treats one of the key issues of modern Italian history with admirable penetration. **Russia:** Theodore Von Laue, *Why Lenin? Why Stalin?,** Isaac Deutscher, *Stalin, A Political Biography,* George F. Kennan, *Russia and the West Under Lenin and Stalin,** Hugh Seton-Watson, *From Lenin to Khrushchev: The History of World Communism,** Edward Hallett Carr, *A History of Soviet Russia,* Vols. IV–V, may all be recommended. **Eastern Europe:** Hugh Seton-Watson, *Eastern Europe Between the Wars, 1918–1941,* and Robert L. Wolff, *The Balkans in Our Time* offer suitable introductions to the region. **Spain:** Hugh S. Thomas, *The Spanish Civil War** promises to become a classic.

The 1930s saw a rash of fascist governments spread through much of Europe. Efforts to understand and compare these regimes provoked three interesting books: Ernst Nolte, *Three Faces of Fascism,** Eugene Weber, *Varieties of Fascism,** and F. L. Carsten, *The Rise of Fascism.**

Our own national history is too well known to need suggestions here. Asia and Africa are difficult for the opposite reason: a general lack of familiarity. Jan Romein, *The Asian Century: A History of Modern Nationalism in Asia* offers an overview. For the **Middle East** Bernard Lewis, *The Emergence of Modern Turkey,* and George Antonius, *The Arab Awakening* are good starting points. **India** is perhaps best approached through two autobiographies: Gandhi's autobiography, *The Story of My Experiments with Truth,** and Jawaharlal Nehru, *Toward Freedom: The Autobiography of Jawaharlal Nehru.** For **China,** Edgar Snow, *Red Star over China** treats the Communists rather sympathetically, while Emily Hahn, *Chiang Kai-shek, An Unauthorized Biography* treats her subject rather unsympathetically. A useful survey is O. Edward Clubb, *Twentieth Century China.** John King Fairbank, *The United States and China** explores the relations between the two countries. For **Japan,** Edwin O. Reischauer, *Japan Past and Present* is a good starting place. Richard Storry, *A History of Modern Japan,** Hugh Borton, *Japan's Modern Century,* and William W. Lockwood, *The Economic Development of Japan: Growth and Structural Change, 1868–1938** may also be recommended. For **Africa,** Lord Hailey, *African Survey* offers a storehouse of information, and Roland Oliver and J. D. Fage, *A Short History of Africa** gives an excellent summary.

The period from World War I to World War II was a fruitful one in literature as in the other arts. This additional list of books gives a selection of the most representative works about that period.

Asia. Yukichi Fukuzawa, *Autobiography;* Rabindranath Tagore, *Mashi and Other Stories;* Junichiro Tanizaki, *Makioka Sisters,** Some Prefer Nettles.**

Europe. Ivo Andric, *The Bridge on the Drina*;* Maurice Barrès, *La Colline Inspirée*;* Bertolt Brecht, *The Caucasian Chalk Circle,** Mother Courage*;* Louis-Ferdinand Céline, *Journey to the End of Night*;* Alfred Döblin, *Berlin Alexanderplatz;* Ilya Ehrenburg, *Memoirs*;* T. S. Eliot, *The Waste Land,** The Hollow Men*;* E. M. Forster, *A Passage to India*;* Federico García Lorca, *Poems of F. García

*Available in paperback edition.

Lorca; Maxim Gorky, *Autobiography,* Lower Depths*;* Robert Graves, *Goodbye to All That*;* Hermann Hesse, *Steppenwolf,* Siddartha*;* Aldous Huxley, *Brave New World*;* James Joyce, *Finnegan's Wake*;* Franz Kafka, *The Castle, The Trial*;* Alexander Kerensky, *Memoirs of the Russian Revolution;* D. H. Lawrence, *Women in Love,* Lady Chatterley's Lover*;* Thomas Mann, *Dr. Faustus,* The Magic Mountain*;* François Mauriac, *The End of the Night, Thérèse Desqueuyroux*;* Vladimir Nabakov, *Despair,* Invitation to a Beheading*;* George Orwell, *Animal Farm,* 1984*;* Boris Pasternak, *Dr. Zhivago*;* Charles Péguy, *Basic Verities*;* Erich Maria Remarque, *All Quiet on the Western Front*;* Jules Romains, *Death of a Nobody,* Knock*;* Virginia Woolf, *Mrs. Dalloway,* To the Lighthouse,* Jacob's Room and The Waves*;* William Butler Yeats, *Collected Poems.*

North America. James Agee and Walker Evans, *Let Us Now Praise Famous Men*;* Frederick Lewis Allen, *Only Yesterday*;* Sherwood Anderson, *Winesburg, Ohio*;* W. H. Auden, *Age of Anxiety;* Ruth Benedict, *The Chrysanthemum and the Sword*;* Pearl Buck, *The Good Earth*;* E. E. Cummings, *The Enormous Room*;* John Dos Passos, *Three Soldiers,* U.S.A.*;* James T. Farrell, *Studs Lonigan*;* William Faulkner, *The Sound and the Fury,* Light in August*;* F. Scott Fitzgerald, *The Great Gatsby,* This Side of Paradise*;* Ernest Hemingway, *A Farewell to Arms,* For Whom the Bell Tolls,* The Sun Also Rises*;* Sinclair Lewis, *Babbitt,* Main Street*;* Margaret Mead, *Coming of Age in Samoa*;* John Steinbeck, *The Grapes of Wrath*;* Robert Penn Warren, *All the King's Men*;* Thornton Wilder, *The Bridge of San Luis Rey*;* Edmund Wilson, *To the Finland Station*;* Richard Wright, *Black Boy,* Native Son.**

Chapter 3

World War II and Aftermath
1939–1949

THE WAR

World War II was much more advanced technically than World War I. This was true in the military sense, for the weapons and strategy of World War II's campaigns were more complex and demanded far more skillful coordination than had the dreary trench warfare of World War I. It was true also of the energy and precision with which the various combatants organized their home fronts. Both aspects of the war demonstrated the tremendous advances which a generation had brought to the theory and practice of social management and control.

Nevertheless, in Europe and the Western world generally, the first war was far more of a landmark than the second. In spite of the vast destruction involved in World War II, its ravages were as skilfully repaired as they had been inflicted. The net shock to people's minds and styles of life—save always for Europe's Jews—was therefore far less than the disruption which World War I had brought to Western nations. But in most of the rest of the world, World War II had much the same effect in breaking down familiar ways and smashing established social patterns of deference and expectation that World War I had had in Europe. China and India underwent fundamental political change; the Moslem peoples, Africans, and southeast Asians lagged only slightly behind in throwing off European political domination. The rise of indigenous independence movements was an index of the breakup of traditional village and artisan patterns of behavior. When the cake of custom cracked, resentments and aspirations previously suppressed, or not even felt, boiled tumultuously to the surface. People everywhere started eagerly along the perilous path of trying to rule themselves, reshape their societies, and transform their economies. Asians and Africans in their millions sought to escape by deliberate—sometimes frenzied—action from everything that had made them weak and poor in the past and prevented them from becoming great and powerful in the future.

First Campaigns. When World War II began on September 1, 1939, such consequences were entirely unforeseen. Germany attacked Poland to get back the corridor that had separated East Prussia from the rest of Germany since 1919. Despite the occasional gallantry of Polish units, they had no chance against German tanks and airplanes, so that within four weeks the German *blitzkrieg* (lightning war) was over. On September 17, the Soviet Red Army began to advance into Polish territory to take possession of what Stalin's deal with Hitler on the eve of the war had secretly assigned to the Russians. Shortly thereafter, the Baltic states signed a series of "mutual defense pacts" with Russia. Lithuania, Latvia, and Estonia accepted these pacts and, with them, the presence of Russian soldiers on their territory, without more than a desperate glance in Germany's direction. Within a year they were incorporated into the Soviet Union. The Finns, however, fought, and to everyone's surprise succeeded in repelling Russia's initial attempt to occupy their country.

Meanwhile, on the Franco-German frontier nothing happened. Desultory exchange of shots signified the presence of rival armies, but the French had no intention of trying to breach the German defenses, and assumed that the Germans could not break through those they had themselves so carefully prepared. During the winter of 1939–1940, therefore, Allied strategists preferred to make plans to aid Finland by going across Norway and Sweden instead of butting headlong against the defended German frontier. The fact that this would involve France and Britain in war against the Russians was not the deterrent later events suggest it should have been. Russian economic and political collaboration with Germany had made the U.S.S.R. into an enemy of sorts already, and Western military men, reacting to the Finns' successes, assumed that the Russians could offer no effective resistance to well-equipped Allied troops—and might even welcome them as liberators.

These plans were scotched by two German moves: first the Nazis overran Denmark and Norway (April 9, 1940), seizing all critical points within twenty-four hours. A month later (May 10, 1940) the Germans struck again, this time attacking Holland, Belgium, and France with all the concentrated force of the German armies. No eastern front against the Russians required attention as in 1914, and trucks and tanks could move much faster and farther than men and horses had been able to do in World War I. As a result, the German plan this time succeeded, taking no more than six weeks to accomplish what four long weary years, 1914–1918, had failed to achieve. French morale cracked early in the fight. The British withdrew a tattered expeditionary force from the beaches near Dunkirk. They were left with little heavy equipment and no battle-ready troops. The war, obviously, was over. It remained only for the defeated French and British to make terms with the victor.

The French government did indeed submit to an armistice which divided the country into an occupied and unoccupied zone, the one controlled directly by Germans, the other semiautonomous under Marshal Henri Philippe Pétain, the aged hero of World War I. The British, however, refused to consider negotiations, despite the plain facts of German superiority. Winston Churchill had become prime minister in April 1940 and brought with him a defiant spirit that proved contagious. German air attacks in the fall of 1940 only hardened the British will to resist. Preliminary German efforts to prepare an expeditionary force to cross the Channel underlined how difficult such an undertaking would be. Across the ocean the American government and public reacted to the British plight by accelerating rearmament at home and by creating loopholes in the neutrality laws to allow emergency shipment of weapons and other urgently needed supplies to Great Britain. No responsible American public figure advocated direct participation in the war, but genuine neutrality was out of the question. Indeed, when British credit became exhausted, the U.S. Congress passed a Lend-Lease Act (March 1941) authorizing the President to make deliveries to Britain (and other countries) on a loan basis, without requiring immediate payments of any kind.

American support of Great Britain "short of war" certainly galled Hitler. His inability to cross the Channel in strength was equally frustrating. There were, however, other theaters of action calling for attention. For one thing, Hitler's ally, Italy, needed help. Having declared war just as France collapsed, Mussolini found his African empire exposed to British attack. Italian counter-efforts to dislodge the British garrison from Egypt met with embarrassing failure.

Hitler was even more concerned by a second Italian failure—this time in Greece. Mussolini attacked that country in October 1940 only to see his soldiers driven back inside Albania, whence they had launched their assault. After a few British planes had gone to aid the Greeks, Hitler decided that he would have to subdue the entire Balkan peninsula to make sure that larger British forces did not follow. This decision was a logical corollary of another, and far more important, decision which Hitler had made in November 1940: namely, that he would attack Russia instead of pursuing the war with Britain to its conclusion. Safeguarding his Balkan flank for a thrust into Russia seemed all the more vital, therefore, in the early spring of 1941.

The German War Machine. German campaign plans unfolded with their customary efficiency. The drive into the Balkans was as dramatically successful as the previous campaigns against Poland, Scandinavia, and France had been. A British expeditionary force sent from North Africa to help the Greeks was destroyed; Bulgaria entered the war on the German side, soon to be followed by Rumania; and the Italian troops in North Africa, reinforced with a few German divisions, and placed under the command of General Erwin Rommel, were soon knocking at the gate of Alexandria.

The attack on Russia began well too. Without even bothering to declare war, German troops crossed the Russian frontier on June 21,

1941, taking Stalin completely by surprise. The Nazi forces drove deeper and deeper into the Russian countryside, taking enormous numbers of prisoners as they advanced. Russia's size, however, blunted the *blitzkrieg*. Even with tanks and trucks, supplies gave out after a thrust of fifty to seventy-five miles. A pause for regrouping had to take place before the advance could be resumed. Each mile deeper into Russia required greater effort for mustering fresh supplies and this, in turn, required a longer pause between offensives. The Russians thus had vital breathing space, and after each defeat they were able to re-form a front.

The Germans had not counted on such tenacity. The Nazi advance began to fall seriously behind schedule. Despite repeated victories, the Germans had not broken the Russian will to resist nor seized the vitals of the Soviet state. As summer turned into autumn the German situation became precarious, for Hitler's army was not equipped for winter. Severe weather set in earlier than usual, and this helped the Russians, who were trained to conduct field operations even in the bitter cold of winter. On December 6, 1941, therefore, Hitler reluctantly called the offensive off, only a few miles short of Moscow, and with Leningrad (the former Petrograd) almost completely besieged. His knockout blow had failed. A two-front war of attrition against Britain in the west and against Russia in the east again confronted Germany, as it had confronted the kaiser a generation before.

The Japanese Offensive. On the very next day, December 7, 1941, the Japanese attacked Pearl Harbor in Hawaii and crippled the battleships of the American Pacific Fleet. Simultaneously, other Japanese forces attacked the Philippines, Malaya, and Indonesia. In spite of a formal treaty of alliance which had been concluded between Germany, Italy, and Japan in 1940, Hitler had not been informed of the Japanese war plan ahead of time. Nevertheless, he decided to take the opportunity offered by the Japanese attack on the United States to declare war against the Americans also. He had ample provocation, for President Roosevelt had done everything he could "short of war" to help Britain. It was, nevertheless, a mistake from Hitler's point of view, for it brought down upon him the full might of the United States, whereas, under the conditions created by the Pearl Harbor attack, the Japanese would almost certainly have become the prime target of American wrath if Hitler had not taken the initiative in declaring war. His act was all the more gratuitous since it was not required by any treaty. (Not that Hitler was a great respecter of treaties.) For their part, the Japanese stubbornly declined to reciprocate Hitler's gesture by declaring war against the Russians.

Henceforward, therefore, the alignment of belligerents differed in the two main theaters of war. In the Pacific, Japan opposed the United States, whose allies included China and Britain, Australia and New Zealand, but not Russia; whereas in Europe, the three major powers

WORLD WAR II
Greatest extent of Axis expansion

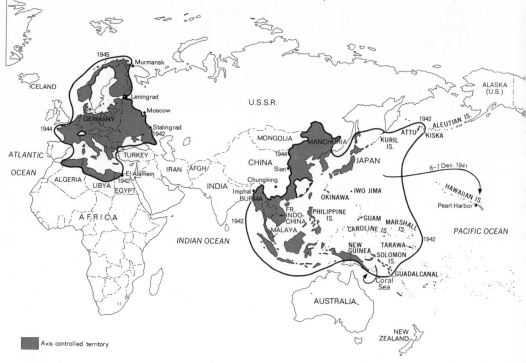

Neutral and unconquered areas surrounded by Axis territory are shown in white. In southeast China, while the Japanese conquered the major ports, they were never able to defeat the Chinese in the area shown in white.

opposing Germany were Britain, the United States, and Russia. Numerous lesser allies clustered on both sides. The Nazis had military help from the governments of Italy, Bulgaria, Rumania, Finland, and (later) Hungary. Indirectly, they drew upon the manpower and economic resources of almost the entire European continent. As for the Japanese, when they had completed their rapid initial conquests, they had Burma, Indonesia, Malaya, the Philippines, most of China, Manchuria, and lesser islands of the Pacific, as well as Korea and their home islands from which to derive the sinews of war. Their opponents, before the war ended, numbered more than forty nations, including most of the republics of Latin America and exile governments from most of the occupied countries of Europe. The United Nations, as this grand coalition was formally christened on January 1, 1942, when the "United Nations Declaration" was promulgated to the world, drew upon the resources of the rest of the earth for its war effort.

Allied Advantages. Given the preponderance of numbers and industrial resources which this global lineup secured for the Allies, it is not surprising that the tide of battle eventually turned in their favor.

82

The further fact that the Americans were in a position to allocate their war production and military manpower at will among the various theaters of war gave the United States the critical and usually decisive role in shaping overall Allied strategy.

The first fundamental success was on the seas. Throughout 1941 and most of 1942 Allied shipping losses exceeded new construction. Shortages of shipping limited every move. American strategic potential could not be deployed unless the supply of shipping increased rapidly. By August 1942, however, mass production in American shipyards began to show results. In that month for the first time more tonnage was launched than was lost. Thereafter each month saw an increase in Allied tonnage, while American submarines began to play havoc with Japanese shipping. As a result, from 1943 onward shipping shortages became as critical a limiting factor for the Japanese as they had been for the Americans in 1942.

As the overseas deployment of men and supplies became assured, the tide of battle turned on one front after another. In the Pacific, the Battle of Midway Island in June 1942 was a defeat for the Japanese navy; in August began a long, desperate fight for possession of Guadalcanal, ending in American victory by February 1943. At the other side of the world, victory at El Alamein started the British Army of Egypt marching westward across the North African desert toward an eventual meeting in Tunisia with an Anglo-American expeditionary force that landed in Morocco and Algeria on November 6, 1942

But the principal theater of war in 1942 was the Russian front. After a dreadful winter, the Germans started to drive eastward again with the return of warm weather. This time their main thrust lay to the south through the Ukraine. Late in the summer they reached the Volga city of Stalingrad. Here the Russians decided to stand fast. Bitter block-by-block fighting proved indecisive; then in November 1942, just two weeks after the Anglo-American armies had landed in North Africa to open a second front of sorts against the Germans, the Russians launched a massive counteroffensive on the flanks of the Nazi spearhead, and quickly cut off the German forces attacking Stalingrad. Attempts to break out of the Russian encirclement having failed, the remnant of the German Sixth Army surrendered in February 1943. German morale and resources never recovered. Initiative on the eastern front passed permanently to the Russians.

The appearance of an American expeditionary force in North Africa in 1942 attested to the fundamental Anglo-American strategic decision of the war: namely, to give priority to the defeat of Germany, and turn major attention to Japan only afterwards. This decision also made it possible to conduct the war on the Allied side as a genuinely joint effort, since American, British, and Russian offensives against Germany could be—and to a considerable degree actually were—made to support one another. Even more important was the effective intermeshing of war economies which arose through the lend-lease administration.

Allied Mobilization. The provisions of the Lend-Lease Act were designed to avoid the recriminations arising after World War I from interallied war debts. Anything actually consumed during the war was to be written off, and equipment remaining at war's end could either be repossessed by the United States or sold at prices to be negotiated at that time. This did in fact reduce postwar frictions, but did nothing to resolve the immediate question of who got what and for what purpose. Only careful integration of strategic plans with the flow of supplies could make rational decisions possible; but when the Americans asked Stalin to tell them his plans and give figures for his home production of key items, the suspicious dictator refused to do so. Perhaps he calculated that the Americans wished to regulate the lend-lease supplies they sent to Russia in such a way as to allow Russians and Germans to bleed one another white, meanwhile keeping back their own troops until the time for decisive action arrived. Confronting such suspicion, the Americans simply decided to give Stalin what he asked for, without trying to fit the Russian requirements into the overall Anglo-American strategic plan. Since delivery to the Soviet Union was long, slow, and difficult, the actual amount of material that could be shipped kept Russian demands upon American productive capacity to relatively modest proportions. In effect, the Russians had to decide what they needed most and could cram into the holds of the few ships available for making deliveries to Russia. This may have mollified Stalin's suspicions, but they were never completely erased.

Planning, of course, was never so exact that changes and adjustments along the way did not have to be made. There were many close squeaks. The great landing in France in June 1944, for example, was almost held up by a shortage of landing craft. But the shortage was discovered in time and emergency efforts were brought to bear so that the right number of landing craft were in fact ready when needed.

The main guidelines for strategic and supply allocations were laid down at a series of conferences between Roosevelt and Churchill, with their respective military chiefs of staff and other advisers in attendance. The first of these took place in August 1941, before the United States became a belligerent, in the harbor of Argentia off Newfoundland. Its principal product was the Atlantic Charter—a formal statement of war aims. Far more fruitful was the second such conference, held in Washington immediately after Pearl Harbor, where the basic principle of "Germany first" was affirmed, and detailed arrangements for the joint administration of the Anglo-American war effort were sketched out. In January 1943, at the North African town of Casablanca, the Allied planners made the decision to invade Sicily after completing the conquest of North Africa. This was later expanded to an invasion of the Italian mainland, which took place in September 1943.

The first conference which Stalin also attended was at Tehran, in November 1943. The key strategic decision here was to invade northern France in the late spring of 1944. This marked the high point of

Allied amity and effective cooperation. Later conferences at Yalta (February 1945) and Potsdam (July 1945) were concerned mainly with political issues, trying to lay down the conditions of a future peace. As Hitler's strength waned, quarrels multiplied, for without a common foe to unite them, the Allies drifted rapidly apart.

The Anglo-American achievement of coordinating their wartime economic and military planning stands out in bold relief when compared with the failure of the Axis nations to achieve anything like the same level of coordination. The Japanese and Germans never concerted strategy; and for geographic reasons their respective war economies had to work separately, save for rare cargoes carried from one side of the world to the other by submarine.

Axis Mobilization. Within the regions dominated by Germany, war mobilization was archaic at first. Until 1942, the Germans planned each campaign meticulously, but acted on the assumption that all, or substantially all, needed supplies would be on hand before military operations began, so that there was no point in trying to link the process of industrial production to the process of waging war. In principle, everything was prepared for ahead of time, on the model of the Prussian war plans of the nineteenth century. A campaign that had to be revised while being fought was a badly planned campaign, and German staff officers saw nothing to admire in such imprecision. As a result, when German troops marched into Russia in 1941, war production in German factories was actually cut back, since everything needed had already—so they assumed—been produced! When victory according to plan eluded the German armies in 1941, it therefore took several months to reorganize the economy for all-out war production. Resulting shortages in German army supplies during 1942 proved critically important, since they limited the Nazi striking force at a time when victory in Russia still seemed possible.

By the latter part of 1942, however, German war production had begun to spurt upwards. In spite of Allied bombing and a long series of military setbacks, war production in Germany continued to increase, and actually reached its peak as late as June 1944. By that time no fewer than 7.1 million foreigners and prisoners of war had been recruited to keep the German factories and farms in full operation. The resources of all the parts of Europe under Nazi control were ruthlessly exploited to fit German war needs. Thus the German war economy had a genuinely transnational base, just as the Allied war effort did. The difference lay in the far readier resort to compulsion which characterized the German system, for many of the foreign laborers were recruited by force.

Nazi doctrine also introduced some remarkable irrationalities. Thus, for example, the female half of the adult population was very imperfectly mobilized because, according to the Nazis, woman's place was in the home and not in factories. This was merely silly, but Hitler's Jewish policy was savage, for he systematically set out to murder the millions of Jews who found themselves within his reach. Individuals and whole communities were hunted down and sent off to special extermination camps where gas chambers killed thousands daily. The whole enterprise was both cold-bloodedly brutal and fanatically stupid, for the Nazis systematically destroyed manpower and squandered skills which, under other circumstances, might have contributed greatly to the German war effort.

The Japanese war economy was less tightly coordinated than the German. Everything depended on shipping, for the distances from Burma to Japan and from Manchukuo to Guadalcanal were enormous. From the beginning Japanese shipping was inadequate to link these far-flung lands together efficiently. As a result, the industrial heart of the East Asia Co-Prosperity Sphere, as the Japanese proudly dubbed their new empire, remained where it had been, in the home islands and Manchuria. Japanese transport and capital could make only occasional use of the manpower and resources of east Asia. As the war years passed an even more critical failure became apparent: the Japanese were not able to keep abreast of the radically new technologies that began to come to the fore toward the end of the war.

In this respect, the Germans acquitted themselves rather well. Their jet airplanes and rockets, both developed during the war, became operational in 1944 and gave England a nasty scare. On the other side, radar and the atom bomb were the two most spectacular technical advances made by the Allies, though it is arguable that the remarkable medical advances of the war—uses for blood plasma, antibiotic drugs, DDT, etc.—will turn out to have more importance for humanity than any of the new weaponry. At any rate it is a fact that in World War II fewer soldiers died of disease than from enemy action, whereas in all previous wars the ratio ran the other way.

The most remarkable innovation of all was the definitive demonstration of the practicability of planned and deliberate invention. Time and time again it was discovered that if highly trained people were set to work to solve a definite technical problem, they could do so. Performance characteristics of tanks and airplanes were revolutionized as a result; so were many other weapons. Manufacturing processes were simplified and speeded up. Vast savings in material and labor were introduced. In small things and in great there arose an apparently endless stream of significant technical improvements. Indeed, industrial technology as a whole began to appear to be a vast process, subject to indefinite alteration as human desire and intelligence might choose to shape and reshape it. Things impossible today might become possible tomorrow—and, in an amazingly large number of cases, did become possible when suitably skilled task forces were set to work to make them so.

World War I faintly foreshadowed the achievements of World War II in these respects. But between the wars the organization and financing needed to assemble and maintain high-powered research and development teams had been withdrawn or severely restricted because the captains of industry and military staff officers had not fully learned the lesson of World War I. Or perhaps it would be fairer to say that the comparatively astronomical costs involved and the uncertainty of achieving any worthwhile result deterred nations from pursuing planned invention between the wars. The numerous successes that came during World War II made those years a sort of critical takeoff period—or so it seems from more than a quarter of a century's perspective. Certainly since the war there has been no surcease from planned and deliberate technical invention, accelerated as never before by national rivalries. This situation, if long continued, will bring enormous changes to everyday human experience—so much so that the normalization of deliberate invention may turn out to be the most significant single achievement of World War II.

The Allied Advance. At the time, of course, such long-range by-products of the secret, sometimes desperate struggles of scientists and engineers to solve particular problems were scarcely realized. To anticipate the enemy in some critical breakthrough was important; to equip and supply the next campaign was also important; and the general goal of winning the war seemed to nearly everyone to be a self-evident and adequate goal toward which to strive.

After the great turning points in the fall of 1942, Allied advance toward the vitals of the German empire never faltered. In 1943 North Africa was conquered, Italy was invaded, and, just as the Allied troops landed, the Italian government withdrew from the war. On the eastern front the Russians recovered most of their lost territory during 1943, but were unable to deliver a knockout blow. In 1944 France was liberated by American and British forces, and the Russians crossed their prewar border into Poland, East Prussia, and the Balkans. Next spring the Russians drove onward toward Berlin and Vienna, while the American and British armies crossed the Rhine and met the Russian vanguard at the Elbe.

As Germany's utter collapse loomed closer and closer, awkward problems of postwar settlement could not be postponed. At Casablanca President Roosevelt had proclaimed "unconditional surrender" as the only terms the Allies would accord their foes. He was anxious to avoid any repetition of 1918, when Germans accused the Allies of having failed to lived up to Wilson's Fourteen Points. But in practice "unconditional surrender" was a meaningless phrase. The end of a war in which millions of people have been engaged must always involve commands and conditions, directing the defeated forces as to what to do, and instructing the victors in how to treat the defeated nation. Nevertheless, the Allies did not come to terms with Hitler. When defeat stared him in the face, he committed suicide. The victors received the surrender of the defeated German forces a few days later, on May 8, 1945. The war in Europe was at an end. Germany's cities had become smoking piles of rubble, occupied by millions of frightened, hungry people who were almost as ravaged as the buildings in which they once had lived and worked.

ALBERT SPEER AND JEAN MONNET

Speer: AFP-Pictorial Parade

Even enemies sometimes serve the same cause. This can be seen in the lives of the German Albert Speer (1905–   ) and of the Frenchman Jean Monnet (1888–   ).

Monnet came from a wealthy business family. He had a quick mind and the right connections, so while still in his twenties he represented France on the World War I Maritime Commission. This body controlled the shipping needed to supply the western front. The problem was technical: calculation of priorities, productive capacities, manpower, and other factors of production could increase the flow of war supplies enormously. Monnet saw more clearly than others what could be done if national jealousies and "business as usual" were put aside.

After the war he played a variety of roles as an idea man and negotiator. He was deputy to the general secretary of the League of Nations, 1919–1923. Later he advised China on railroad finance, Austria on bank regulation, and American bankers on investment overseas. Obviously, Monnet was a businessman and financier, not a revolutionary. Yet he became Europe's most successful revolutionary during and after World War II.

His first personal impact on the course of World War II came when he persuaded American officials, while the United States was still at peace, to calculate what America would have to produce to defeat Germany and Japan. The resulting "Victory Program" was just ready by December 1941, when Japan's attack on Pearl Harbor brought the United States into the war. This program, constantly revised to fit changing strategic plans, guided actual American war production until 1945.

Later, Monnet took charge of planning France's postwar economic recovery. The result was extraordinary. After 1945 France became one of the most dynamic countries in the world in technical and economic matters. Monnet's greatest revolutionary impact, however, came through his role as advocate, organizer, and manager of the Iron and

Coal Community, which prepared the way for the Common Market. Between them, these organizations revolutionized European economic and political life.

Albert Speer's profession and goals were completely different from those Monnet pursued. Starting out as an architect, Speer joined the Nazi party in 1931. He soon came to Hitler's attention and was given the job of building a series of vast structures meant to symbolize the greatness of the Third Reich. Hitler was always in a hurry, and Speer won his confidence by the efficiency with which he organized manpower and supplies to erect enormous buildings.

This was the experience Speer had behind him when Hitler put him in charge of armaments production in 1942. German manpower was insufficient to supply the Nazi war machine, so Speer turned to the conquered peoples of Europe. Some workers came voluntarily, but many were recruited as slave laborers. Despite Allied bombing, Speer was able to repair damages and even increase production of war materiel until June 1944. He did so by treating all of Europe as a single economic unit, ruthlessly subordinating all competing interests to the German war effort. In 1945 Allied judges found Speer guilty of crimes against humanity and sentenced him to twenty years in prison. He was released in 1966.

The irony of Speer's achievement was that, although he believed in race purity, he flooded Germany with foreigners—Slavs, Greeks, Frenchmen, and others. Mobilization on a continental scale inevitably meant massive intermingling of peoples and the dwarfing of the German nation.

Nevertheless, it is clear that Monnet's success in forwarding European economic integration after World War II built directly upon Speer's no less successful management of Europe's wartime economy. Their methods differed: Speer used force lavishly, while Monnet relied on persuasion and the price system. But both worked in the same direction—a direction defined less by personal preference or ideals than by the dictates of technical efficiency.

Monnet: Paris Match-Pictorial Parade

The Battle in the Pacific. For geographical and political reasons, the war against Japan divided into widely separated theaters. In China proper a long, desultory, and indecisive battle sapped Japanese strength. In Burma, Indian and British troops slogged through jungle and rice paddies and eventually (1945) reconquered Rangoon. In the southwest Pacific, American troops, initially aided by Australians, hopped from island to island, beginning in New Guinea and Guadalcanal and ending with the invasion of the Philippines in October 1944. The U.S. Navy simultaneously mounted an attack across the central Pacific, beginning with the capture of Tarawa in November 1943 and culminating in the seizure of Okinawa, after a bitter struggle, in April-June 1945.

By August 1945, even the most hardened Japanese militarist had to admit that heavy bombing raids, launched now from nearby Okinawa, and an ever tightening naval and submarine blockade, which had already destroyed most Japanese shipping, made further fighting entirely hopeless. Yet unconditional surrender, the only terms Japan's enemies offered, remained unacceptable until after two crowning blows descended upon Japan during the first half of August 1945. First, the Americans dropped an atomic bomb on Hiroshima (August 6) which destroyed the center of the city and snuffed out scores of thousands of lives in a twinkling. When this produced no immediate response the United States delivered a second and still more powerful atomic attack against Nagasaki three days later. The Japanese government was still reeling from the first of these demonstrations of American power and ruthlessness when the Russians declared war and started to march into Manchuria on August 8. Clearly, capitulation could not be put off any longer, but negotiations took time, so that a formal armistice did not take effect until August 15, and the final ceremonial surrender occurred only on September 2, 1945, six years and one day from the time when Hitler's armies had started World War II by crossing the Polish frontier.

As the war years drew to their close, shortages and suffering were everywhere severe, yet intelligent and farseeing individuals had already spent a good deal of thought on postwar reconstruction. Because of this, the shift from war to peace actually went very much more smoothly than in 1918–1919.

THE PEACE

The United Nations. President Roosevelt and his advisors set great store by correcting Wilson's World War I errors. Chief among these, Roosevelt believed, was Wilson's failure to carry popular sentiment with him in support of the League of Nations. Roosevelt therefore decided that the thing to do was to establish a new international body, the United Nations Organization, while the war was still going on and

90

before any sort of postwar reaction could assert itself. Stalin reluctantly agreed at Yalta (February 1945). Accordingly, a full-dress international conference, attended by representatives of fifty nations, met in San Francisco from April to June of that year to establish the rules for the new international body. Roosevelt himself died soon after the San Francisco Conference had assembled, but his spirit dominated the proceedings, and the agreements that emerged bore the mark of American idealism and aspiration for a peaceable, lawful world.

The structure of the United Nations that emerged from the San Francisco Conference resembled the defunct League of Nations in many respects. A veto power was accorded to each of the permanent members of the Security Council, i.e., to each of the great powers. Lesser powers found their voice through the General Assembly, where each member nation had a single vote. Specialized functions were handed over to other assemblies, and an international secretariat, owing allegiance to the United Nations rather than to any single state, was created to administer all the affairs entrusted to the various new international organizations. Headquarters were located in New York.

By subscribing to the United Nations, Russia as well as the United States repudiated its prewar policies of isolation and autarchy. The world had become too small for such an alternative to seem safe any longer. The only conspicuous discrepancies between legal relationships as defined in the United Nations Charter and the facts of political power were that the defeated enemy nations were excluded, and China, though still seriously distracted by civil broils, was accorded the dignity of ranking as one of the four great powers of the world. This was a far more auspicious start than the League of Nations had enjoyed, and in fact the United Nations handled some prickly issues during the first postwar years with considerable success.

While the United Nations was struggling to birth, Allied relations degenerated. The British and Americans disliked what the Russians were doing in eastern Europe, particularly in Poland, where the effort to impose a government "friendly" to Russia required open and flagrant violation of the Polish popular will. The Russians, for their part, were anxious both to secure themselves against any future attack and to plunder the regions they had occupied in order to help relieve the desperate shortages at home.

The new American President, Harry S. Truman, allowed most of the wartime economic controls to lapse, and demobilized the armed forces very rapidly. Yet the retreat towards "normalcy" never got very far. Lend-lease was indeed halted suddenly with war's end, but some of the most vital lend-lease functions were transferred to UNRRA (United Nations Relief and Rehabilitation Administration). American goods, purchased and distributed by UNRRA, continued to flow into most of the war-ravaged Allied countries after lend-lease came to an Moreover, generous settlements were negotiated with most of the recipient nations. The Russians, however, refused even to account for the very large deliveries they had begun to receive near the end of the war.

ROOSEVELT AND DE GAULLE

FDR: UPI-Compix

Franklin Delano Roosevelt (1885–1945), four times elected President of the United States, and Charles André Marie de Gaulle (1890–1970), twice elected president of France, did not like each other. During World War II FDR once said that De Gaulle thought he was Joan of Arc, and De Gaulle often made clear his distaste for American interference in French affairs.

Franklin Roosevelt was born to wealth and social distinction. His early career paralleled that of his distant cousin, President Theodore Roosevelt, with the difference that Franklin was a Democrat. During World War II he served as assistant secretary of the Navy. He was later elected governor of New York and then, in 1933, he became President at a time when the Great Depression had almost paralyzed America.

Roosevelt promptly proclaimed a New Deal, trying to relieve economic problems by energetic government action. War mobilization during World War I offered the only model for massive official intervention in what had previously been private business and finance. Later, when World War II overtook the United States during Roosevelt's third term, governmental control of the economy was reinforced by the renewed need for war mobilization.

But FDR never relied on military methods of command to accomplish his purposes. He believed that enduring results could only be attained by first persuading Congress and the public. He used the radio and press conferences to put his case before the American people; but when his proposals failed to meet with positive response, he often hesitated and drew back. On the other hand, because FDR did win public support for key policies of the New Deal, they soon became irreversible. As a result, he was elected President four times in a row and died in office, honored around the world as a champion of democracy and of the common man.

Charles de Gaulle, son of a professor of philosophy, chose to become an army officer. In World War I he served under Marshal Pétain at the Battle of Verdun, but he was captured and spent the rest of the war in prison. In the 1930s he wrote a book advocating tank warfare, and criticizing the French for fortifying the frontier. Then, in 1940, when his friend and former commander, Pétain, presided over the French surrender to Hitler, De Gaulle flew to London and organized the Free French movement. Thereafter he did all he could to assert the dignity of France against both British and American slights. In 1945 he returned in triumph to Paris as head of a provisional government. Two years later he resigned when he found that he lacked support for measures he judged necessary. He tried to build up a political party to return himself to power, but this proved unsuccessful, so in 1953 he retired to write his memoirs.

Five years later civil war threatened to break out in France. De Gaulle returned to office with extraordinary powers to reorder the constitution. After a plebiscite had ratified a new constitution, he was elected president of the Fifth French Republic and used the powers of his office to disengage France from war in Algeria and from dependence on the United States. He was reelected to a second term in 1965. Yet when he failed to win a plebiscite on a change in the constitution, De Gaulle again resigned and retired to write another installment of his memoirs. A few months later he died, having saved France not only from the Germans and the Americans, but from his fellow Frenchmen as well.

Yet, however much De Gaulle sometimes found himself out of sympathy with other Frenchmen, he never tried to solve political differences by force. Like Roosevelt, he held that politics ought to be conducted by persuasion and compromise. Only so, they both believed, could crises be resolved without sacrificing the strength that active popular support can give to governmental policies.

De Gaulle: Culver Pictures

In 1945 everyone assumed that American troops would return home within a few months, as soon as peace treaties had been arranged. But the effort to close the books on the war by concluding treaties of peace with the defeated nations proved unexpectedly difficult. At Potsdam, in July 1945, while the war with Japan was still in progress, President Truman, Premier Stalin, and the new prime minister of Great Britain, Clement Attlee, agreed to divide Germany into zones of occupation, but declared that they would concert policy for the country as a whole through an Allied Control Council, located in Berlin, in which each occupying power would be represented. They also explored peacemaking procedures. The task of working out the specifics was then assigned to the foreign ministers of the three great powers, who met repeatedly between September 1945 and December 1946 trying to reach agreement.

Allied Discord. Early in the game it was decided to concentrate first on the lesser enemy powers: Italy, Rumania, Bulgaria, Finland, and Hungary. Quarrels arising over Russian policy in Poland, and above all over how to handle Germany, quickly envenomed relations. Painfully drawn out haggling over the treaty texts reflected these irritations. Eventually, however, treaties were drawn up, submitted to a conference at Paris (July-October 1946) at which the lesser Allies were represented, modified slightly in response to their suggestions, and then signed on February 10, 1947.

In the short run this looked like a victory for the Russians, for the British and Americans in effect acknowledged the legitimacy of Communist power in eastern Europe. Yet in the longer run, Stalin's ruthless bargaining was shortsighted. Prolonged and petty haggling over the peace treaties roused the apprehension and hostility of the American public, dramatized the high-handed ways in which the Russians sought to protect themselves in the lands under Red Army occupation, and made painfully clear to all the world the existence of an "Iron Curtain" extending across Europe, behind which liberty and justice, as understood in the West, were cruelly and systematically denied.

In Germany, China, and Japan, the rising climate of suspicion thus created meant that initial agreements among the Allies soon broke down. As far as Europe was concerned, the critical point came in May 1946, when the American commander of the U.S. Zone of Occupation in Germany decided to stop all further reparations deliveries to the Russians until they submitted a detailed accounting of what they had taken from their own zone. This the Russians refused to do. As a result, efforts to concert Allied policy for Germany as a whole were given up, and each zone went its own way.

The situation in the Far East also provided ground for quarrels. The Americans occupied Japan with only nominal representation of the other Allied powers. The Russians did not try very hard to gain a foothold in Japan, but on the Chinese mainland the situation was much more precarious. At the Yalta Conference, in return for Stalin's promise to enter the war against Japan, President Roosevelt endorsed Russian demands for joint control over the Manchurian railroads and for special rights at Dairen and Port Arthur. In return, Stalin undertook to support Chiang Kai-shek's government, thereby tacitly abandoning the Chinese Communists to Chiang's not very tender mercies.

When informed of this deal, Chiang was very loath to agree. What Stalin demanded amounted to restoration of the rights Imperial Russia had enjoyed before the Russo-Japanese war of 1904; but the Chinese hoped to throw off rather than to reimpose foreign shackles. Nevertheless, after long haggling Chiang yielded, and signed a Sino-Soviet Treaty of Friendship and Alliance, which confirmed the Yalta arrangements, on August 14, 1945, just a few days after Russian troops had begun to march into Manchuria.

Americans thought it vital for Chiang Kai-shek to come to terms with Stalin, for if the Russians should back the Chinese Communists while the Americans backed Chiang and the Kuomintang, major disaster for China and perhaps for the world would clearly ensue. With the treaty of August 14 in hand, however, it looked as though Stalin would refrain from helping the Chinese Communists. Corresponding-ly, the Americans intended to refrain from helping the Kuomintang. Wise policy seemed to call for conciliation, so that the two Chinese parties might be persuaded to compromise their quarrel and set up a coalition government.

A fatal flaw soon ruined this well-intentioned policy. The Chinese Communists and the Kuomintang were not ready to listen to counsels of moderation at a time when each side saw the possiblity of seizing power from the Japanese. Moreover, wartime treaties tied the United States to Chiang's government, and in the moment of victory it seemed wrong to leave Japanese garrisons in charge of most of China until such time as the Kuomintang and the Communists agreed to cooper-ate. Hence the Americans decided to help Chiang's troops reoccupy the cities of China that had been under Japanese control, while at the same time urging compromise and cooperation with the Communists. But as Chiang's troops advanced, equipped with American weapons and aided by American air transport, the practical pressure for compromise with the Communists decreased day by day. After all, why should Chiang give up his twenty-year-long struggle against the Communists when American military supplies seemed sure to bring total victory within sight?

Not surprisingly, negotiations languished. Chiang Kai-shek and his foes thoroughly distrusted one another. Neither side believed in the sovereign remedy of free elections and administrative legality upon which American advisers tended to rely. As a result, negotiations broke off fruitlessly by the middle of 1946. Civil war flared anew. With extensive American military supplies still at their disposal, Chiang Kai-shek's troops at first enjoyed the upper hand. By the end of 1946 they had in fact occupied all the important cities of China and had everywhere driven the Communists back into the countryside.

Russian policy remained noncommittal. Stalin probably expected the United States to install an obedient puppet regime in China as he himself was doing in the countries of eastern Europe, and felt there was no use in backing the Chinese Communists, since he was not prepared to risk a military clash with the United States. At any rate, the Chinese Communists got no direct help from Stalin. The Russians did, however, permit large quantities of Japanese arms to fall into Chinese Communist hands. They did so by evacuating Manchuria (April 1946)—actually in response to a request from Chiang Kai-shek's government—more rapidly than the Chinese troops could advance, thus leaving Japanese arsenals open to the first comers, who in every case proved to be Communist forces that had been permitted to infiltrate the Manchurian countryside while the Russians still held the towns.

The Breakup of the Grand Alliance. Incipient civil war in China ruffled Russo-American relations. The struggle over Germany, which by the end of 1946 had led Russians and Americans to bid against each other for the sympathy and support of the German public, was an even more important irritant. Yet it took a while for the "Cold War" to emerge as the dominant political reality of the postwar world. Many Americans clung to the hope that somehow cooperation with the Russians could be achieved. Others were reluctant to accept the idea that Americans should use their money and manpower to garrison Europe and other parts of the earth indefinitely. The Russians, too, were desperately war-weary, and in no condition to undertake any new struggle against their erstwhile allies. The war had wrought massive destruction in Russia; some twenty million people had died as a direct result of the German attack, and severe shortages hindered everyday life.

Stalin's overriding preoccupation appears to have been the military security of the Soviet Union—or what he conceived that security to be. He must have decided to give highest priority to the construction of atomic weapons. Among other measures calculated to achieve this end, he set the Soviet spy system the task of trying to discover how the Americans had made the bombs they dropped over Japan in 1945. Stalin also wanted "friendly" governments in all of eastern Europe and would have liked to create a similar protective glacis southward in Iran, Turkey, Sinkiang, Outer Mongolia, and Manchuria as well. When Russian forward moves into Iran, Turkey, and Sinkiang aroused emphatic diplomatic protests, Stalin withdrew without much argument; and, as we have seen, he also pulled Russian troops out of Manchuria in April 1946 when asked to do so. But in eastern Europe he held fast. This was the avenue along which German assault had come, and along which any future attack from the West would come. Friendly governments in Poland, Czechoslovakia, Hungary, Rumania, and Bulgaria seemed vital. Such a band of states would buffer any future attack a revived Germany might someday attempt, and make forever impossible the sort of surprise that had nearly toppled Stalin from power in June 1941.

Stalin perhaps thought that by allowing the Americans to do what they wished in China and Japan, and by giving the British a similarly free hand in Greece and in western Europe, he was according his allies the sort of respect and freedom he wanted for himself within the Russian sphere of influence. If so, American references to free elections and democratic self-determination in eastern Europe, and their efforts to liberalize trade relations over the entire earth, must have seemed to Stalin like unwarranted pinpricks. He reciprocated such unfriendly gestures by allowing the Greek and Yugoslav Communists to resume guerrilla war in Greece, directed this time against a government backed by British rather than German arms. Communist parties in western Europe likewise became more intransigent in domestic politics in proportion to the cooling of relations between Russia and the Anglo-Americans.

The breakup of the Grand Alliance of World War II was therefore not the work of any one person or nation. The hopes and fears of the great powers were so much at odds that effective communication between them simply broke down. Russians could not believe that Americans meant what they said; Americans could not understand why their good intentions were not self-evident, whether in China, Germany, eastern Europe, or the United Nations. By the end of 1946 each side could—and did—feel that its own good faith had been betrayed by the other's cynical double-dealing. Americans saw how Stalin had made mockery of free elections and democracy in eastern Europe. Stalin saw how the Anglo-Americans kept meddling in the affairs of his part of the world despite the fact that he had scrupulously left them to their own devices in the parts of the globe assigned to them by the fortunes of war and treaty arrangements.

The End of Imperialism. This rapid transformation of relations among the three great powers of the postwar world was certainly the dominating political phenomenon of the time. But the disintegration of European empires in Asia and Africa was of almost equal importance, and promises to be a good deal more permanent.

War operations destroyed the Italian empire in Africa. Emergency military administrations replaced the Italian regimes on an interim basis, except in Ethiopia, where with British help Emperor Haile Selassie, the victim of Mussolini's attack in 1935–1936, returned to his throne in May 1941. In Somaliland, Eritrea, and Libya, the victors had no particular desire to institute a new colonial regime. Both the United States and the Soviet Union opposed "imperialism," though each meant different things by the term; and even the British had begun to find that the burdens of empire outweighed any benefits it might bring. The solution was to turn the former Italian colonies into United

Nations trusteeships, an arrangement that substantially duplicated the League of Nations mandates of the interwar period.

The French empire also suffered erosion during the war years. The necessity of choice between obedience to the Pétain government in France and the upstart authority of Charles de Gaulle, the self styled leader of the "Free French," confronted colonial administrators with awkward decisions. At first almost all the French colonies recognized Pétain, but by 1943 De Gaulle headed a provisional government that effectively controlled all of French Africa. In Syria, a brief but sharp military campaign in 1941 dislodged the Pétainist administration. The Australian troops who carried the brunt of this campaign did not withdraw until De Gaulle, much against his will, agreed to promise Syrian and Lebanese independence. These two states achieved their new status in 1944, though French troops did not leave until 1946.

The situation of French Indochina was especially complicated. By agreement with Pétain's government the Japanese moved troops into Indochina early in 1941, and the Pétainist governor remained in office until March of 1945. But despite the continuity of French administration in Indochina, the French position in Indochina was irretrievably undermined during the war. Imperial Japanese propaganda, intended to rouse Asians against Europeans, and an underground Communist-directed resistance movement led by Ho Chi Minh agreed on only one thing: the French must go.

The British, Dutch, and American empires in southeast Asia also suffered what proved to be irreparable damage as a result of the Japanese victories of 1941–1942. The American capitulation at Bataan and the British capitulation at Singapore punctured the myth of the white man's invincibility, and the Japanese sought systematically to parade this fact among the "liberated" peoples of southeast Asia by publicly humiliating prisoners of war.

There were differences of opinion within the Japanese government as to what sorts of regimes should be set up in conquered regions, and policy shifted as the fortunes of war altered. To begin with, interim military governments supplanted the ousted colonial administrations everywhere. In the Philippines and in Burma, however, local national-ists were ready from the beginning to cooperate with the Japanese, and in 1943 each of these countries was officially declared independent. These moves did not, of course, lead to the evacuation of Japanese troops. On the contrary, the new independent governments of Burma and the Philippines remained Japanese puppets.

In Indonesia and Malaya Japanese policy fluctuated. At first the conquerors planned to annex these lands to the Japanese empire; later, Indonesian nationalists were encouraged to prepare for independence by organizing and arming themselves. Japanese plans for announcing the independence of Indonesia were checked only by the imperial rescript of August 15, 1945, accepting Allied terms of surrender. But an Indonesian nationalist and revolutionary, Sukarno, whom the Japanese had recognized as head of an Independence Preparatory

Committee, went ahead (with tacit Japanese backing) and declared Indonesian independence on August 17, 1945, anyway. Three weeks later, when British troops arrived in Indonesia as representatives of the Allied southeast Asia command, they intended only to accept the surrender of Japanese troops and supervise their repatriation. In fact, however, they soon found themselves fighting against Sukarno and his makeshift Indonesian forces. By the time the Dutch were able to arrive in force, Indonesian nationalists were too well organized and too well armed with Japanese weapons to yield. Nevertheless, it took nearly three years, until 1949, to convince the Dutch that it would be too costly to reconquer their lost empire of the East Indies.

Much the same situation met the British in Burma, where a remarkable number of rival revolutionary and nationalist parties disputed power. Unlike the Dutch, the British made little attempt to enforce public order in their former colony. They had decided to grant Burma independence and declined to get involved in the political struggle. A very shaky regime therefore took over between 1946 and 1948, beset by revolt and rebellion from every side, but indisputably and undeniably free from British tutelage.

In Malaya, on the other hand, the British reestablished a colonial regime. They did so with the acquiescence of the Malay portion of the population, which feared the enterprise of Chinese immigrants who dominated the economic life of the country. The Chinese, however, were not pleased, and hotheads among them took to the jungle and organized guerrilla units. Not till 1955 did their venture end in failure.

The postwar political experience of the Philippines resembled that of both Burma and Malaya. The Filipinos, like the Burmese, achieved political independence rapidly and without having to overcome any resistance from the ex-colonial power—in this case the United States. An exile government fled from the Philippines in 1941 with General Douglas MacArthur; its shadow returned. But the substance of power soon devolved upon men who had remained in the islands during the Japanese occupation, and who had in some degree or other collaborated with the Japanese. Nevertheless, the American government never deviated from the plan, announced before the war, of establishing Philippine independence in 1946. But the new government, like that in Malaya, had to face a Communist-colored guerrilla movement almost at once. Only after prolonged effort and some strenuous agrarian reform did armed revolt die out.

In general, both the American and Russian governments welcomed Asian independence during the immediate postwar years. The two powers looked with suspicion on any recrudescence of imperialist policies among the west European nations. Except in China, Russian patronage of Communist and American preference for nationalist rebels did not make much practical difference. Communism and nationalism regularly mingled and merged in the Asian context where the local peoples usually saw no discrepancy between the two ideals.

British policy was mixed. In addition to restoring something like prewar conditions to Malaya, the British repossessed the trading city of Hong Kong, despite American (and Chinese) disapproval. But in the far more important question of India, the British government made no attempt to preserve or prolong their political control. On the contrary, London hurried the pace toward Indian independence.

India: The Question of Partition. The war years had brought new complications to India. The British had raised a vast army of over two million Indians. Yet the overwhelming proportion of the soldiers and officers of the Indian army sympathized with the demand for independence which the Congress Party had voiced at the beginning of the war. In 1942, British authorities had jailed Mohandas Gandhi, Jawaharlal Nehru, and many thousands of other political activists when, having rejected an offer of dominion status, they advocated passive resistance in the face of the Japanese advance toward India. Soon after this crisis, the Japanese advance came to a halt. Most Indians saw real advantages in cooperating with the British to build up a large Indian army. Outward political calm therefore set in that lasted until the end of the war.

Nevertheless, one very important change did take place: the Muslim League, under the leadership of Mohammed Ali Jinnah, gathered strength as more and more Indian Moslems became politically convinced of their separate identity from the Hindu majority. Consequently, when bargaining over the postwar status of India resumed, the Congress Party with its demand for an independent India faced the Muslim League demanding an independent Pakistan with the same unbending intransigence which the Congress had long exhibited in its dealings with the British. Agreement proved difficult. Only after the British government announced its intention of withdrawing from India within a fixed time limit did the rival Indian parties reluctantly agree to partition. The innumerable difficulties of partition were swept hastily toward settlement when the British advanced the date of their withdrawal by eight months, creating an almost panic pressure for speedy, irrevocable decisions. In August 1947 these birth pangs duly and on schedule produced two new, independent states: India, and a Pakistan divided into two territorially separated parts by the intervening bulk of northern India.

Relations between the two new governments were far from cordial. Brutal riots broke out between Moslems and Hindus in regions where the two religious communities lived side by side. Thousands died and hundreds of thousands fled for refuge across the new frontier lines. Gandhi, the patron saint of Indian independence, lost his life to an assassin's bullet in 1948 when he tried to stop riots between Hindus and Moslems. His dramatic death checked Hindu violence in India, whereupon the riots subsided almost as suddenly as they had arisen.

A second and more enduring irritant to relations between India and

Pakistan was a by-product of the overthrow of the princely governments which had survived in many parts of India under British protection as a sort of decorative archaism. Most of the princes were Moslems, and Pakistan tended therefore to sympathize with them. In Kashmir, however, the situation was reversed. There a Hindu ruler presided over a Moslem population. When Pakistani troops tried to annex his principality, the prince appealed to India for help. The Indian army went to his rescue, with the result that Kashmir came to be divided between the two rival states along a line defined by the place where their respective troops happened to collide. Neither would yield its claim to the whole province. As a result, Kashmir has remained a bone of contention ever since.

Dismantling the British Empire. Indian independence implied the independence of Ceylon. Arrangements proceeded fairly smoothly since, despite serious divisions between rival ethnic groups, the British were resolved to withdraw. Ceylon's formal independence came in 1948.

The various British colonial possessions in Africa remained for the time intact, since the war had brought no particular political disruption to those lands. All the same, enhanced prosperity, arising from brisk and expanded demand for African products during the war years, allowed commercial farming and mining to penetrate the fabric of African life more thoroughly than had been the case before the war. As a result, new relationships and new horizons created a political audience for the bright young men who had acquired a Western-style education between the wars. Aspirations for independence and national dignity began to resonate among large enough segments of the population to make nationalist and revolutionary movements a factor to be reckoned with. French and Belgian colonies in sub-Saharan Africa experienced a similar quickening of political life. Far to the south, the Union of South Africa felt the same surge. Fearing it, the white inhabitants rallied behind Dutch-Afrikaner nationalists, whom an election in 1948 brought to power. The new government set out to assure white rule by disfranchising black voters.

The victory of Afrikaners in the 1948 elections in South Africa also signified the political retreat of the English element in the white population of that dominion. Henceforward, neither sentiment nor personal connections with England played any important role in South African affairs. The other dominions, Canada, Australia, and New Zealand, also weakened their ties with Britain in the postwar years, despite (or perhaps in part because of) the fact that each of them had declared war promptly in 1939 and had sent troops to fight under British command.

Reaction was strongest in Australia, where the Japanese victories of 1942 demonstrated both how weak the Australians were when thrown back on their own resources, and how unable Great Britain had become to maintain the sea guard upon which Australia's security traditionally depended. The United States soon came to the rescue. In 1942 General MacArthur established his headquarters on Australian soil, and the United States Navy presently filled the vacuum created by the withdrawal of British naval units from the Pacific. But this merely underlined the fact that British protection was gone.

Just a few months before the Japanese attack dramatized this revolution in military and international relations, the Australian domestic scene underwent a corresponding, though less catastrophic, change. The Labour party came to power, bringing to office Irish and other elements in Australian society which were vigorously critical of Britain. During the rest of the war, therefore, the Australian government was eager rather to accentuate than to diminish the distance between their nation and Britain. Instead of providing men to fight far from home, as during World War I, the Australians concentrated, once the crisis of checking Japan's expansion had been surmounted, on producing supplies for the (mainly) American forces operating in the southwest Pacific. A rapid industrial expansion was one result; decay of the Australian share in military operations was another.

Unlike Australia, New Zealand did not become an American headquarters and base; and, being farther away, it feared the Japanese less than the Australians did. New Zealanders remained correspondingly more attached to Great Britain, especially since Britain continued to constitute the principal market for New Zealand's wool and butter.

Canada's experience of World War II underlined the sense of separate nationhood which had been growing among English-speaking Canadians ever since the Statute of Westminster (1931) had accorded to Canada and the other British dominions the legal substance of sovereignty. Canadian troops, stationed in Britain for long months before the invasion of France in 1944, had ample time to discover how different British ways were from their own; and the fact that Canadian factories (as well as farms) poured out a flood of war supplies for British (as well as Canadian) use altered the traditional economic relationship between the dominion and Britain in a fundamental fashion. Like the United States after World War I, Canada emerged from the war as a creditor nation, exporting industrial as well as agricultural commodities.

The result, therefore, of World War II was to weaken economic, military, and psychological ties that had previously linked the principal British dominions with the mother country. In some respects the United States moved into the place Britain vacated. In the immediate postwar period both Australia and Canada sheltered behind American air defenses as once they had sheltered behind the British navy. Culturally, economically, and psychologically, too, the United States tended to supplant Great Britain, although the British dominions often preferred to try to counteract or escape rather than to submit to American influence in these fields of activity.

Palestine-Israel: Birth of a Nation. Palestine was another place where British imperial power came to an end immediately after the war. In the 1930s armed struggles had already broken out between Arabs, who had inhabited Palestine for centuries, and immigrant Jews, who were attempting to build a new nation in a land their ancestors had left in ancient times. The British were unable and unwilling to repress renewal of this struggle after the war. Hitler's policy towards Europe's Jews during World War II enormously intensified the Zionist drive in 1945 and 1946, for the horrors of the Nazi extermination camps had uprooted all the Jews of Europe. Palestine looked far more attractive to the survivors than return to a life that no longer existed. Zionist organizations moved energetically into this situation and arranged, both legally and extralegally, for thousands of Jews to come to Palestine. Simultaneously, an underground army gathered equipment and organized the entire manpower of the Jewish community in Palestine for the task of seizing power and proclaiming a new sovereign Jewish state as soon as conditions seemed ripe.

British administrators made some effort to adjudicate the quarrel between Jews and Arabs, but it soon became clear that remonstrance and conciliation were useless. Mainly through American initiative the case came before the United Nations, which recommended partitioning Palestine into two nations. Despite an Arab boycott, this solution achieved formal ratification in November 1946. When the British withdrew a few months later, war instantly flared between the two communities. By the time United Nations agents were able to arrange a truce, several hundred thousand Arabs had fled from their ancestral lands, and the new state of Israel faced a hostile ring of Arab neighbors across an exposed and lengthy frontier. Jewish pride in their accomplishment and their demonstrated efficiency in peace and in war only offended Arab sensibilities the more.

No Arab state or ruler was able to wipe out the injury they felt at Israel's birth. A great outburst of anti-Jewish agitation spread throughout the Arab world and broke up Jewish communities in Morocco, Yemen, and similarly remote places. Large numbers of these "oriental" Jews fled to Israel, whose agents stood ready to assist all co-religionists in entering the new Zion.

America Reacts to the New Order. Zionist sympathies were very strong among the Jewish communities of the United States, and the Palestinian policy of the American government reflected this partiality. The way in which the Palestine question was handled through quasi-parliamentary procedures in the United Nations also conformed to the official American view of how international issues should be disposed of. In its early sessions the United Nations discussed other controversies: the Dutch role in Indonesia, the Russian role in Azerbaijan, the British role in Greece, and the American role in China. Despite indignation at finding the activities of American troops in China criticized as imperialistic, all this accorded well with the official expectations of the American government, and gave no cause for reconsideration of the policy of rapid and radical demobilization which had been assumed—rather than decided—to be the natural, proper, and inevitable consequence of the end of the war.

Actually, American demobilization went rather well. As was to be expected, rapid withdrawal of controls and rationing increased prices. But consumer goods surged into the market within a few months, and the demobilized soldiers found plenty of jobs waiting for them on their return. Important residues of the wartime experience of a controlled economy remained. Government guarantees of full employment were written into the statute books in 1946, and the awesome power of atomic energy stayed under governmental jurisdiction. American troops also remained in Germany and Japan, pending the conclusion of peace treaties with these nations.

Despite these and similar exceptions, in general—and certainly in intent—the United States tried to get back to normal, in the hope that the new agencies for international discussion and control would bear the burden for which they had been designed and permit each nation to attend to its own affairs with reasonable confidence in the way the world as a whole was being run. Only reluctantly and with serious doubts and reservations did the American Congress and public decide, in the course of 1947, that this idyll would not work. Fresh initiative and new commitments of American economic and even military resources seemed called for.

They came in swift succession: first an emergency loan to Great Britain, then support of the Greek and Turkish governments against Communist pressures, next a general plan for assisting European nations towards economic recovery. These new American commitments in Europe coincided with radical decay of the American position in China. By 1949, the lines of the Cold War had become sharp and clear both in Europe and in the Far East, where China had become Communist and Japan alone remained firmly within the American sphere of influence.

The fact that Communist-led guerrilla movements cropped up in many disturbed regions of the earth, and that Communist parties in almost every country spoke harshly of American "imperialism," convinced most Americans that a world-girdling Communist conspiracy, centered and controlled in Moscow, lay behind all the difficulties and troubles that confronted the United States overseas. This was, however, a half-truth at best. Stalin and his fellows certainly set guidelines for the Communist parties of the world, and sometimes may, in fact, have been able to command dramatic turnabouts. But between 1945 and 1949, the Russians were in general far too concerned with their own problems at home to invest much time, energy, or money in forwarding world revolution. In the 1920s Lenin had indeed believed in imminent world revolution; but Stalin had seen Lenin's dreams burst like bubbles. Like others, Stalin learned from experience; and what he learned was that foreign Communists were not to be depended on. Instead of overestimating revolutionary potential, as the Russians did in the 1920s, Stalin in the 1940s seems to have underestimated it in China and perhaps in Europe as well. Where Communist movements succeeded, as in China, it was without direct Russian help, and where they failed, as in western Europe, it was equally without Russian help.

Matters were very different within the countries occupied by the Russian armies. There Communist revolution from above seemed to Stalin the only way he could be sure of a "friendly" government in lands which traditionally bore small love for Russians. In the course of 1947, as relations with the West worsened, Stalin set out to purge the governments of eastern Europe of undependable, i.e., non-Communist, elements. Agrarians and socialists who collaborated with local Communists in the first postwar governments were driven from office and some were executed. Out-and-out party dictatorship quickly displaced the "peoples' democracies" which had initially disguised Communist power. But the means by which Communist governments were erected in Bulgaria, Rumania, Poland, and Hungary violated everything the United States recognized as democratic procedure. Hence, Russia's conduct in eastern Europe gave new substance to American and western European fears of Communist world conspiracy.

The Marshall Plan. In the face of such dangers the United States Congress decided, in the course of 1946–1947, that special and extraordinary actions would have to be undertaken to check the spread of Russian power. The test case was the long debate over a loan of $3.75 billion to Great Britain. This was proposed to Congress in January 1946, but was not approved until July, after long and impassioned discussions. The issue was whether the United States should lend Britain special support, and why. The clinching arguments that came into play in May and June of 1946 were political. At that time Britain was Communism's main opponent in Europe. American power had been, or was soon supposed to be, withdrawn. France and Italy were both under coalition governments in which Communists played an important part. Germany was helpless. Britain alone remained as a counterweight to Russia, but conversion of the British economy from war to peace required special help. The loan was intended to ease and hasten economic reconversion, keeping Britain strong and stable and capable of playing an active military-diplomatic role on the European continent.

Yet in spite of the loan, by the spring of 1947 the British government had reached the conclusion that its resources were so seriously overextended that retrenchment would be necessary. The most exposed and embarrassing British commitment was in Greece, where guerrilla activity had revived in the summer of 1946 and now threatened to topple the government. Military and economic aid on a massive scale seemed necessary if the Greek government was to recover morale and begin to fight back effectively. Britain was unable to provide the needed subvention. What would the United States do?

President Truman responded by inviting the United States Congress to authorize a special aid program for Greece and Turkey. Turkey was then also under heavy pressure from the Russians, who had suggested to the Turks that they should cede two eastern provinces to the Soviet Union and grant the Red Army special rights to garrison the straits as well. The President took this occasion (March 1947) to proclaim what was later called the Truman Doctrine: to wit, that the United States would use its resources to aid any people anywhere in the world who requested help in stemming Communist attack. This time debate was briefer. In May Congress approved Truman's proposal for special aid to Greece and Turkey, and soon military and civilian supplies were again flowing from American ports to aid an ally in war.

The situation in Greece was particularly acute, but the difficulties other European nations confronted in recovering from the ravages and dislocations of the war were everywhere enormous. If checking the spread of revolution was in the American national interest, then it soon seemed evident that systematic assistance to European-wide reconstruction might be a very good way to head off further Communist uprisings. In June 1947 Secretary of State George C. Marshall made this suggestion in a public speech; European statesmen seized the suggestion eagerly, and at a conference in July set machinery in motion to estimate requirements and coordinate separate national recovery plans. American officials collaborated closely from the start, and the U.S. Congress acted quickly, so that in April 1948 the European Recovery Program was ready to go into effect.

Initially, the Americans invited all European nations to take part in this coordinated effort. The Russians were not specifically invited, but neither were they excluded. Stalin, however, reacted negatively, and decided that this was a capitalist trick for enslaving all of Europe to American bankers. The Russians, clearly, were not ready to share their economic secrets with the world, nor to expand national planning of the sort Stalin's Five-Year Plans had pioneered to a continent-wide or worldwide scale.

Yet this was precisely what the American initiative aimed at. From a transatlantic point of view the separate countries of western Europe looked too small to be viable as separate economic units. Transnational coordination and planning of economic development seemed the obvious answer. American experts set eagerly to work, therefore, to encourage Europeans to think and plan in continent-wide terms. Most European nations outside the Russian sphere were ready enough to participate. Austria, Belgium, Denmark, France, West Germany, Britain, Iceland, Italy, Luxembourg, the Netherlands, Norway, Sweden, and Switzerland all took part; and the special American aid programs in Greece and Turkey were also later brought under the umbrella of the general European Recovery Program, or Marshall Plan as it was commonly called.

As the program came into operation, comparatively vast sums of American capital were put at the disposal of European nations, and large quantities of American goods crossed the ocean to replenish and expand European stocks. The criteria by which particular investments were made were not those of traditional banking. Economic recovery and advance beyond prewar levels was a political desideratum. Whether invested capital returned the highest possible interest or profit was merely a secondary, though not irrelevant, consideration. The Marshall Plan's return to political economics was especially notable because Germany was included as a full partner and beneficiary. Europe's economic recovery without Germany was impossible; and when the aim was to forestall revolution, systematic discrimination against the defeated foe seemed obviously unwise.

The recovery plan was a smashing success. Within four years European economic production surpassed prewar levels almost everywhere, save in such unfortunate lands as Greece, where guerrilla war raged until 1949. The contrast with the prolonged economic dislocations and stagnation of the post-World War I years was especially striking. This time American capital irrigated all of western Europe, not Germany alone, as had been the case in the 1920s. In addition, Keynesian notions of how governments could and should cope with unemployment and manipulate credit permitted officials to evade the paradoxes of the interwar years, when idle workers and idle machines had stared at one another, and no one knew what to do about it.

The Soviet Union and Its Satellites. Stalin's response to the dramatic return of American power to the European continent was to draw tighter the reins he already held in his hands. At home this meant a renewal of efforts to police thoughts and feelings, as well as resumption of the Five-Year Plans. Prewar emphasis upon investment in heavy industry and armaments persisted. Consumer goods, while far more abundant than they had been during the war, remained scant and often of poor quality. But Russian armament and related technologies soon attained a level of excellence inferior to none. The detonation of Russia's first atomic explosion in 1949 showed how rapidly it was possible to catch up with American techniques when all the resources of the Russian state were harnessed to the task. And in rocket design the Russians soon were to prove that they surpassed all others, including the Americans.

Stalin was also at some pains to tighten his control over satellite governments of eastern Europe. This presented special problems in both Yugoslavia and Czechoslovakia. In Yugoslavia, a vigorous and self-confident Communist party, tempered by four years of successful guerrilla operations against the Germans, came to power in 1945. Tito, the party leader, was unwilling to become Stalin's puppet, and when he discovered Russian agents conspiring against him inside Yugoslavia, he unceremoniously expelled them. Stalin objected, and the quarrel soon broke bitterly into the open. One result was the defeat of the Greek Communists, who had depended heavily upon supplies from Yugoslavia. A second result was a convulsive effort on the part of other east European Communist parties to search out and punish any potential "Titoists" in their own ranks. The most outspoken, independent, and nationally minded Communists of Poland, Hungary, and Rumania lost their lives as a result of these purges.

Until 1948 Czechoslovakia differed from its neighbors in preserving some of the substance of multi-party political life. In the immediate postwar months, the Czechs had hoped to constitute a link between East and West, and welcomed Russian support. Correspondingly, the Russians did not find it necessary to resort to high-handed methods in Czechoslovakia to keep a "friendly" government in power. All Czech parties, remembering how the Western powers had betrayed them to the Germans in 1939, were pro-Russian. But when the Marshall Plan was first proposed, the Czech government wished to take part. Stalin vetoed the idea, and decided that Communist political monopoly would have to be imposed in Prague, too, if Russian influence were to remain secure. Accordingly, the Czech Communists staged a particularly squalid coup d'état in February 1948.

The Czech coup made Germany's fate the next critical issue. Allied promises to administer Germany as a whole had broken down early in 1946. Both the Russians and the Western powers then proceeded to organize their separate parts of Germany as best they could. The American and British zones were merged for economic purposes in December 1946, and plans for the creation of local German governments proceeded smoothly. Anglo-American plans called for the eventual emergence of a federal German government along democratic lines; but for a long time the French hesitated and held back, fearing renewed German power and hoping, perhaps, for some sort of accommodation with the Russians if the unification of the western zones of Germany did not proceed too rapidly. But instead of accommodation, relations worsened. In June 1948 the Russians cut off access routes which had been used by the Western powers to supply their troops stationed in Berlin. The emergency was met by organizing an airlift, which managed for nearly a year to supply not only the Allied garrisons but also the German population of the western half of the city.

The Organization of NATO. The Czech coup swiftly followed by the Berlin blockade put a fresh urgency behind negotiations already in progress for the conclusion of a military alliance between the United States and the nations of western Europe. The danger of Communist subversion and attack seemed real indeed. The need to coordinate military plans was just as urgent as the need to coordinate planning for economic recovery. Accordingly, in April 1949 twelve nations signed the North Atlantic Treaty. By its terms, the United States, Canada, Great Britain, France, the Netherlands, Belgium, Lux-

108

embourg, Italy, Norway, Denmark, Iceland, and Portugal all agreed to come to one another's aid in case of attack. The treaty further provided for periodic consultation on political and military questions, and set up a united NATO (North Atlantic Treaty Organization) command to which the separate member nations were expected to contribute military units. The idea was that perpetual guard against sudden surprise attack was necessary. Only if an adequate force stood ready to react at a moment's notice and in accord with carefully prearranged plans, could the danger of Russian aggression be minimized.

As NATO plans took shape, the political reordering of West Germany also hastened to a conclusion. In September 1949 a new basic law, defining the legal and constitutional basis of German government, entered into force. This constitutional document was drafted at Bonn by German regional representatives and then approved by the occupying powers. It created a federal republic, with a strong executive and full parliamentary responsibility. Chancellor Konrad Adenauer, a veteran of pre-Nazi politics, emerged as the dominant figure of the new government, and soon rallied German national feeling to the side of the West. The rival German People's Republic in the East, on the contrary, could not command either the support of its own people or the trust of the Russians.

Political Polarization. The increasing polarization between East and West was felt everywhere in Europe. Communist parties, which in the first postwar months had joined government coalitions in western Europe, passed into opposition. Efforts to rouse insurrectionary strikes in France, Belgium, and Italy uniformly failed, but Communist voting strength remained important in each of these countries. The Communist tide in western Europe began to ebb decisively after April 1948, when elections in Italy returned a clear majority for Christian Democrats. Italy, it became clear, would not go the way of Czechoslovakia. Then, within a few months, Stalin's public controversy with Tito disrupted and disheartened Western Communist parties as well as contributing directly to Communist failure in Greece.

British political life remained apart from the storms of continental politics. In 1945 a Labour government came to power, determined to carry through a sweeping socialist program. Key industries were nationalized, but did not run much better for it. The government also organized the National Health and other social services, making the nation much healthier and perhaps somewhat happier. But other persistent problems of British society were not faced: in particular, habits of hard work upon which, in the long run, the prosperity of a nation must rest were not reinforced. The interwar experience of prolonged unemployment had burnt itself too deeply into the memories of the trade unionists of Great Britain. Instead of trying to get on with the job in hand as quickly and economically as possible, efforts to stretch out the task and spread the work prevailed, with the result that

British production lagged, export prices remained above world levels, and the remarkable élan which German and French economies were soon to show failed to emerge in postwar Britain.

Obviously western Europe's recovery gave the Russians little upon which to congratulate themselves. Stalin's efforts to make Russia strong and secure had succeeded merely in rousing the American giant, and sealing an alliance between West Germany and the other peoples of western Europe. Mastery over Czechoslovakia was balanced by the defection of Yugoslavia. The noisy exchange of insults and accusations between Belgrade and Moscow, and the Yugoslavs' continued impunity, were profoundly subversive of Russia's power over the east European Communist parties. Only pervasive fear of attack from the West and an equally pervasive distrust of their own people kept local Communist parties obedient to Stalin's will.

All in all, the Russians had botched things badly in Europe. On the other hand, within the Soviet Union itself transition from war to peace had gone smoothly and without seriously straining the regime. No military hero tried to seize power; no faction disturbed Stalin's hold upon the Communist party; and reconstruction of war damage proceeded rapidly without work stoppages or any other indiscipline on the part of the workers. Agriculture lagged, to be sure, but Russia had proved again its capacity to go it alone, without American or any other type of foreign aid. If the Russian people endured a lower standard of living than they otherwise might have been able to enjoy, they at least had the psychic satisfaction of knowing that they were citizens and subjects of a great world power, whose strength was matched only by that of the United States of America. Communist conviction and idealism were also undoubtedly factors in sustaining Russian morale. To be building a better life for the future made present hardships endurable; and the damages of the war adequately excused all present shortcomings. Thus the heroic, self-sacrificing spirit of the 1930s continued to inspire the politically active elements of the Russian population in the 1940s. As long as this remained true, and the rest of the population acquiesced in Stalin's policies, his power remained firm. By comparison, failures in Europe, short always of a move that might actually provoke war, remained trifling.

The Fall of Chiang: Communism in China. Moreover, if Stalin needed consolation for his own setbacks in Europe, he needed only to glance at China, where American plans and hopes backfired spectacularly. The key fact was that Chiang Kai-shek's soldiers proved to be unwilling to fight very hard against the Communists, who won over the peasantry of China by taking land from absentees and rentiers and awarding it to the people who actually cultivated the soil. Such simple policies alienated landowners, who looked to the Kuomintang and Chiang's soldiers to protect their property rights. But the rank and file of Chiang's armies were not particularly interested in defending the rights of landowners, since most of them were peasants too, and sympathized with Communist land policies.

In such a situation, the more equipment and supplies the Americans put at Chiang's disposal, the faster Communist strength increased. Over and over again Kuomintang units surrendered their arms without more than token resistance, thus enormously accelerating the pace at which Communist armed strength increased. The process, once set in motion, ran very fast throughout the length and breadth of mainland China. In the fall of 1948 Kuomintang troops in Manchuria, who had been cut off from any but sporadic access to the outside world ever since their arrival on the ground in 1946, surrendered to their Communist besiegers. This was a serious blow to the morale of Chiang's government and armies. Thereafter the surrender of large units and strategic strongholds in the face of Communist attack became common. The advancing Communist armies reached and crossed the Yangtze in April 1949 and before the year was out all of south China had fallen into their hands. Chiang and a remnant of his forces retired to Taiwan; but the mainland belonged to Mao Tse-tung, the Communist chief, and his followers. On October 1, 1949, the Communists duly proclaimed the Chinese People's Republic. The Soviet Union recognized the new government at once, but the United States retired from the fray, wondering what had happened so suddenly to American plans for a peaceful, democratic, grateful China.

The Russians had almost nothing to do with Mao's victories, but initially seemed in a position to profit from them. Communist China needed help and supplies to start industrial reconstruction and had only one source from which to borrow: the Soviet Union. In return, Russian influence and advice might be expected to have controlling importance. In other words, the role the Americans had reserved for themselves in postwar China was suddenly assigned to the Russians. Correspondingly, American power in east Asia retreated to the water's edge.

Japan: The U.S. Occupation. In Japan, to be sure, the American occupation regime met with substantial success. Instead of remaining sullenly hostile, the Japanese enthusiastically took up some of the superficial characteristics of American culture, and submitted gracefully enough to democratization and reeducation, American style. Perhaps the most important change brought about by the occupation regime was land reform, analogous to, though less sweeping than, the land reform Chinese Communists were simultaneously bringing to the Chinese countryside. The end result was to give farmland to those who worked it. Landlords lost all importance in Japanese as well as in Chinese society. Economic recovery came slowly; still no disastrous famine nor extreme deprivation resulted from the occupation. Emperor Hirohito remained on the throne, but the Japanese constitution and system of law were drastically revised. This was done by the Japanese

Chiang: Keystone Press

Chiang Kai-shek and Mao Tse-tung began life in a traditional Chinese environment. Each became a revolutionary and rose to command a party that espoused a foreign ideology. Yet a massive carry-over from China's past was assured when individual lives, like those of the two leaders themselves, bridged the gap between the Confucian past and the bewildering present.

Chiang was born in 1887, son of a small land-owner. After attending a military academy in Japan, he returned to China and joined Sun Yat-sen's Kuomintang party of revolutionaries. Despite the support of intellectuals, the party met with little success until the early 1920s, when Russian advisers arrived in Canton to reorganize the party along Bolshevik lines. The Russians also offered aid in building up an army to challenge the local warlords who controlled most of China. Accordingly, Chiang went to Russia for advanced military training, and on his return became commander of the Kuomintang's new army.

This gave him a key position after Sun Yat-sen's death in 1925. Chiang set out to unite China by force. His victories soon provoked bitter quarrels about exactly how to revolutionize newly conquered provinces. In 1927 Chiang decided to break with the Russians and the Communist wing of the Kuomintang. Several hundred Communists and their sympathizers were killed in the purge that followed. Survivors fled to the countryside of south China.

Among these survivors was Mao Tse-tung. Six years younger than Chiang, he also came from a small landholding family, and embraced Marxism as a young man while attending Peking University. After 1927 he applied his Marxism to the situation in China by urging peasants to stop paying rent and interest. Most peasants liked Mao's message, and he rose rapidly in the Chinese Communist party, becoming chairman in 1931.

Chiang, meanwhile, consolidated his personal power over the Kuomintang, and in 1928 won control of north China. He still faced Communist rivals in the south and soon collided with the Japanese, who occupied Manchuria in 1931, in the north. Between 1931 and 1935 he was able to drive the former from their strongholds, forcing them to make a three-thousand-mile march northward towards the Russian border. It took more than a year and only one in ten of those who started survived.

Nevertheless, once in a position to get a few vital supplies from Russia, Mao found northern peasants just as eager for his message as those of the south. The Japanese occupation of north China, beginning in 1937, did not prevent the spread of Communist organization through the countryside. But Chiang's defeats by the Japanese hurt his prestige and forced him to retreat far up the Yangtse. There he depended on supplies brought over "the Hump" from India by U.S. fliers. This made it easy, after the Japanese defeat of 1945, for the Communists to call him a cat's-paw of foreign imperialists.

Mao: Keystone Press

Mao's success, however, depended on the fact that he had won over the vast Chinese peasant mass. Chiang's soldiers were sons of peasants, and simply would not fight against Mao's program for dispossessing landlords and usurers. Hence, American aid to Chiang backfired, and by 1949 Mao controlled all of mainland China.

Chiang withdrew to Taiwan, where he showed how much he had learned from his defeat by carrying through a radical land reform. In the following decades he also presided over a remarkably successful program of industrial development. Meanwhile, on the mainland, like the founder of any new dynasty in China's past, Mao organized a successful effort to make China a great power once more.

The two rivals, growing old, each stubbornly claim the right to rule all China. Each seeks to outlast the other, hoping, perhaps, to see his claim finally vindicated in the confusion that seems sure to follow the death of the other. And as each grows older, the reverence he commands from his followers increases, for all the world like the reverence accorded to Chinese emperors of old as they grew ripe with years.

themselves acting under directives and in accordance with informal advice from the occupation authorities.

By the terms of surrender, Japan gave up Korea as well as all other imperial possessions. The Russians and Americans then divided the peninsula at the 38th parallel, establishing their respective military administrations on either side of that demarcation line. The surrender terms also divided Vietnam along the 17th parallel between Chinese and British zones of occupation. In the north the Chinese permitted an insurrectionary Communist-led regime to organize itself under the leadership of Ho Chi Minh. When the French returned in 1946 they found it impossible to agree through negotiations, but equally impossible to defeat Ho Chi Minh's insurgents by military force. Given the climate of opinion generated by the Cold War, it was all too obvious that neither of these Asian countries was in a very happy or stable position.

American policy in the Far East adjusted itself reluctantly to the loss of China. Naval bases, such as Okinawa, guaranteed a continued American military presence in the area, and this the United States proposed to retain. But there were serious doubts about commitments on land. When American forces withdrew from Korea in 1949, no American troops remained behind on the Asian mainland.

It seems best, however, to break off the narrative of postwar events at this point, when the lines of the Cold War were drawn sharply in Europe, leaving only minor ambiguities in the Far East. Not all the world's population was caught up in the Cold War. The date 1949 has no particular significance for India, Africa, or Latin America. But for world affairs as a whole 1949 does mark the achievement of a stalemate of mutual terror—or something approaching terror— between the Russians and the Americans. A postwar world very different from that imagined either by Stalin or by Roosevelt had defined itself. We shall try to survey what was made of it in the next chapter.

SUGGESTED READING

On the background of World War II see J. W. Wheeler-Bennett, *Munich, Prologue to Tragedy,** L. B. Namier, *Diplomatic Prelude, 1938–39,* and Herbert Feis, *The Road to Pearl Harbor.** For the war itself, two excellent books stand out amidst thousands: Gordon Wright, *The Ordeal of Total War, 1939–45,** which is admirably brief, and the longer and more exclusively military study by Basil H. Liddell-Hart, *History of the Second World War.**

*Available in a paperback edition.

Wartime diplomacy is treated in Herbert Feis, *Churchill, Roosevelt and Stalin,** John L. Snell, *Illusion and Necessity: The Diplomacy of Global War,** and William H. McNeill, *America, Britain and Russia: Their Cooperation and Conflict 1941–46.* The Axis side is dealt with in F. W. Deakin, *Brutal Friendship: Mussolini, Hitler and the Fall of Italian Fascism,** Johanna Menzel Meskill, *Hitler and Japan: The Hollow Alliance,* John Toland, *The Rising Sun: The Decline and Fall of the Japanese Empire, 1936–45,** and F. C. Jones, *Japan's New Order in Asia: Its Rise and Fall.*

Memoirs abound, of which Winston Churchill, *The Second World War,** 6 vols., is the greatest. D. D. Eisenhower, *Crusade in Europe,** Harry S. Truman, *Memoirs,** 2 vols., and Charles de Gaulle, *War Memoirs,* 4 vols., command special interest because of their authors' high position in world affairs.

Specialized topics are dealt with interestingly in Hugh Trevor-Roper, *The Last Days of Hitler,** and R. J. C. Butow, *Japan's Decision to Surrender.* Cornelius Ryan, *The Longest Day,** and Hans Speidel, *Invasion 1944* tell the story of the Allied landing in Normandy from opposite sides. Alexander Dallin, *German Rule in Russia 1941–1945,* and *Hitler's Europe,* ed. by Arnold J. and Veronica M. Toynbee, treat Europe's internal history under the Nazis.

Postwar settlement in Europe may be investigated with the help of Hugh Seton-Watson, *The East European Revolution,** Gordon Wright, *The Reshaping of French Democracy,* Gabriel A. Almond, ed., *The Struggle for Democracy in Germany,* Muriel Grindrod, *The Rebuilding of Italy,* and H. Stuart Hughes, *The United States and Italy.* W. Diebold, Jr., *The Schuman Plan: A Study in Economic Cooperation,* and J. P. Nettl, *The Eastern Zone and Soviet Policy in Germany, 1945–1950* are also interesting.

In the Far East, Kazuo Kawai, *Japan's American Interlude,* and G. C. Allen, *Japan's Economic Recovery* treat admirably of Japan. China's troubled history can be studied through Herbert Feis, *The China Tangle: The American Effort in China from Pearl Harbor to the Marshall Mission,** Tang Tsou, *America's Failure in China, 1941–1950,* and Benjamin Schwartz, *Chinese Communism and the Rise of Mao.**

Three books on recent Indian developments may be recommended: T. G. Spear, *India, Pakistan, and the West,* Selig Harrison, *India: The Most Dangerous Decades,* and C. H. Philips, *Politics and Society in India.* For the Middle East, George Kirk, *The Middle East 1945–1950** surveys developments as a whole. Edgar O'Ballance, *The Arab-Israeli War,* and William R. Polk, D. Stemler, and E. Asfour, *Backdrop to Tragedy: The Struggle for Palestine* deal with the conflicts between Jews and Arabs in that region.

For Latin America, W. Shanahan, *South America,* H. A. Holley, *A Short Introduction to the Economy of Latin America,* and William W. Pierson and Frederico G. Gil, *Governments of Latin America* survey the scene satisfactorily. Edwin Lieuwen, *Arms and Politics in Latin America,** and John J. Johnson, *The Military and Society in Latin America** analyze the role of the military.

Chapter 4

Postwar Perplexities

As we approach our own time, problems of shifting perspective become acute. Events keep changing their meaning as new developments crowd in after them. Consequently, any effort to generalize is likely to seem silly within a short time as some unexpected occurrence alters the tone and direction of public affairs. Yet only by seeking general lines of historical development can we avoid confusion amidst all the details of daily happenings. So the attempt to understand is necessary, even though we can be sure that subsequent events will compel revision, perhaps far-reaching revision, of present judgments.

The post-World War II world seems to have passed through two fairly distinct periods. From the time the Cold War alignment became sharp and clear, about 1949, until 1962, when the United States and the Soviet Union collided sharply over Cuba, the rivalry and mutual fear between the two "superpowers" dominated the globe. Nevertheless, there were limits to the power Russia and the United States commanded even in those years; and from at least 1958, when General de Gaulle returned to power in France and set out to reassert the full independence of his country, there were growing rifts in the alliance systems the two superpowers had created. The Cuban crisis of 1962 showed that in an emergency the United States and the Soviet Union were both prepared to disregard the interests and wishes of their allies. Consequently, after 1962, the two alliance systems rapidly decayed. After the turn-around years of 1958–1962, a more complicated political pattern asserted itself in which China, Japan, and western Europe (the Common Market) acted as great powers, along with Russia and the United States. Moreover, the polycentric character of international politics after 1962 allowed greater scope for local movements, aspirations, and quarrels. Increasingly, matters such as these preempted attention, domestically as well as across the borders of the world's sovereign states.

Open rivalry between the Soviet Union and the United States of America, publicly announced and fully organized by 1949, implied a twofold competition. On the one hand, the two superpowers engaged in an arms race, each seeking to improve its weapons systems to assure security against sudden and devastating attack. The critical choices were nearly all kept secret, even when they affected the economies as well as the security of the two countries involved—and of all the world. Publicly, on the other hand, the Cold War revolved around rival alliance systems and aid programs designed to strengthen either the "free world" or the "socialist camp."

These self-chosen names for the two sides point up the ideological side of the struggle. The United States set out to defend democracy and freedom against Communist subversion everywhere on the earth, while the Marxist-Leninist philosophy inherited from the revolution of 1917 committed the Soviet Union, at least vaguely, to forwarding the cause of socialist revolution around the world. Their rival ideologies certainly affected the decisions of American and Russian leaders, especially in the early stages of the Cold War. Eventually, however, the cynicism with which the Russians had used socialist ideology in foreign policy ever since the 1930s became apparent, as did the way the United States supported a number of dictatorial police regimes and called them part of the free world simply because they were not Communist.

The Arms Race. From the start, however, appeals to ideology were only part of the picture. The massive arms race bit deeply into both American and Russian economic resources. Within both societies special interests—what President Eisenhower called the military-industrial complex—came to depend upon the continuation of the arms race for their prosperity. And nonideological calculations of national interest couched in terms of access to military bases, strategic materials, and reliable allies always played a significant part in directing the decisions of the rival governments.

Ideological rivalry and the pursuit of national interests were nothing new in politics, and the fierce arms race that set in between Russia and the United States after the Russians exploded their first atomic warhead in 1949 had a precedent in the naval race that had broken out between Britain and Germany before World War I. But the massive destruction atomic warheads were capable of made this new arms race far more fateful, and the extraordinary complexity of the new weapons systems made the arms race of the 1950s and 1960s so expensive that even the United States began to find the price hard to pay.

Despite the veils of secrecy that surrounded all important decisions, two turning points in the arms race stand out clearly. The first came in 1950, when President Truman announced that the U.S.

government would try to build a new and far more powerful atomic warhead using hydrogen instead of plutonium as the nuclear fuel. Scientists had long been aware of this technical possibility, and knew also that the result would be vastly more powerful than anything attainable with plutonium. What triggered this American decision was fear that the Russians would soon begin, if they had not already done so, to design such a bomb. The fact that the U.S.S.R. had been able to explode a plutonium warhead only four years after the Americans had done so indicated that Russian technology and productive capacity were far superior to anything the Americans had expected. If Russian scientists and engineers could make an A-bomb, why couldn't they make the far more powerful H-bomb, too?

This calculation proved quite correct. The first American hydrogen explosion occurred in November 1952, and the Russians exploded their pilot hydrogen warhead less than a year later, in August 1953. These were "devices" rather than bombs, however; and several more years were required before suitably small and stable packaging made the tremendous new weapons safe for handling. The United States had such a bomb ready in 1956, when a test explosion destroyed the Pacific atoll of Bikini.

The Russians were not especially interested in designing bombs, for they lacked the airplanes and forward bases necessary to drop them on the United States. Hence, their energy went into a different line—the design of long-distance, intercontinental rockets, powerful enough to travel around the earth and deliver their deadly force anywhere on the surface of the globe. Such rockets had the further advantage that the hydrogen warheads they carried did not need to be made small and safe to handle, as bombs dropped from airplanes did.

Exactly when the Russians began investing in big rockets remains secret; but in 1955 President Eisenhower, stimulated in all probability by intelligence reports of what the Russians were doing with rockets, announced that the United States would embark on a program of rocket development aimed at penetrating outer space and reaching the moon. Scientific exploration and improved worldwide communication were part of the payoff expected from such a program, but no one doubted that the main consideration prompting the United States government to spend the vast sums of money needed for rocket development was military. For if the Russians were building rockets powerful enough to fly from somewhere in Siberia to attack any and every American city, then it seemed vital that the Americans should have similar rockets that could retaliate by threatening Russian cities with instant destruction. This, then, constituted the second major phase of the arms race.

For a few years in the late 1950s it looked as though the Russians had an edge over the United States in rocketry. Premier Nikita Khrushchev announced in August 1957 that the Russians had successfully tested an intercontinental ballistic missile capable of reaching any part of the globe; and two months later the Russians sent *Sputnik*,

COMMUNICATIONS, 1969–71*

Radio, Newspapers, Telephones, & T.V.

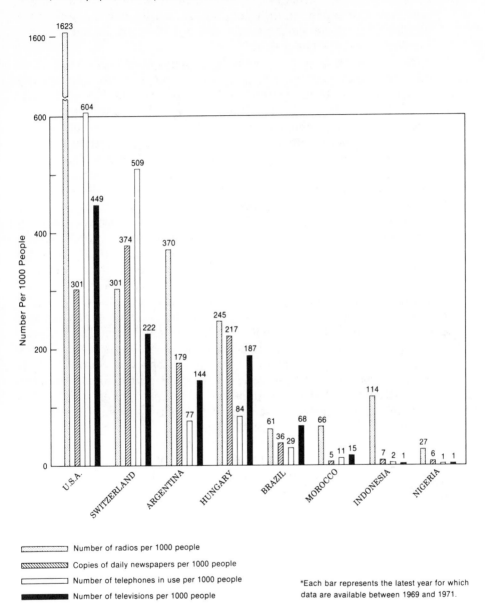

Number of radios per 1000 people

Copies of daily newspapers per 1000 people

Number of telephones in use per 1000 people

Number of televisions per 1000 people

*Each bar represents the latest year for which data are available between 1969 and 1971.

Despite the rapid growth of communications media, there are still vast numbers of people, particularly in the underdeveloped world, who never will see a television or use a telephone or read a newspaper (as much because they cannot read as because they cannot obtain or afford one). To take one example, whereas in America there is one television for every two people, in Indonesia there is only one for every 1000. One might not expect television to be universal by now, but radio surely comes much nearer to being so—and yet, while there is better than one radio for every person in the U.S., there is only one for every 37 people in Nigeria. The communications gap—and with it the ignorance gap—is still far from being closed.

119

the first artificial satellite, into orbit around the earth, proving that they had developed rockets swift enough to escape Earth's gravity entirely. The Americans were a mere three months behind in launching their first earth satellite, but the American payload was much smaller than those the Russians had put into space, and this gap persisted until the late 1960s.

Size by itself was not necessarily a measure of performance, and the Americans had the advantage of a ring of bases near Soviet borders that had been constructed for airplanes in the 1940s and early 1950s. In addition, the United States began producing atomic-powered, missile-launching submarines in 1954. These could rest on the sea bottom for months on end or move about underwater at will, all the while threatening almost instant destruction to Russian cities, rocket installations, and other strategic targets. Hence, Russian superiority in rocket size and power, though real, did not necessarily mean any tangible advantage over the United States in war; but it did scare the American public and raised the question for both superpowers of whether there was any effective defense against rocket attack. Despite enormous investments in early warning systems and the like, no workable system has yet been devised, and the costs of trying to bombproof cities or even to secure the survival of a governmental command system in time of all-out atomic attack seems so astronomical—and of such dubious value—that neither side has really tried.

The result by the late 1950s was a balance of terror. The Russians and the Americans found themselves at each other's mercy, in the sense that buttons pushed in the command posts that controlled their strategic rockets could theoretically wipe out all the important cities and kill at least half the populations of both countries within a few minutes. Atmospheric poisoning from such a blowup might even destroy all higher forms of life on Earth.

Such dire possibilities profoundly altered all earlier meanings of war. No rational person could take the risk of launching rockets that would invite instant and deadly retaliation by the other side. The billions of dollars and rubles poured into the arms race thus created an extraordinary stalemate. Neither side felt it could do without its nuclear capability; at the same time, neither side felt it could use such weapons, even in "local" wars, for fear of sudden and irreversible escalation and ultimate disaster.

The costly futility of the Soviet-American arms race did not entirely prevent other nations from embarking on a similar course. Britain exploded an atomic warhead in 1952, for instance, but did not pursue atomic armament vigorously thereafter. France and China, however, came along in the 1960s and 1970s with their own atomic weapons development, designed to give them the means to act independently as great powers even in the face of Russian and American force. Other states may have secret atomic programs in various stages of development—Israel and India, for instance—but only the United States, Russia, Britain, France, and China have tested warheads; and the extreme costliness of the sort of atomic armament Russia and the United States built up in the 1950s and 1960s makes it almost certain that other states will not duplicate their actions. Other weapons systems—biological and chemical agents in particular—may become critical; but by 1962, when the Cuban crisis showed how much both superpowers dreaded using their costly nuclear weapons, the arms race precipitated by the American A-bombs dropped over Japan in 1945 had reached a deadlock that seemed likely to last a long time.

The Revolution of Rising Expectations. The stalemate into which the arms race degenerated was one limitation on the power of the United States and of Russia. Those muscle-bound giants, afraid of their own strength, were not in a position to control other peoples very effectively. Another limitation sprang from the fact that most of humanity in the post-World War II years underwent a profound revolution of rising expectations. The upheavals of the war years disrupted traditional social structures in many areas, including most of Asia and Africa. Within Europe and the Americas, too, groups that had previously existed under various kinds of disadvantages awoke to the possibility that things could be changed by deliberate action and organized protest. As these movements gained momentum, the military command systems and political-strategical calculations of the Russian and American governments became increasingly irrelevant to popular feeling and behavior. Moreover, since the leaders of the great powers failed at first to recognize the force of popular sentiment aroused by rising expectations at home as well as abroad, their calculations often proved mistaken.

Manifestations of this profound change in human affairs were not lacking within both the Soviet Union and the United States. The Soviet government ever since the 1930s had had to struggle with pervasive and troublesome peasant discontent. This discontent was critical because efficient agriculture was next to impossible as long as those who produced the food on which the society depended felt aggrieved in fundamental ways. The Soviets also may have had some problems with non-Russian nationalities, but repression and the real opportunities for personal advancement the Communist regime offered these people muted such complaints. In the United States, the most important element in the population that responded to the revolution of rising expectations was the blacks, whom white Americans regularly treated as second-class citizens despite constitutional guarantees of civil rights that had been enacted after the abolition of slavery in 1863. A Supreme Court decision in 1954 declaring separate schools for blacks and whites to be illegal was an important landmark in the development of the civil rights movement. This movement, led in large part by Dr. Martin Luther King, Jr., emphasized nonviolent forms of protest, and became the principal vehicle of the early phase of collective black self-assertion within the United States.

In southern and eastern Europe, response to the revolution of rising expectations was also very vigorous. In lands with Communist governments, discontent found only occasional, sporadic, and unorganized expression. But riots demanding better consumer goods and working conditions broke out from time to time on a scale that could not be handled by ordinary police action. In non-Communist countries, where the controls of party and police were less strict, discontent characteristically took the form of voting for the most extreme available party of protest, i.e., for Communists. As a result, Italy and southern France had substantial Communist parties that drew their main strength from peasants who objected to the traditional backwardness and poverty of Mediterranean agriculture.

Outside of Europe and North America, the revolution of rising expectations took an even more emphatic form. In Asia and Africa, peasant hostility toward landlords, tax collectors, usurers, and other traditional social elites was brought to especially intense heat by the fact that these hated groups had all collaborated to some degree with European and/or Japanese imperialists. Hence, race feeling and a powerful hatred of foreigners of every kind merged into and reinforced revolutionary impulses. In many lands, the ideas that best articulated these revolutionary impulses were more or less Marxist. This was so because Marxist doctrine seemed to offer scientific reasons for believing what the rebels most wished to believe: i.e., that poverty, ignorance, and helplessness, which had traditionally been the lot of the majority of mankind could be remedied by deliberate, revolutionary action. This sort of Marxism, already divorced from its original industrial context, was further transformed by nationalist and racial feelings, and by youthful rebelliousness against parental control.

The local course of events depended on two variables: the vigor of the opposition encountered by the revolutionary movements and the extent to which the revolutionary leaders succeeded in mobilizing genuine mass support. Where opposition was weak, success generally came to the revolutionaries before they had to do the hard and tedious work of organizing most of the population behind them. This was the situation in much of Africa, where first British and then French imperial administrators decided to abdicate rather than fight. Ghana was the first African state to attain independence in this fashion. Transfer of sovereignty occurred in 1957, when British colonial authorities released Kwame Nkruma from prison to make him prime minister of the new government. Only where there were a significant number of European settlers, as in Kenya and Algeria, did strong resistance to revolutionary nationalist movements arise. But there, too, the British and French governments decided by 1962, after some hesitation and periods of painful guerrilla war, to withdraw. Belgium withdrew from the Congo rather abruptly in 1960. By the early 1960s, therefore, all of Africa north of Rhodesia and the Portuguese colonies of Mozambique and Angola had seen white imperial administrators replaced, usually without prolonged or violent struggle, by local political or military rulers who had emerged from among the black Africans.

122

In South Africa and Rhodesia, however, withdrawal of British authority transferred power to whites, who, finding themselves in a minority position vis-à-vis black Africans, set out to assure their political and military supremacy by enacting laws to keep the two races apart, while reserving the best lands and jobs for whites.

The new black governments of Africa were all relatively weak. Most had come to power before more than a small proportion of the entire population had been mobilized for common public action, and they all inherited problems of poverty, complex tribal and ethnic rivalries, and technical backwardness. Hence, the intense dislike black African rulers felt for what the whites of South Africa, Rhodesia, and the Portuguese colonies were doing found little more than verbal expression in the United Nations and elsewhere.

In Asia and Latin America, the revolution of rising expectations developed in a more complex way. Local elites divided sharply over whether or not to accept Marxist doctrines. In countries like Korea and Vietnam, Communist revolutionaries were counterbalanced by nationalist groups that rejected the ideas and ideals of the Communists, and were willing, with varying degrees of success, to use military force against their revolutionary rivals.

In some countries, religion played a decisive role. Thus, in Moslem lands, the traditional faith of Islam strenuously and systematically opposed Marxist atheism. Among Arabs, the special heirs of Mohammed, the appeal of a return to the original unity of Islam, when all believers had united into one great and glorious community of the faithful, rivalled the attractiveness of the secular Marxian faith. In Latin America, the white element in the population that traditionally dominated the Indians and blacks found an ally in the Roman Catholic church, which also bitterly opposed Marxist atheism.

In India, on the other hand, there was no systematic religious intolerance of Marxism—just a traditional scepticism of any doctrine that promised worldly salvation. Communist ideas found strongest response among the linguistic minorities of the south, who felt excluded from full participation in the Hindi-speaking government operating from the capital city of New Delhi in the north. In Japan, Marxist ideas appealed mainly to students and other youths. But as individuals assumed adult social roles, most of them seemed to shed their Marxist ideology and rebelliousness. Parallels to this pattern of behavior were recognizable in western Europe and the United States. What was mainly remarkable in Japan was the intensity with which the same persons pursued different and conflicting goals at different times in their lives.

American Misunderstanding of the Revolution of Rising Expectations. Swept by such powerful emotions and revolutionary ideas, postwar social and political structures heaved and gyrated from day to day. Nothing seemed secure. The American public was completely unprepared for such multiple uncertainties, concerned as it was with the terrible threat of atomic war. Subversive intellectuals, loyal to

Communism rather than to the United States, were widely believed to have given the Russians essential atom-bomb secrets; others were accused of having handed China over to the Communists. And when revolutionaries using Marxist phrases cropped up here, there, and everywhere, it became easy for Americans to believe that a worldwide Communist plot to revolutionize the world really commanded the life and loyalty of thousands upon thousands of skilled agents. Many Americans, including high officials of the government, came to this conclusion and set about doing all they could to stop the Communist tide in its tracks, if not to roll it back.

The Truman Doctrine, enunciated in 1947 in connection with the President's request to Congress for military as well as economic aid for Greece and Turkey, was the first official statement affirming this policy. Almost in passing, Truman declared that the United States would come to the aid of freedom-loving peoples everywhere who found themselves endangered by Communist subversion. In 1950 this view of international reality acquired new plausibility when the Communist government of North Korea attacked South Korea. In 1945 Korea had been divided along the 38th parallel into American and Russian zones of occupation. Half-hearted efforts to unite the whole peninsula failed, and the occupying powers proceeded to set up governments in their halves that claimed the right to rule the whole land. Then the Russians and Americans withdrew, and in January 1950 the U.S. secretary of state, Dean Acheson, made a speech in which he described a United States defense perimeter in the Pacific that failed to include South Korea.

Stalin may have interpreted this to mean that the Americans were prepared to sacrifice the government they had set up in South Korea. At any rate, he apparently authorized transfer from Russian stocks of enough war materiel to equip the North Korean army for an offensive against the south. When all was ready, the North Koreans attacked in June 1950. The exact timing was probably governed by the confused result of an election in South Korea, held May 30, 1950, in which Syngman Rhee, the U.S.-appointed leader of the South Korean government, failed to win a clear majority. Before negotiations for setting up a new government were complete, the North Koreans invaded.

Syngman Rhee promptly appealed to the United States and to the United Nations for help. The American response was speedy and, to Stalin, must also have been surprising. But from the American point of view, here was an unusually clear case of naked Communist aggression. If the United States meant what it had been saying about a world in which international law would be enforced through the United Nations, now was the time to act. Accordingly, President Truman instructed General Douglas MacArthur to use American forces stationed in Japan to come to the aid of the South Koreans. Truman also put the full weight of the American government behind the South Korean appeal to the United Nations. At that time, the Russians were boycotting the Security Council, so when the Korean question came up for a vote, there was no veto. The United Nations formally censured the aggression of the North Koreans and recommended military sanctions. In the following months a total of sixteen members of the United Nations sent detachments to fight in Korea, but the brunt of battle was borne by South Korean and American troops.

The struggle was dramatic. The North Koreans first seemed on the verge of success, for the South Korean army almost disintegrated under the force of their initial attack. But enough American troops arrived at Pusan in the extreme south to hold a bridgehead. Then the tables turned. General MacArthur carried through a landing far to the north at Inchon, and the North Korean army, suddenly endangered from the rear, began to collapse. Before American and other U.N. troops reached the Korean border with China, however, the Red Chinese army intervened and won unexpected victories over MacArthur's advancing columns. By the time the front stabilized again, a battle line snaked across Korea not far from the 38th parallel. Truce conversations began in 1951, but a cease-fire was not finally arranged until 1953.

As the Korean War settled toward stalemate, indignation and frustration in the United States became explosive. General MacArthur wished to pursue total victory, by bombing China if necessary and despite the risk of Russian intervention. This President Truman refused to approve, and when differences of opinion persisted, the President dismissed MacArthur from his command. Faced for the first time with the ambiguities of waging war in an atomic age, the American public found it hard to believe that the master weapons scientists had fashioned could actually hamstring American armed might. Cries of treason and accusations that the government was "soft on Communism" gained wide currency, but the extremism of such charges eventually discredited Senator Joseph McCarthy and others who had sparked the campaign.

Abroad, the Korean War helped the United States to draw the lines of alliance against Communist aggression tighter than before. In Asia, Japan and the Chinese Nationalists on Taiwan became American allies, and Japan began a spectacular period of economic expansion by serving as a main supply base for the United Nations forces in Korea. In Europe, the Korean War helped to galvanize efforts at transnational consolidation. The NATO alliance became operational, and the Marshall Plan continued until 1952 to stimulate the European economy. In 1950 a "Coal and Steel Community" had been proposed, and during the following three years it gradually came into being. This community acted as an international authority with power to regulate production and prices of coal and steel in France, Belgium, the Netherlands, Luxemburg, and West Germany. Such economic consolidation across national lines proved a success, but parallel efforts to found a European army and to set up some sort of European political authority came to naught.

The Communist camp, too, experienced a tightening of control from Moscow during the Korean War. East European Communist parties were systematically purged of real or suspected "Titoists," i.e., members who preferred to follow an independent line in dealings with the Russians. Stalin even got ready to launch a new purge inside Russia itself. Then, suddenly, he died in March 1953. Three months later came the truce in Korea, and a period of comparative relaxation in Cold War tensions ensued.

The one place where active fighting continued was in Indochina, where French forces were vainly trying to suppress a Communist-led guerrilla movement. Following their victory in Korea, the Chinese felt ready and able to extend greater amounts of help to the embattled Vietnamese Communists. Accordingly, the scale of fighting increased, and in 1954 at Dien Bien Phu a substantial French garrison found itself cut off and surrounded by enemy forces. When the United States refused to send help, surrender became the only alternative. The French will to fight never recovered. In the following months a truce was patched up, Vietnam was divided in two, and future elections to settle the form of government for the whole country were agreed upon. But before the elections occurred, the United States decided to back the establishment of a separate, non-Communist regime in the south. The Communist response was to resume guerrilla war in 1957, with Chinese and some Russian support.

Russian Misunderstanding of the Revolution of Rising Expectations. The course of events in Vietnam matched Communist expectations nicely. Imperialists—first the French, then the Americans—acted like imperialists, and Communists took the lead in organizing popular resistance. In other words, in Vietnam Communists were able to ride the wave of the revolution of rising expectations, and to interpret it in terms of their Marxist-Leninist faith. In eastern Europe, however, doctrine and reality collided harshly. The Communist regimes there were unable to satisfy popular demands for more consumption goods and greater personal liberty, and were unwilling to equalize discomfort and deprivation by making Communist bosses live as poorly as the majority had to. Thus, in eastern Europe, the revolution of rising expectations worked against Communists, and made their claim to act as the vanguard of the revolutionary workers and peasants sound absurd.

Popular discontent came to a boil in 1956. The precipitating factor was a speech delivered in January of that year before the Twentieth Congress of the Communist Party of the Soviet Union by Premier Nikita Khrushchev. Khrushchev had only recently emerged as the principal leader of the Russian government, and he took this occasion to denounce his predecessor, Stalin, for having abused his power. Khrushchev's impassioned account of Stalin's crimes against Communist party members set off a widespread retreat from the rigors of Stalinism within the Soviet Union. As the news spread to Poland and Hungary, local Communists took Khrushchev at his word and concluded that slavish obedience to instructions from Moscow was one of the heritages from Stalin's tyranny that should cease. In Poland, the result was the rise of a new leader, Wladislaw Gomulka. Gomulka had been imprisoned for "Titoism" in the early 1950s. Once in power, he proceeded to run the Polish state in his own independent, but dogmatically Communist, way. He became, in fact, a second Tito. In Hungary, however, control quickly passed out of Communist hands. This the Russians decided was too dangerous to be tolerated. Other Communist governments of east Europe might come tumbling down if the Hungarians made good their revolt. Accordingly, during the first weeks of November 1956, Soviet tanks rolled into Budapest and suppressed the Hungarian experiment.

The Suez Crisis. By coincidence, the crisis within the Russian empire of eastern Europe coincided with another sharp military clash over the control of the Suez Canal. To understand what happened, one must go back to 1947, when Zionist Jews roundly defeated Palestinian Arabs and established the new state of Israel. Throughout the Arab world this defeat rankled shamefully, especially among young military men who blamed their rulers for what had happened. The indignation they felt at betrayal from the top coincided with the feelings generated in Arab society as a whole by the revolution of rising expectations. Major Gamal Abdel Nasser came to power in Egypt in 1954, two years after an army coup d'etat in 1952, because he was able to voice both the indignation Arabs felt everywhere at their defeat by the Israelis and the burning hope for better days ahead that was the essence of the revolution of rising expectations.

Once in power, however, it became necessary to act. Nasser found an easy target in the British, who had retained the right to garrison the Suez Canal Zone when they withdrew from the rest of Egypt after World War II. At first the British agreed to evacuate their troops; but when Nasser proceeded to make a deal with Russia exchanging Egyptian cotton for armaments, and then declared that the Suez Canal Company would be run by Egyptians and its shares nationalized, it looked as though in withdrawing from the Suez the British might be handing Egypt and the canal over to the Russians. France was also eager to check Nasser, for he was enthusiastically supporting his fellow Moslems in a guerrilla war against the French in Algeria. The Israelis, too, felt it was better to attack Nasser before he grew too strong. They therefore eagerly entered into secret negotiations with the French and British for a combined attack on Egypt.

The plan was kept secret from the United States, as well as from other foreign powers, on the theory that American scruples about international law might interfere with the swift accomplishment of the goal of overthrowing Nasser and his government. Accordingly, when military operations began in October 1956, they came as a surprise to Washington. International aggression, which the United States had tried to stop in Korea, was again taking place; but this time it was America's most important allies who were the aggressors!

127

President Eisenhower decided that principle was more important than alliances. Accordingly, the United States government again turned to the United Nations as a means of checking international disorder. This time the Soviet Union and the United States agreed: both opposed the British, French, and Israeli attack on Egypt.

With the two superpowers acting in concert, the British and French quickly backed down and the Israelis eventually withdrew their troops from the part of the Sinai peninsula they had occupied. Peace was promptly restored; the United Nations and the American program for managing international affairs had won a clear victory. Or had they? After all, the crisis in Egypt had so distracted attention from Europe that the United States had failed to lift a finger to help the Hungarians in their struggle to throw off Soviet rule. Moreover, the estrangement between the United States and France arising from the Suez crisis never healed. Instead, in 1958 General Charles de Gaulle returned to power with the intention of making France once again fully independent. His plan was to balance America off against Russia in such a way as to allow Europe to emerge under French leadership as a new, fully independent world power. Though De Gaulle was only partially successful, his policy nevertheless substantially curtailed American influence in western Europe.

Moreover, Nasser did not become a convert to the American way of settling international disputes as a result of what happened in 1956. On the contrary, he prepared as rapidly as he could for a new struggle against Israel; and since the Russians had agreed to construct a great dam at Aswan, and continued to supply Egypt with arms, it seemed likely that Nasser would become more and more dependent on Moscow.

Hence, in the years that followed, the 1956 victory for principle began to seem appallingly costly to many Americans. As a result, American faith in the United Nations and its quasi-judicial methods for imposing peace evaporated. A new, tougher-minded mood took over in Washington. The shift was consummated with the election of President John F. Kennedy in 1960, who felt that the way to wage the Cold War was to behave like the Soviet Union and other states, i.e., to use propaganda and idealistic appeals when it seemed advantageous to do so, but to act in strict conformity to calculations of national interest.

The Cuban Crisis. The most important testing ground of the new American policy came in Cuba. In 1959 Fidel Castro came to power in that island after a victorious guerrilla campaign in the mountains. Before long he quarreled with the American government and, as relations worsened, Castro leaned more and more on the Communists among his followers until his government became an out-and-out party dictatorship. Meanwhile the Americans began to organize and equip a force of Cuban exiles to overthrow Castro's by now openly Communist government. Subversion on such a scale was indeed a far cry from earlier American support of international legality. Nevertheless, in the first days of his presidency, Kennedy authorized the Cuban exiles to land at the Bay of Pigs on Cuba's southern shore. The invasion failed miserably, but not before official American involvement in the attempt became clear to all the world.

Castro was, no doubt, both gratified and alarmed. The Cuban people had not rallied to the invaders; on the other hand, he had to fear lest the Americans return to the assault with far more formidable forces. He therefore appealed to the Russians for aid, and for reasons that remain unclear, Premier Khrushchev decided to send Soviet rockets to Cuba. Perhaps Khrushchev was pushed into this adventure by criticism from the Chinese and other Communist doctrinaires to the effect that the Russians were gaining nothing from their superiority in rocketry. Against a background of such reproaches, Castro's appeal for support probably looked like a golden opportunity to tip the balance of power between the United States and the Soviet Union decisively in the Russian favor. Khrushchev may have figured, for instance, that once American cities came under the threat of rockets based in Cuba, he would be able to force the Americans to withdraw from Berlin, where the garrisons of American and other western troops left over from the wartime occupation had long troubled the Russians. At any rate, Khrushchev again heated up the Berlin question in 1961 by declaring that the Russians could not allow existing arrangements to endure much longer.

Soviet plans were upset by the fact that, in October 1962, the United States government discovered what was afoot in Cuba before the rockets had been emplaced, and indeed before all essential parts had even been delivered to the island. As a result, when President Kennedy declared that the U.S. Navy would intercept Russian ships enroute to Cuba in order to prevent delivery of the remaining hardware required to make the launching sites operational, there was little the Russians could do. No one was prepared to start an all-out war over the matter; and after a few tense days the Soviet government backed down and ordered the ships carrying the missing rocket parts to turn around and return to Russian ports. An agreement was quickly reached for the dismantlement of the launching pads that had been built and for the withdrawal of Russian technicians needed to maintain (and presumably to launch) the weapons. In return the United States promised not to try to invade Cuba again.

Castro was furious at what he felt to be Russia's betrayal. Russian prestige suffered a serious blow, and Khrushchev's hold on supreme power within the Soviet Union was shaken, though he was not compelled to surrender office formally until 1964. Yet the reputation of the United States among its allies was not enhanced by Russia's discomfiture. On the contrary, during the tense days of crisis over Cuba, President Kennedy did not consult his European allies nor show much concern for their interests, even though the upshot, one way or the other, was bound to affect the lives of all Europeans, and, indeed, of all the peoples of the world. The memory of how, when the chips were down, the superpowers acted by and for themselves lingered on, and made General de Gaulle's arguments for European self-reliance a good deal more convincing than before.

Sino-Soviet Quarrels. Radical weakening of the Russian alliance system actually preceded the Cuban crisis, for the uneasy relations between the Soviet Union and the People's Republic of China had degenerated into open quarrel by 1960. Stalin had done next to nothing to help Mao Tse-tung to power in 1949. Thereafter, the Russians' long-standing claim to head the socialist camp always ran afoul of Mao's habit of making his own decisions and conducting his own policy according to a party line that he defined. After their success in driving the Americans out of North Korea, the Chinese Communists busied themselves with asserting firm control over the old imperial borderlands of China. Tibet, for instance, was brought to heel in 1959 by an armed expedition, and disputed frontier zones were seized high in the Himalayas, even when this involved armed clashes with Indian troops in 1959 and again in 1962. This aggressive policy embarrassed Indian Communists and openly challenged the Russians, who had conspicuously befriended India a short time earlier.

Chinese policy at home went even further, for in 1958 Mao Tse-tung announced a "Great Leap Forward" which, he declared, would allow the Chinese to advance directly to the stage of communism predicted by Marx. This program implied a radical doctrinal reproach to the Russians, who, a full generation after their revolution, had only been able to achieve the socialist stage of production, a mere halfway house on the way to Marx's communism.

The Russians also had difficulty with the Chinese over borders, for Mao made it clear that Chinese lands seized by the tsarist government between the seventeenth and twentieth centuries were not rightfully ruled from Moscow. The Russians retaliated in 1960 by withdrawing all the forms of aid they had been giving the Chinese. Several thousand Soviet technicians returned home, leaving the various projects on which they had been working unfinished. The blow to Chinese plans for industrial and military production was severe, and partly as a result Mao's Great Leap Forward fell far short of expected goals. Mao naturally blamed the Russians for China's failures, and launched a worldwide propaganda campaign denouncing them as traitors to the revolutionary cause. In radical circles everywhere Maoism tended to supplant other versions of Marxist doctrine. Everywhere the Communist cause experienced new tensions and many Communist parties split into pro-Chinese and pro-Russian factions.

Titoism in the 1940s and 1950s had been troubling enough to the Russians, but Maoism in the 1960s and 1970s was far more damaging. China's size and potential power were only part of the reason. What really hurt the Russians was ideological, for Mao was able to portray the Russians as conservatives who preferred the status quo to fresh revolutionary adventures. This meant that all the restless peoples of the world who were stirring in their own ways to the revolution of rising expectations had nothing to look forward to from Russia, insofar, that is, as they believed Maoist propaganda. That propaganda, however, was strikingly successful because so many facts agreed with it. Russia's revolution had indeed come of age. By creating its own kind of ruling class among the privileged ranks of Soviet society, the Soviet Union had become extremely vulnerable to reproach for betraying the real communist ideals of the revolution.

Domestic Problems Among the Great Powers. Within China itself similar problems existed. Efficient management of large factories and smooth supply and distribution of the many items needed to keep a technologically sophisticated economy going required elaborate networks of command and obedience. Moreover, when supplies were short, some had access to rare goods while others went without. Managers and workers who handled rare commodities were obviously in a better position to secure those commodities than others were. Under such circumstances, even Mao's teachings could not prevent selfishness from finding ample scope.

Nevertheless, Mao and some of the people closest to him profoundly deplored the decay of the true communist spirit. In 1966 they called upon the youth of China to reassert the old ideals by launching a "Cultural Revolution" aimed at bureaucrats, experts, and other privileged elements in the society. For more than two years extensive purges and some disorder resulted from the efforts of youthful Red Guards to enforce a higher dedication to the principles of Maoism. By 1969 the Cultural Revolution had tapered off. In some cases the Red Army, where discipline had never been relaxed, had to be called upon to check overzealous Red Guard youths. A good deal of economic disruption seems to have occurred at the height of the Cultural Revolution; and in the early 1970s China had to buy food abroad, mainly from Canada, to feed its enormous and growing population.

While Mao and his followers were thus experiencing some of the costs of trying to live up to revolutionary, equalitarian principles, the two conservative superpowers, Russia and America, confronted growing internal problems and unraveling alliance systems. To take the Russian case first: Khrushchev's dismissal from office in 1964 was occasioned as much by his inability to get better performance from Russian agriculture as by his failure in Cuba. Yet the two men who divided principal authority in Russia after Khrushchev's ouster, Leonid Brezhnev and Alexei Kosygin, were also unable to solve the long-standing problem of getting maximum productivity from a sullen and often unskilled agricultural labor force. Consequently, after a disastrous growing season in 1972, Russia, too, had to go shopping abroad for vast quantities of grain. It was also difficult for the industrial plant of the Soviet Union to produce and distribute enough consumer goods to keep up with the rising expectations of the Russian public. Even more troublesome, perhaps, was the fact that writers and scientists were making clear their discontent with the restrictions imposed on thought and expression by Soviet authorities. Such discontent, at least by implication, challenged the truth and adequacy of official Marxism, which in turn legitimized the authority of the Communist party and of the government itself.

Abroad, too, the Russians faced mounting costs and no very tangible returns. Their quarrel with the Chinese continued unabated through the 1960s, and as a result they lost their revolutionary momentum all around the world. Foreign governments allied with Russia sometimes showed signs of restlessness. This was particularly true of Czechoslovakia, where a Communist government experimented with milder controls only to provoke a Russian invasion in 1968, followed by a sharp change of party line as new men, acceptable to Russia, took command. Elsewhere in eastern Europe the Russians avoided resort to armed force, but they could not prevent Communist governments from following an increasingly independent line, especially in Albania, Rumania, and Poland.

In the Arab lands the Russians found themselves saddled with expensive and not very grateful "friends." Egypt depended mainly on Russia for armaments, for instance, but had little to offer in return. The costly futility of this policy was brought home to the Russians in 1967 when a new war between Israel and Egypt led to the abrupt collapse of Egyptian forces. After a mere six days of combat, the Egyptians lost control of the Sinai peninsula, as well as most of the equipment the Russians had given them. The Russians, perhaps reluctantly, decided to reequip the Egyptians; yet after Nasser's death (1970), his successor, Anwar Sadat, quarreled with the Russians and banished their technicians from Egypt. As a result, when war with Israel again broke out in 1973, the Egyptians (with their Syrian and other Arab allies) fought alone, but did so more successfully than before, achieving a military stalemate with Israel. The most active role in negotiating a settlement devolved upon the United States; and when Secretary of State Henry Kissinger arranged for an Israeli withdrawal from the Suez Canal (1974), allowing the Egyptians to resume control of that vital waterway, the Russians seemed to have lost influence and had remarkably little to show for their past investments in Egypt. (At the same time, a temporary cutoff of Arab oil reminded the West of the need for cultivating Arab goodwill.)

The United States, too, met a series of disappointments and disagreeable surprises in the 1960s and early 1970s. The assassinations of President Kennedy in 1961 and of Dr. Martin Luther King, Jr., in 1968 reminded the world of an ugly, violent side of American life. Manifestations by blacks of their discontent also became sharper and sporadically riotous. Even more corrosive was the polarization of opinion over military involvement in Vietnam, a polarization that provoked bitter rhetoric, massive demonstrations, and a few outbreaks of violence in the late 1960s. No sooner had President Nixon brought some sort of settlement to the Vietnam War than a fresh crisis arose. Evidences of corruption and illegal exercise of power in the President's entourage broke tumultuously into the open as ·a result of legal investigations of a burglary of Democratic Party headquarters at

Watergate in Washington, D.C.

After a series of shocking revelations, based partly on admissions of wrongdoing by close advisers of the President and partly on the tapes of conversations between the President and members of his staff, President Nixon resigned his office in August 1974. His decision was triggered by the overwhelming threat of impeachment and removal from power. He was succeeded by Gerald R. Ford, who had replaced Spiro Agnew as Vice President. (Agnew himself had been forced out of office under the threat of criminal prosecution.) The new President announced a policy of renewed cooperation with the Congress in an effort to solve the rising domestic crisis of inflation. He also promised to continue Nixon's policy of détente with the Soviet Union and China.

In foreign affairs, the record of the United States in the 1960s was like that of the Soviet Union. That is to say, alliances came apart; intentions miscarried. NATO suffered a serious blow when France withdrew from the alliance lock, stock, and barrel in 1966. Then, in the early 1970s, the Federal German Republic (West Germany) concluded treaties with Poland and other countries of eastern Europe, including even the German Democratic Republic (East Germany). Apparently the governments of Europe, both Communist and non-Communist, were developing independent policies of their own, deliberately bridging the Iron Curtain that had once divided Europe into rival armed camps. The United States did not oppose the "opening toward the east"; on the other hand, Americans did not initiate it, nor do anything to hurry it along. The old pattern whereby American and Russian advisers hovered over every move on the European chessboard no longer held true.

A major reason for Europe's new independence in diplomacy was the remarkable economic upsurge that took place in all of western Europe following the gradual elimination of tariff barriers that had previously divided each nation from its neighbors. As set up initially in 1957, the European Common Market included France, West Germany, Italy, Belgium, the Netherlands, and Luxemburg. Its spectacular success attracted Greece and Turkey as "associates"; and in 1971 the British gave up their tradition of imperial detachment by joining the Common Market, too. Denmark and Ireland followed soon after. As in diplomatic matters, the United States did not oppose the development of the Common Market, and had even, through the Marshall Plan (1948–1952), done much to lay the basis for its later success. But by 1973 it was clear that Europe's prosperity was creating problems for the American balance of payments, because sales of United States goods were falling short of American expenditures in Europe. No United States government could welcome this reversal of the post-World Wars I and II pattern, when Europe had been financially dependent on American loans.

The War in Vietnam. Europe's increasing wealth and strength was, in a sense, not a setback but a success for American foreign policy, even if it meant a diminution of United States influence and (at least relative) power. No such description applied to American actions in southeast Asia. The effort to build a stable, non-Communist government in South Vietnam proved immensely more costly than anyone had anticipated. After 1965, when President Lyndon Johnson decided that the only way to defeat the Communist forces was to send substantial numbers of American troops to fight on the ground as well as from the air, the Americans looked more and more like imperialists, not merely to the Vietnamese, but to all the world.

The Communist government of North Vietnam claimed that South Vietnam was not a separate country and that the real will of the entire Vietnamese people, north and south, was for national liberation from the imperialist yoke represented before 1954 by the French and thereafter by the Americans. North Vietnam therefore sent troops and supplies southward to make good its claim. The North Vietnamese, in turn, received military equipment from China and Russia which enabled them to mount an amazingly successful resistance, even in the face of more than half a million well-equipped American soldiers backed up by substantial South Vietnamese armed forces.

American officials saw things very differently. The United States government repeatedly declared that it was not imperialistic because it sought only to allow a free expression of the political will of the people of South Vietnam. This was merely a reaffirmation of the Wilsonian ideal. The difficulty was that, if massive and prolonged fighting were necessary to defeat the Vietnamese Communists and hold free elections, the people who remained in the shattered villages and devastated towns under the shield of the American armed forces were not really free to vote against their "liberators." Hence, the election of 1967 which ratified General Nguyen Van Thieu's power in South Vietnam did not end the controversy, in spite of American efforts to make the election honest. Sporadic fighting continued between Communist guerrilla forces and President Thieu's army even after the withdrawal of American troops had been completed in 1973.

The futility of American policy, seeking to export democracy by force and provoking instead antiforeign, nationalist feelings among the Vietnamese that strengthened the Communist side, became apparent slowly, and not before sharp and bitter controversy had broken out within the United States. It is, however, still too soon to assess the historical significance of what happened in Vietnam. Perhaps the Wilsonian democratic ideal has been lastingly discredited as a basis of United States foreign policy. Perhaps, the Marxist vision of world revolution as a necessary preface to social betterment has also been effectively discredited as a guide for Russian and Chinese policy making. At any rate, it seems likely that the ideological simplicities that have played so prominent a role in public affairs ever since 1917, when the world was first offered a choice between Leninist and Wilsonian revolutions, will never again command deep and wide conviction among the world's peoples.

Decay of the Revolutionary Ideal. One reason for making such a statement is that revolution has lost most of its charm throughout the ex-colonial world where new, independent sovereign nations sprang up so rapidly in the 1950s and 1960s. African and Asian governments, whatever their ideological principles or historic traditions, regularly found that one of the tasks of running a government was to keep order at home; and, as even Mao Tse-tung had to admit when he called off his Cultural Revolution, it is impossible both to keep order and simultaneously to conduct a revolution. Confronted by such a choice, the new governments of Asia and Africa jettisoned their revolutionary ideals. Those who dissented and accused government officials of betraying the faith were jailed or killed.

Instead of nourishing the hope of a world made new by revolutionary change at home, rulers of the newly independent lands often found it preferable to mobilize against some neighboring enemy. The most bitter and prolonged of these confrontations has been that between Israel and the Arab lands—a confrontation that eclipsed Cold War ideologies in the Middle East from the start. In addition, however, the ill feeling between India and Pakistan, dating back to the partition of British India into two states in 1947, seems to have increased with time. The revolt of East Pakistan in 1971 to set up a new state, Bangladesh, added fresh fuel to the fire, for the successful assertion of the independence of Bangladesh owed a good deal to Indian help.

In Africa, the discrediting of grandiose schemes for revolutionary change may perhaps be dated to the overthrow of President Kwame Nkruma of Ghana in 1966. Nkruma had aspired to become spokesman for all of black Africa, as well as to promote far-reaching social and economic changes within Ghana, by high-handed methods when necessary. The army officers who overthrew him discovered many scandalous abuses of power and privilege by Nkruma and his followers. The gap between the ideals they preached and their self-serving use of power, plus the fact that Nkruma had bankrupted Ghana by his ambitious building program and other expenditures, did much to discredit revolutionary rhetoric. Moreover, the need of the new governments of Africa for trained people was so great that almost everyone with a suitable education could find a government job. Student revolutionaries easily became busy bureaucrats, too concerned with everyday crises to think about making a revolution.

A major problem for the new African governments has been the ethnic pluralism they inherited from European empire builders. Differences of language and custom offer ready-made lines of cleavage and invited the expression of discontent. The most dramatic example of this problem was the revolt of the Ibo peoples of Nigeria, 1967–70. But the effort to create a new state of Biafra on the basis of Ibo national consciousness failed, largely, perhaps, because the Biafrans were unable to find anyone to supply them with enough arms to meet the Nigerian army on more or less even terms. Other new African states have confronted similar potential unrest. Sporadic outbreaks of local violence between rival ethnic groups have occurred widely.

Latin America is the one area of the world in which the impulses generated by the revolution of rising expectations have not yet lost their dynamism. To be sure, efforts to export Marxist revolution from Castro's Cuba have met with no success, and the principal Latin American apostle of people's wars of liberation, Che Guevara, died in the Bolivian jungle in 1967 when he attempted to act on his own principles by starting a guerrilla war. Nevertheless, it seems clear that hope of transforming existing arrangements of society is still strong among important segments of society in many Latin American countries, and the governments have not been very successful in either suppressing or satisfying malcontents. This hope is likely to grow as literacy spreads. In five years (1965–1970), the illiteracy rate in Latin America dropped from over 40 to less than 25 percent.

It would be a mistake to leave the impression that public affairs since 1962 have registered nothing but a series of failures, disappointments, and frustrations. In some parts of the world, the 1960s and early 1970s were a time of unusual success. This was most strikingly true in Japan, where an extraordinary rate of economic growth allowed a rapidly rising standard of living. Moreover, the economic boom did not disrupt Japan's political order, as dramatic economic change often does in lands where institutions have not adjusted successfully to the requirements of industrial society.

Similarly spectacular economic development characterized France, West Germany, and Italy. Canada, Australia, and South Africa also prospered notably as industrial lands, as well as in their traditional roles as suppliers of raw materials to the European and Japanese markets. The same was true of Brazil, despite (or perhaps because of) a very high rate of inflation. Rapid changes in the economic aspects of life in these lands certainly strained traditional political systems, most notably in South Africa, where the Africaans element (descendants of Dutch settlers) not only excluded black Africans from participation in politics, but also cut off all ties with Great Britain and almost silenced the British element in the population. In Canada, likewise, the French element in the population grew restless at its traditional rural and subordinate role in Canadian society. But the strains were mild compared to those in South Africa, and the Canadian government and political process mollified all but a few French extremists.

In addition to these lands where the standard human desire for greater wealth achieved some satisfaction in the 1960s and early 1970s, there were also a few lands where the white heat of ideological commitment continued to sustain hopes of a better future in spite of actual disasters. This was true in North Vietnam, for instance, where an intense revolutionary faith in the future was vital in sustaining the long strain of war against foreign "imperialists." Revolutionary underground groups in Latin America and the Irish Republican Army in Ulster were inspired by a similar faith, even while their members led

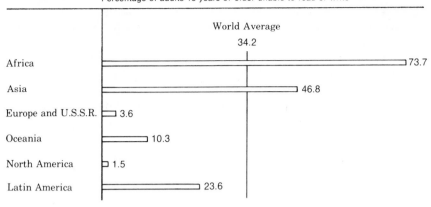

WORLD ILLITERACY, 1970

Percentage of adults 15 years or older unable to read or write

World Average
34.2

Africa — 73.7

Asia — 46.8

Europe and U.S.S.R. — 3.6

Oceania — 10.3

North America — 1.5

Latin America — 23.6

A high rate of illiteracy is another mark of the underdeveloped area. Witness the fact that over 70% of the people in Africa are illiterate, while in western Europe and North America, illiteracy is virtually nonexistent.

hunted lives and inflicted various forms of violence upon others.

Yet on the whole it seems fair to say that these pockets of ideological commitment were exceptional. Overall, the dominant trend was the decay of ideology as a guide to political behavior. Governments fell back on routine or appealed to the national interest and, in many instances, to the narrower self-interest of rulers and officials as against that of the general public. Soviet embarrassment at revelations of police brutality through Alexander Solzhenitsyn's novels and American embarrassment at the Watergate revelations of corruption in high places are symptomatic. Illegal actions to protect those in power may be hard to resist, but they are even harder to justify in public and can only occasionally be kept secret.

The great secular faith of modern times, nationalism, seemed in retreat in western Europe; the success of the Common Market could scarcely have been as great as it was if that were not true. A similar weakening (or at least a transformation) of nationalism may also be taking place in other industrially developed lands, such as the United States and Japan. At any rate, appeals to patriotism did not have their usual success in the United States during the Vietnam War, and the Japanese remain remarkably indifferent to military matters.

President Richard Nixon's striking initiatives in foreign policy, including his reestablishment of diplomatic contacts with Communist China in 1972 after a spectacular visit to Peking, and signing of an agreement with Russia limiting the proliferation of strategic armaments (i.e., atomic rocketry) in the same year after a visit to Moscow, certainly attest to the decay of ideology as a guide to political behavior, for Nixon was a leading crusader against Communism early in his political career. Nevertheless, it remains to be seen whether tough-minded calculations of national interest will succeed in containing the arms race, which has been so costly to both Russia and America since

1949. Some of the economic difficulties which began multiplying in both countries in the late 1960s clearly stem from the high proportion of resources they have been putting into armaments.

A remarkable and dramatic move towards collaboration in outer space, whereby Russian and American astronauts will meet in an orbiting space laboratory and share the tasks of conducting experiments from that vantage point, was announced during President Nixon's visit to Moscow in 1972. If this should go smoothly, the fateful competition in space and rocketry that loomed so large throughout the post-World War II years will enter a new and far more hopeful phase. The vested interests in both societies that have grown up around the enormous production and support systems needed to send rockets into space might thus discover a new outlet for their expertise, and would not find diversion of resources from the arms race to be an immediate personal and collective disaster, as would otherwise be the case.

For the world at large, such political-military questions are certainly of the highest importance. Yet there are other important dimensions to the human condition. Growing populations pressing against food supplies set limits to political action; the possibility of irremediable ecological disaster as a by-product of industrial activity demands swift political intervention. Population growth and industrial growth, proceeding at different paces in different parts of the earth, also raise the question of whether human societies and standards of living are becoming or ought to become more nearly equal. And if equalization is either inevitable or desirable, one must ask whether it will or ought to be equalization upward or downward. Can the world's poor attain the level of consumption characteristic of the United States today without creating ecological disaster, or should those who today command a disproportionately large share of the world's energy and material goods instead learn to live more cheaply? Is economic development a good thing? What, in short, is life for?

Clearly the political ideas and ideals we inherited from our predecessors are not adequate answers to questions such as these. Leninism and Wilsonianism have both worn themselves out as credible faiths and prescriptions for the future. It looks like the end of an era, but what will follow, who can say?

SUGGESTED READING

It is always hard to understand recent times because the rush of events does not of itself present a pattern for our comprehension. Hence books that make the attempt to find an intelligible pattern are needed, even at the cost of oversimplification. Among such may be recommended Kenneth Boulding, *The Meaning of the Twentieth Century: The Great Transition,** Hans W. Gatzke, *The Present in Perspective: A Look at the World Since 1945,** Robert L. Heilbroner, *The Future as History,** Harrison Brown, *The Challenge of Man's Future,** Geoffrey Barraclough,

*Available in a paperback edition.

*An Introduction to Contemporary History,** and Theodore H. Von Laue, *The Global City: Freedom, Power and Necessity in the Age of World Revolution.*

No thoroughly informed account of the A-bomb and H-bomb balance of terror can yet be written, but several efforts in this direction have been made. Cecil Van Meter Crabb, *American Foreign Policy in the Nuclear Age,** Henry A. Kissinger, *Nuclear Arms and American Foreign Policy,** Arnold L. Horelick and Myron Rush, *Strategic Power and Soviet Foreign Policy,* Herman Kahn, *Thinking About the Unthinkable,** and P. M. S. Blackett, *Atomic Weapons and East-West Relations* are among the more interesting and better informed. A related topic, the exploration of space, is handled by E. M. Emme, *A History of Space Flight.**

The origins and responsibility for the Cold War came under sharp debate among historians in the United States during the 1960s, when the high cost of trying to police the world became apparent. Much was written in a partisan spirit, but the following are among the more judicious efforts to treat the issue: John Lewis Gaddis, *The United States and the Origins of the Cold War, 1941–1947,** Lloyd C. Gardner, Arthur Schlesinger, Jr., and Hans Morgenthau, *The Origins of the Cold War,** Martin F. Herz, *Beginnings of the Cold War,** Walter LaFeber, *The Origins of the Cold War.** A related problem is how to understand world Communism. Here Robert V. Daniels, *The Nature of Communism,* and Richard Lowenthal, *World Communism: The Disintegration of a Secular Faith** may be recommended.

Three efforts to analyze the troubled pattern of international affairs deserve mention here: Peter Calvocoressi, *International Politics since 1945,** which is basically narrative; W. W. Rostow, *The Diffusion of Power: An Essay in Recent History,* and Morton A. Kaplan, *Great Issues of International Politics: The International System and National Policy** are more interested in a political science approach. J. D. B. Miller, *The Politics of the Third World** looks at the scene from the point of view of the underdeveloped nations.

The following books may serve as introductions to the recent political scene.

Europe. Robert E. Osgood, *NATO: The Entangling Alliance;* George Liska, *Europe Ascendant: The International Politics of Unification;* Walter Laquer, *Europe Since Hitler*;* M. M. Postan, *An Economic History of Western Europe, 1945–64.*

Middle East. Majid Khadduri, *Political Trends in the Arab World*;* Michael Curtis, ed., *People and Politics of the Middle East.**

Far East. James Chieh Hsiung, *Ideology and Practice: The Evolution of Chinese Communism*;* Peter Van Ness, *Revolution and Chinese Foreign Policy: Peking's Support for Wars of National Liberation*;* David Rees, *Korea: The Limited War*;* Chong-sik Lee, *The Politics of Korean Nationalism;* G. F. Hudson et al., *The Sino-Soviet Dispute*;* John T. McAlister, Jr., and Paul Mus, *The Vietnamese and Their Revolution*;* Frances FitzGerald, *Fire in the Lake.**

Africa. Arnold Rivkin, *The African Presence in World Affairs;* Vernon McKay, *Africa in World Affairs;* J. B. Webster and A. A. Boahen, *History of West Africa: The Revolutionary Years, 1815 to Independence*;* Manfred Halpern, *The Politics of Social Change in the Middle East and North Africa.*

Latin America. Magnus Mörner, ed., *Race and Class in Latin America*;* Hugh Thomas, *Cuba: The Pursuit of Freedom;* William L. O'Neill, *Coming Apart: An Informal History of the Americas in the 1960s;* Eric Williams, *From Columbus to Castro: The History of the Caribbean, 1492–1969;* Arthur P. Whitaker and David C. Jordan, *Nationalism in Contemporary Latin America.*

RISING EXPECTATIONS

The 1970s continued the "great leap forward" of underdeveloped countries into modernity that was so accelerated by World War II. Ancient ways of life bypassed by the industrial revolution of the nineteenth century are now frequently changing. Even in countries which have rejected Western political systems, the products and processes of the industrial West have been eagerly sought after, with sometimes amusing but more often amazing results.

Southeast Asian rice farmer. *Photo: Exxon Corporation*

The first pair of landscapes suggest the fundamental transformation taking place in agriculture as mechanical power is applied to farming. The extraordinary pattern produced by this covey of gigantic combines and tractors responsible for making such marks on the landscape utterly dwarf the older scale of human and animal effort which still exists in places like Asia. Only such mechanization permits the feeding of the modern megalopolis and the emptying of the countryside— a flight to urbanism which constitutes the most novel aspect of recent social history.

Mechanized farm, U.S.A. *Photo: Loomis Dean, LIFE Magazine © Time Inc.*

Indian construction workers. Photo: Howard Sochurek, LIFE Magazine © Time Inc.

Computer, U.S.A. *Photo: Exxon Corporation*

As urbanization grows so does industry, spreading into different areas at different rates. Modern ends—like this great dam which will provide water for hitherto parched regions of India—are sometimes still achieved by quite traditional means, i.e., hand labor on heavy construction work. When factories become more modern, however, hand labor is often assigned to mechanical and repetitive tasks on the assembly line. When human hands are thus used as machines instead of as the brain's exploratory tools, great psychological strains enter workers' lives, but long-range consequences of this deformation of human experience will probably never be known since automated controls have begun to transfer nearly all merely repetitive tasks to precise and tireless machines.

This, in turn, opens the question of what work is. In an automated world, how can and should a man earn his living? The uses of leisure, and the just apportionment of income among groups and individuals offer unsolved problems for industrially developed regions of the world which are almost as difficult and in some respects far more insoluble (since human societies have little experience with affluence) as the problems of the poor and underdeveloped lands, where the population presses hard upon the food supply and living standards hover close to the starvation level.

Assembly line worker, U.S.A. *Photo: Gjon Mili for FORTUNE © Time Inc.*

Economists and social engineers know, at least in principle, how poverty can be overcome, through programs of investment, training in new skills, and population control. But even the most intelligent and energetic efforts to escape from poverty and acquire the rudiments of modern technology introduce a tremendous range of discrepancies into non-Western societies. With new machines come new ideas, and as traditional patterns of living break up and disappear, popular hopes and expectations are liable to outrun the level of progress which can be achieved by even the greatest efforts of that society.

Social control, too, becomes difficult, and, as the contagion of deliberate rapid change spreads from one region of the earth to another, the gap between generations widens. Old and new, in Japan as everywhere else, turn their backs and walk away from each other. It is not easy for us to imagine the disruption of the links between generations that results from the arrival of even elementary literacy in a society where folk tales and face-to-face communication between elders and youth had previously been the way in which traditional values and social discipline were preserved. Liberation and wider horizons opened for the young by being able to read automatically mean a repudiation of the authority of community elders and local tradition. Novelty can easily

Television school, Niger. *Photo: Marc Riboud, Magnum*

Story-teller, Botswana. *Photo: N. R. Farbman, LIFE Magazine © Time Inc.*

145

become so alluring that older local patterns of deference and guides to conduct give way, with the result that there is sometimes no peaceable way to hold a people together and get them to work toward common ends. In such a situation, wholesale resort to military rule and party dictatorship is only to be expected.

It is far easier to import the outward trappings of a foreign culture than it is to adjust local values and social patterns to assimilate the new. As a result, initial borrowings are almost always and necessarily superficial. The lovely bridge and super-modern buildings of Kuala Lumpur, Malaya's capital, as well as the old sheik and his telephone, are strangely incongruous. The three Indian women, carrying their bundles in the same way they have for centuries, are symbols of the

University of Malaya, Kuala Lumpur. *Photo: Brian Brake, Magnum*

Sheik and grandson, United Arab Emirates.
Photo: Bruce McAllister, Black Star

Women on their way to work, India. *Photo: Werner Bischof, Magnum*

human situation as it exists in many parts of the world. The old ways are more familiar: the women walk on an ancient cobbled road instead of the paved one. But even as they cling to some aspects of the old life, the new surrounds them, bringing hope for a higher standard of living, along with the threat of a dying environment. For the present, at least, the hope is stronger than the threat.

As the world shrinks and the walls of tribe and village come tumbling down, men begin to know their neighbors—across the street and across the world. But knowledge is neutral. It may be used for good or evil purposes with equal effect. Whether envy, fear, and hate will boil up toward uncontrollable violence and war, or whether reason and generosity will prevail among the peoples of the world remain unanswered questions for our age. No doubt, as in times past, both ways will find scope for repeated expression as men continue to stumble toward the future.

Beggars, India. *Photo: Werner Bischof, Magnum*

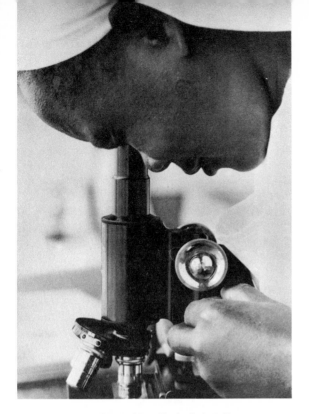

Boy with microscope, Uganda. *Photo: Charles Harbutt, Magnum*

Barefoot doctors, Peoples Republic of China. *Photo: Eastfoto*

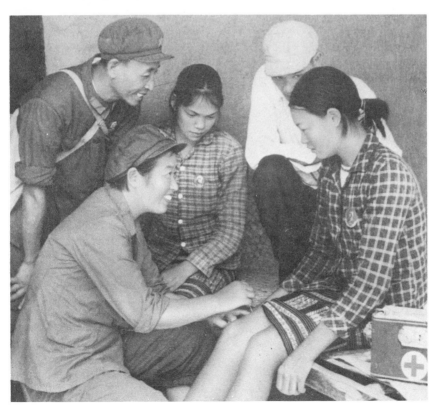

Chapter 5

Social and Cultural Trends Since 1939

TRENDS OF THE FUTURE

The political and military turmoil of recent decades both expressed and provoked rapid changes of social patterns and cultural traditions in all parts of the world. Each nation and each community had its own peculiar experiences; so, of course, did every individual person. Without a longer time perspective it is difficult to assess the significance of these myriad experiences for the general history of civilization. But if we are to understand our world, some effort must be made to generalize. Only so can we hope to guess where we stand and where we are going, and perchance try to use our intelligence to do something about it.

The Ascendance of the City. Broadly speaking, it looks as though the world is now teetering on the brink of a social mutation as vast as the transformation that came to society when humans ceased to be predators and began to cultivate their food, and, presently, to build cities. This is a very radical assertion, the implications of which need to be explored.

Ever since people first started to gather into cities, some five thousand years ago, civilized societies have been built around specializations of function and distinctions of rank. Those at the top enjoyed relative abundance of goods and the rewards of status and power; but the vast majority always tilled the soil, and were compelled to surrender part of what they produced in the form of taxes and rents. These, supplemented in some degree by income from trade and industry, sustained the upper classes, who governed, prayed, fought, and carried on the higher cultural activities that we like to think of as the distinguishing marks of civilization.

This fundamentally hierarchical structure of society now seems to be dissolving all around the world. To be sure, most people are still farmers, and sharp differences of income and function continue to characterize society both in Communist and in non-Communist lands. Nevertheless, the agricultural base of society is being called into question as it has not been since farming first began. This occurs in two ways.

In some technologically advanced lands, a small proportion of the entire population now suffices to raise all the food needed to feed vastly expanded urban communities. In the United States, for example, a mere 5 percent of the population was engaged in agriculture in the mid-1960s, while 95 percent (not to mention those of other lands who helped consume American agricultural surpluses) ate food they had not raised themselves. Obviously, with such a numerical shift the traditional relationship between city and country, food consumer and food producer, citizen and peasant, is destroyed. The fundamental experience of the agricultural seasons, the definition of work in terms of the tasks of plowing, planting, harvesting, and threshing, and the possibility in bad times of getting along for a while on the products of the family's own labor—all these characteristics of a society closely based upon agriculture must clearly wane as agricultural work becomes a specialized and highly mechanized task like any other.

In other parts of the world, modern communications have broken down the former isolation of village life without changing technical, social, or economic realities to keep up with new expectations. As knowledge of how city folk live seeped into the countryside, a radical discontent with the restrictions and hardships of life on the land disturbed the old, traditional basis of village society. Young people wished to leave home and start life in a city, where excitement, variety, wider horizons, and, presumably, a better life seemed possible. Such migration to towns often proceeded without any economic incentive; but when good jobs were to be had in cities, migration from the countryside gathered velocity all the more rapidly. Satisfactory statistics to measure the magnitude of this movement do not exist. Indeed, the proper definition of urban as against rural occupations is hard for census takers around the world to agree on. But the worldwide scope of recent urbanization can be appreciated by considering the following figures:

Percentage of world population living in cities of 100,000 and over[1]

1900	1950	1970
5.5	13.1	23.2

The Peasants' Revolt. However impressive in itself, the recent growth of urban population does not measure the psychological disruption of rural communities. Farmers and peasants have become conscious of how narrow and constricted their traditional lives are, and they resent their disadvantages vis-à-vis city folk. The recency of this phenomenon in most of the world needs also to be borne in mind. Effects are just beginning to show themselves. The revolt of the world's peasantries against their traditional status in society may well prove to be the principal axis of world politics in the second half of the twentieth century.

[1]Philip M. Hauser and Leo F. Schnore, *The Study of Urbanization* (New York: John Wiley & Sons, Inc., 1965), p. 548. 1970 figure an oral communication from Dr. Hauser.

In Asia and Africa—and somewhat less dramatically in Latin America—World War II marked the horizon line for this peasant awakening. Widespread distribution of radios to peasant villages was undertaken during and after the war as a means of diffusing political propaganda. At one stroke, the arrival of a radio and loudspeaker brought the world of the city to the countryside. The effect was often profound. Peasants the world around have always nursed a secret sense of grievance against cities and civilization. From the farmer's point of view, anyone who does not work for a living in the direct and immediate muscular sense of the word is necessarily suspect. How can he eat, save by somehow cadging food produced by the sweat of honest people's brows? In times past, peasant grievances rose to political expression from time to time, when the depredations of tax collectors, overcrowding on the land, or a faltering of authority provoked peasant revolt. Such uprisings were seldom successful; and even if successful in overthrowing one political regime, they met automatic betrayal when victorious leaders faced the task of setting up regular government and started to collect taxes, just like their predecessors.

This age-old pattern is far from dead in our time. There are plenty of circumstances provoking peasant unrest—including, in many parts of the world, naked pressure of population on the land. What is new, of course, is the intimacy of communications between village and city. The forms of expression for peasant discontent obviously depend very much on what sort of views are disseminated from the cities. Incitement to revolution and violence falls on receptive ears. This, in fact, has been the great strength of Communist movements since World War II, for the Marxian explanation of local hardships is a plausible one, and has the great advantage that it points out the enemy: landlords and exploiters, capitalists and bankers, foreigners and imperialists, against whom peasant feeling, as well as nationalistic and racial feelings, are easy to mobilize.

Exhortation to hard work, better methods of cultivation, devices for channeling surplus labor from the village to new industrial undertakings—in general the challenge of trying to solve local problems by intelligence and effort—may also fall on receptive ears, or may not, depending on how easy it is for the villagers to identify themselves with the national goals in question, and what they hear from competing voices.

As so often happens when new technologies impinge on human life, the effect of the changed urban-rural relationship in our time is to expand the range of the possible. At one extreme, brutal civil war and harsh mutual suspicion may divide different classes or ethnic groups. At the other, coordination of social effort on a scale to embrace nearly everybody becomes practicable. What is common to both responses is the decay of customary limits to and definitions of conduct. Old people may grumble and doubt, but the young believe and act. The drama created by the resulting generation gap has been played out in village after village and family after family within the past thirty years.

Wider mobilization of human energies for agreed purposes becomes possible with the breakdown of custom. In the long run this may enlarge wealth and increase the power at mankind's disposal. But in the short run these energies can be and, as we have seen, often have been used to pit nations or classes against one another. No one who has studied history will think this is a new fate for mankind. Only the scale, pace, and mass of the phenomenon is new in our age. But scale and mass, if sufficiently great, can produce differences in kind, and as the peasant majority of mankind enters into the political process and rebels against the traditional disadvantaged and exiled state in which their predecessors acquiesced, who can predict the long-range result?

The Changing Meaning of Work. The peasant rebellion takes on a further significance if we try to survey what is also occurring, or seems about to occur, in industry. In the more advanced countries automation of production lines has already gone very far. Human labor, in the old definition of the term, becomes less and less important; inanimate power, machines, and automatic mechanisms for regulation and control have taken over many of the functions once reserved for human brains and muscles. To be sure, automation of distribution and transport lag, and in most of the world agriculture has scarcely been touched by it. But automated food production is a technical possiblity, and in some (especially American) farms has already come partially into being.

Thus it requires no great stretch of the imagination to believe that in our time the meaning of work is beginning to undergo a fundamental metamorphosis. With this metamorphosis the whole texture of daily experience and the meanings of daily life will also change, but in what directions and how, it is hard to say.

So fundamental a transformation in human society will probably take two or three centuries to work itself out. It seems likely that we in the twentieth century are merely on the verge, unable to recognize the lines along which some future automated and workless society may define a new rhythm and balance of everyday life. When and if humanity survives such changes (and it is always well to remember that atomic or biological warfare may remove us all from the face of the earth long before a new postagricultural age establishes itself), mankind will presumably enter upon an era of history as different from the age of cities and peasants, of civilizations and wars, of social hierarchy and economic inequality, as our age is from that of the human hunters who roamed the earth before techniques of food production first chained people to the ceaseless round of labor in the fields.

The far-reaching transformations of the human scene will come, if at all, only bit by bit. But already some striking characteristics of the way the flight from the land has begun can be discerned. The basic fact is that western Europe, and the lands settled from Europe, started industrialization a century or more before other parts of the world did, and at a time when spacious, thinly occupied frontier regions were

ENERGY: PRODUCTION AND CONSUMPTION, 1971

(Quantities in million metric tons* of coal equivalent)

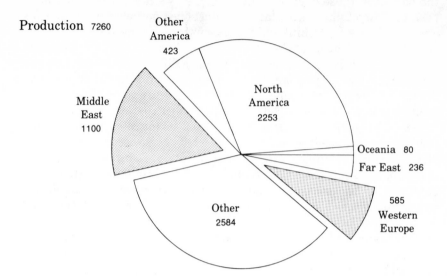

Production 7260

Other America 423

Middle East 1100

North America 2253

Oceania 80

Far East 236

Other 2584

585 Western Europe

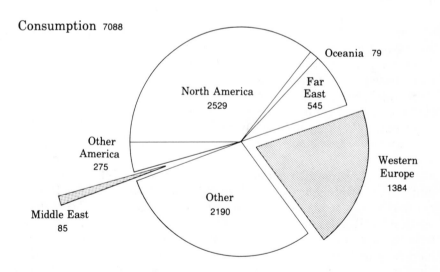

Consumption 7088

Oceania 79

North America 2529

Far East 545

Other America 275

Western Europe 1384

Middle East 85

Other 2190

*A metric ton is a unit of mass and weight equal to 1000 kilograms or 2204.6 pounds.

A region's capacity to produce energy, whether from coal, oil, gas, or other natural resources, gives us some idea of the basis of the economy of the region. For instance, western Europe, an area high in population, which has traditionally exported manpower rather than raw materials, consumes more than twice as much energy as it produces. The thinly populated Middle East, on the other hand, has grown rich on its oils wells, as indicated by the fact that it produces about thirteen times as much energy as it uses.

154

easily available for European settlers to occupy and exploit. Industrialization and urbanization when the Americas and northern Asia, as well as remoter regions like Australia, southern Africa, and New Zealand, lay open for settlement differed from the circumstances confronting crowded Asian countrysides today; and the breakup of rural routines extending across centuries, reaching a climax in the fifty years since World War I, was qualitatively different from the disruption of village life now occurring in Asia and Africa.

New Demarcations. As a result of Europe's priority, the world is divided between what are now often called "developed" and "underdeveloped," or backward, lands. The gap is broad, and in many respects appears to be widening, in spite of various aid programs and the efforts of Asian, African, and other poverty-stricken peoples to escape from their backwardness.

In the more developed lands this world situation has created no special tensions. A relatively thick cushion of corporate groupings continues to function reasonably well, even under the changing conditions of recent decades. The state is the greatest of these corporations; but under its legal umbrella a host of interacting, organized bodies compete for human attention and loyalties with varying fortunes, some rising and some falling, while the system as a whole alters comparatively slowly. Businesses, labor unions, army units, street gangs, political parties, churches, schools, clubs, cooperatives, taverns, fraternal societies, commercial sports and entertainments—taken together—constitute a web within which most individual lives are held in place, so to speak, despite the intrinsic openness and anonymity that big cities and massive population migrations permit. The vitality of such groups, moreover, makes urban living more or less tolerable for most people, and acts as a stabilizing force in society, despite the galloping technological innovation of our age.

Perhaps the most important overall trend in the arrangement of these various corporate groupings has been a tendency to divide along age lines. Prolonged formal education segregates children and youth by age groups in school. Parents usually leave home to go off to their work, where they associate mainly with persons of nearly the same age; and on retirement it is not uncommon, at least in the United States, for the aged to flock together at places where the weather is mild and medical services abundant. Stratification by age in this fashion is likely to have pervasive consequences, particularly when specialized mass media reinforce the self-consciousness of each separate age group. Cultural continuities within families, localities, and social or professional classes are likely to diminish in significance; discontinuities across age lines are almost certain to increase, and may even provide the central issues of domestic politics for the "developed" countries in time to come.

In backward and underdeveloped societies, however, dissatisfaction with the state of affairs, both globally and locally, remains far more acute. In Asia and Africa neither peasant nor university graduate can

155

PER CAPITA INCOMES IN DOLLARS, 1971

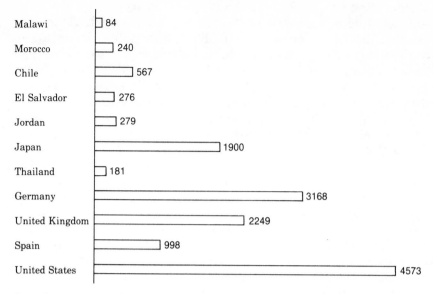

Malawi	84
Morocco	240
Chile	567
El Salvador	276
Jordan	279
Japan	1900
Thailand	181
Germany	3168
United Kingdom	2249
Spain	998
United States	4573

It is rather startling to note that in only seven nations in the entire world do people enjoy an income of over $3000 per year: U.S.A., Canada, Kuwait, Germany, Denmark, Sweden, and Switzerland. The vast majority of the rest of mankind manages to exist on under $500 per year, which, despite differences in the cost of living, is an appallingly low figure, and indicates that most people in the world live on a bare subsistence level.

feel pleased at the enormous gap between the wealth and power of developed lands and local poverty and weakness. This general dissatisfaction is fed by the spreading disorganization of traditional social groupings which seem incapable of coping with the times. In widely scattered regions of the world such formerly significant social links as tribes, village communities, castes, kindreds, religious communities, and the like survive only with difficulty or in confusing diluted forms. New institutions, most notably political parties, tend to be thin on the ground. But precisely because they lack effective competition for the loyalty of their members, newly sprung parties often try to preempt total allegiance. People emancipated from the past lack guidelines and definitions for their daily lives. Authoritarian parties naturally try to fill the gap.

As a result, cliques, in which even such matters as what kind of hat a person wears or how he addresses an acquaintance on the street may be carefully prescribed, have tended to flourish in societies emerging suddenly from traditional peasant life. In the 1960s and early 1970s this has seemed true in much of sub-Saharan Africa, and perhaps also explains much of the behavior of Communist China. In regions where religion has a stronger hold, at least one rival to newfangled political authoritarianism exists. Hence, throughout the realm of Islam, all the way from Indonesia to Morocco, and from Turkestan to Nigeria, there has been a persistent tension between traditional religion, which continues to command wide loyalties, and newer political movements, professing some sort of secular, socialist faith. In Latin America, the

156

Roman Catholic Church has played an analogous conservative role.

The Changed Role of the Military. A trait of recent social development in backward countries deserving particular attention is the rise of armies as instruments of political and technical modernization. The policies of the United States and of the Soviet Union have aided and abetted this development. If we take the internal balances of industrially developed states as a norm, American and Russian military-aid programs have concentrated both technical training and costly machinery in military hands far out of proportion to the resources available to other groups in backward nations.

Yet it would be incorrect to attribute what has happened only, or even primarily, to the policies of the great powers. There is an intrinsic glamor in the possession of arms. They embody power, and in a situation where nearly everything is uncertain, and where personal loyalties and patterns of conduct are in rapid and drastic flux, the possession of arms becomes especially critical. When coup d'état is never far away, whoever has weapons and knows how to use them is in a position to organize or forestall such affairs.

Moreover, army techniques and principles are relatively easy to transplant from one society to another. The simplicity of a military chain of command is readily understood by all; and devices for creating esprit de corps—pay, uniforms, drill, inspections, parades, and the like—are both relatively simple and universally effective. Finally, the more complex materials of war—trucks, tanks, artillery, telephones, and radio, to name only the simplest—require training in techniques that are readily transferable to civilian occupations. Individuals who have learned how to operate and maintain such devices become an elite of talent for societies in the process of emerging from agricultural simplicity; and the armies of the world, by training their soldiers in such skills, automatically confer upon them a measure of prestige and superiority over their fellows.

Modernization through militarization is not unique to our time. In the eighteenth century, Russia did much the same; and as long ago as the fourth century B.C., Macedonia modernized to the level of the classical Greek city-states by methods that seem strikingly similar. But these precedents from the past hardly help define the worldwide impact of recent militarization. Wars may become bloodier, but this is not certain, for as armies and air forces become better equipped they also become more vulnerable, since sources of supply for highly specialized modern military gadgets are usually limited to the depots of the great power from which the equipment originally came. This gives the great industrial and military powers a quite effective veto over the conduct of any prolonged military enterprise. Once committed to action, even the best equipped and stockpiled force requires a flow of spare parts and munitions that quickly reaches back to the factories where such things can be produced. Consequently, any war tends at once to engage the great powers, who must decide whether to withhold military supplies from their protégés or not.

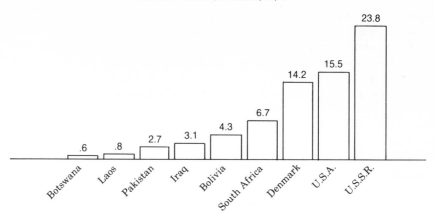

MEDICAL PERSONNEL, 1969–71
Number of doctors per 10,000 people

23.8

15.5

14.2

6.7

4.3

3.1

2.7

.8

.6

Botswana   Laos   Pakistan   Iraq   Bolivia   South Africa   Denmark   U.S.A.   U.S.S.R.

The tremendous inequality in developed and underdeveloped lands is again apparent from this chart, which illustrates the number of doctors for every 10,000 inhabitants in various nations. The U.S.S.R. surpasses the U.S.A and all other lands in this respect, a fact which will surprise most Americans. On the other hand, there are wide differences in the skill and knowledge among doctors and other medical personnel in different parts of the world. The average level of medical training in doctors in the U.S.S.R. is somewhat lower than in the U.S.A. and varies also in other countries. These statistics, in other words, do not show how good medical services are; they do show how unevenly abundant (or scarce) they are in different parts of the world.

Thus, one may conclude that the efforts of the new nations to equip their armies with modern and powerful weapons have actually had the effect of tying them closer to the sources of supply upon which the operation of the new armaments depends. Where modernization has gone furthest, in other words, dependence and inferiority vis-à-vis the great powers has tended rather to increase than to decrease, at least until such time as armaments of high quality can be locally produced on a scale equivalent to the production of the great powers. For most of the world's nations, this means forever, since the resources needed to equip and reequip a modern army are so enormous that only a great power can do so. These facts are bitterly ironic for people who have striven hard to win national independence and equality.

The Haves and the Have-Nots. But this is only the most dramatic case of a far more widespread phenomenon: for as organized invention revolutionizes technology at an ever increasing rate, the backward societies of the world have a harder and harder time staying in the race. Initial costs become enormous, and have to be met over and over again, since no sooner is one level of technology partially domesticated than the research laboratories of the rich nations develop a new and usually more difficult technology, which leaves the old behind.

Complicating the task before the backward peoples of the earth still further is the fact that the first result of improvements in medical care, communication, and economic production is a tremendous spurt in population. Peasant societies survived in the past only because far more babies were born than grew up. Disease, famine, and violent death traditionally decimated the world's peasantries; births had to be numerous to keep population stable. When relatively simple and inexpensive inoculations can check epidemics, and when administrative devices to blunt the edge of famine exist in almost all parts of the world, population growth becomes spectacular. More babies grow up, marry, and give birth to still more children; and this, continued over two or three generations, can utterly transform human numbers.

The magnitude of this problem is familiar and critical, as the following statistics will suggest:

ESTIMATED WORLD POPULATION, 1920–1970

(millions)

	1920	1930	1940	1950	1960	1970	1963–1971 Annual rate of increase	Density per sq. km.
World	1811	2015	2249	2509	3010	3632	2.0	27
Africa	141	157	176	207	257	344	2.6	12
America	208	244	277	329	412	511	2.1	12
Asia except U.S.S.R.	966	1072	1212	1384	1684	2056	2.3	76
Europe except U.S.S.R.	329	356	381	395	426	462	.8	94
Oceania	9	10	11	13	16	20	2.1	2
U.S.S.R.	158	176	192	181	214	243	1.1	11

Figures like these deserve to be pondered, for they show not only that the world's population has doubled in a mere fifty years, but that the rate of growth is increasing. Exponential growth cannot continue indefinitely; soon the earth will not be able to hold humanity if recent population trends continue for very long. Before we reach the point where there is standing room only, population checks of one sort or another will come into play, whether peaceable or violent, spontaneous or imposed from without. Indeed, only strenuous and skillful efforts at increasing food supplies and industrial production can now prevent growing populations from lowering standards of living, particularly in the poorest parts of the earth.

It is easy for well-fed Americans to analyze the world's problems in terms of a race between economic development and population growth, and to try to think of ways to increase the one and slow the other. But from the point of view of the three quarters of mankind who find themselves in parlous danger of losing this race, such cool and detached analysis of the situation and what to do about it can seldom be anything but irritating. If desperate efforts to become rich and strong do not suffice, and if the old style of life seems as hopeless as the new, what then? Anger and frustration, hatred of those who are more fortunate, and irrational behavior on a mass scale is one possible response. Redoubled effort to modernize, even more radically than

BIRTH AND DEATH RATES

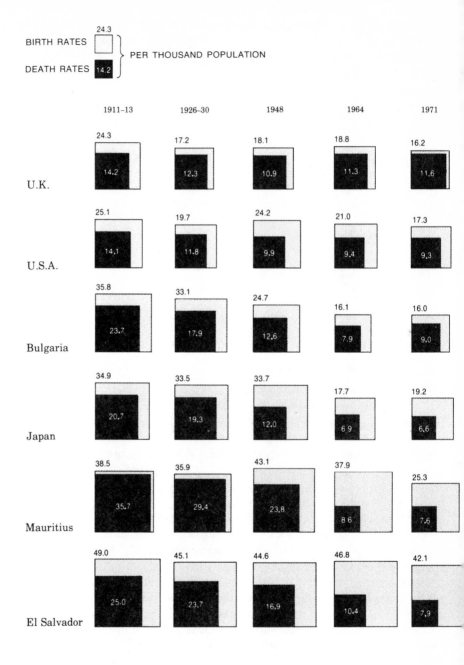

BIRTH RATES ☐ ⎫
24.3

⎬ PER THOUSAND POPULATION

DEATH RATES ■ 14.2 ⎭

	1911–13	1926–30	1948	1964	1971

U.K. 24.3 / 14.2 — 17.2 / 12.3 — 18.1 / 10.9 — 18.8 / 11.3 — 16.2 / 11.6

U.S.A. 25.1 / 14.1 — 19.7 / 11.8 — 24.2 / 9.9 — 21.0 / 9.4 — 17.3 / 9.3

Bulgaria 35.8 / 23.7 — 33.1 / 17.9 — 24.7 / 12.6 — 16.1 / 7.9 — 16.0 / 9.0

Japan 34.9 / 20.7 — 33.5 / 19.3 — 33.7 / 12.0 — 17.7 / 6.9 — 19.2 / 6.6

Mauritius 38.5 / 35.7 — 35.9 / 29.4 — 43.1 / 23.8 — 37.9 / 8.6 — 25.3 / 7.6

El Salvador 49.0 / 25.0 — 45.1 / 23.7 — 44.6 / 16.9 — 46.8 / 10.4 — 42.1 / 7.3

This cross section of the birth and death rates of developed and underdeveloped nations eloquently portrays what is meant by the "population explosion." In every country the death rate has dropped—often dramatically, as in the case of Mauritius—since 1911–1913. The alarming fact, however, is that while the death rate has steadily declined, the birth rate, particularly in underdeveloped areas like El Salvador and Mauritius, has remained virtually unchanged, so that the population is multiplying at an ever increasing rate—not arithmetically but geometrically.

before, and to extend conscious management to such aspects of human life as procreation is a second conceivable line of action. The ex-peasant nations of the world will have somehow to choose a path that falls between these extremes; and we can safely assume that the history of the rest of the twentieth century will turn in large part upon the choices they make.

Communist and Non-Communist Nations: Similarities and Differences. If the initial impact of modern technology and social organization seems likely to widen the gap between the rich and poor, the industrial and agricultural, the white and colored portions of mankind, it seems equally true that the demands of this same technology are propelling the more highly developed industrial nations toward a more and more similar organization of society. This is most obvious in economics. In the mid-1960s the Russians began experimentation with market prices as a device for moving products through the industrial system and regulating quality. The United States and other non-Communist nations have experimented far more boldly with various forms of political regulation of economic processes. The upshot seems clearly to be convergent. Politically controlled capitalism and a market-oriented socialism begin to resemble one another in essentials, particularly since the goals sought through political regulation of economic activities have also converged very conspicuously. In the U.S.S.R. the satisfaction of the private consumer and a higher standard of living for all have begun to compete with the simpler goals of more heavy industry, more armaments, more fuel, steel, electricity, and other basic commodities which sufficed in Stalin's day. Simultaneously, in the United States, ever since World War II the use of extensive resources for the production of armaments has supplemented an economy traditionally keyed to consumer demand. Various other forms of public expenditure—roads, foreign aid, social services—have also played an increasingly important part in the U.S. economy. Similar mixed economies—partly controlled by market demand, partly directed by public policy—prevail in other industrially advanced lands, with different boundaries between private and public sectors in different places.

Politically, the contrast between the Communist and non-Communist worlds remains important, for Communist parties claim and enforce a monopoly wherever they have risen to power. On the other hand, the sort of relationship between public opinion and government policy created by the new mass media may turn out to be quite similar in all industrialized nations. Someone has to decide what to report on radio and television and how to report it, and this makes the management of news inevitable. Democratic and liberal governments are almost as ready to manage news as Communist regimes, and our traditional checks upon official manipulation of information—such things as the availability of other channels and modes of publicity like newspapers, journals, handbills, etc.—by no means nullify the effects skillful news management can achieve.

On still a third level, resemblances between the more highly developed industrial societies also seem to be growing. I refer to public efforts to manipulate socioeconomic structures and patterns of behavior. In the United States, President Johnson's War on Poverty, announced in 1964, offered the most flamboyant American example of an effort to change social reality according to plan. The piecemeal and imperfect implementation of civil rights legislation, aimed at securing real equality for blacks in American life, was a similar attempt; so were programs of urban renewal and agricultural subsidy. Russian efforts to remodel society through official action went back to tsarist times. Under Lenin and Stalin, when the revolution was new and changes were particularly rapid, the government relied more on force than on persuasion or economic incentives. But here, too, recent efforts seem to resemble comparable American programs by showing a greater regard for the wishes of the people whose lives are being changed. Thus, for example, Khrushchev's "Virgin lands campaign" relied on high-pressure advertising to recruit the labor needed to bring several million acres of Kazakstan under cultivation. By way of comparison, in Stalin's day, concentration camps supervised by the secret police provided the labor required in remote and unattractive parts of the Soviet Union. Thus, while Soviet methods have become less brutal, American public officials have taken over functions once largely reserved for private business—with the result that methods and goals of social engineering in the two countries begin to resemble one another more and more closely.

In these and other respects, convergence of American and Russian societies is very striking. In other parts of the world trends are not so simple. In western Europe, for example, the Common Market has allowed the breaking through of old national barriers to the distribution of goods and migration of persons. This has given a remarkable fillip to all aspects of economic life, and has provoked radical social changes which often transcend existing political boundaries. Since there is no single government for the Common Market countries, nothing so strong and all-embracing as the American or Russian government has presided over these transformations. Moreover, in most European countries armament production is less important than it is for the two great world powers. Japan, too, has prospered since 1950 without an armaments industry of any consequence, and with a government which on principle, if not always in practice, resists the impulse to regulate and control economic and social change.

The variety of social and political structures in the world as a whole seems a good deal more apparent today than was the case when colonial administrators dominated the African and much of the Asian scene. Whether modern industrialism and worldwide communications will in time override these differences and create a standard model for all human societies, or whether local, ethnic, and cultural multiplicity will persist indefinitely among mankind, is a still unanswered question. Signs and portents, unsure at best, are flatly contradictory.

General Considerations. Art and thought have a complicated, circular relationship to society as a whole. They reflect society but also act upon it; and separate arts and particular strands of thought may have a real autonomy of development that bears little or no relationship to anything outside. Satisfactory generalizations are therefore difficult to make for any period of history, and particularly so for a time of which we are both observers and products. Yet the high culture of an age is in some respects its most lasting achievement, and the world since 1939 may well strike later generations as more significant for its art and thought than for its political struggles and social transformations.

If we try, first, to take a global view of mankind's cultural posture, it seems safe to suggest that everywhere traditional styles of art and thought have lost their hold on the minds of the creative few who set the cultural tone. This is as true in Western countries as in non-Western ones. The visual and verbal arts, together with the music, produced by Westerners have changed so radically since 1900 as to constitute a break in the overall cultural style of Western civilization. This break into "modernism" was almost as radical—though perhaps not quite so painful—as the interruption every important non-Western artistic tradition suffered in the course of the nineteenth century as a direct result of Western encroachments. The European style of natural science has exhibited greater stability than any artistic tradition; and religion, too, has been a strong conservative force in every society. Yet here, too, the recent changes in these dimensions of human concern have been greater than in most earlier ages.

When so much is adrift, old landmarks inevitably go under. New ones, which may in time become familiar to future generations, are likely to seem mere flotsam in a chaotic sea when first they appear on the horizon. Hence it is difficult to know whether we are merely living through the decay and disruption of an age gone by, or are privileged to witness the birth pangs of some new cultural style or styles that will define the sensibilities of ages yet to come. Perhaps both are in process; but if so, we can scarcely yet expect to recognize the character and importance of whatever it is that will last amid all the confused variety and endless novelties of our time.

Two general reactions are possible in the face of widespread breakdown of old cultural (as well as of social) traditions.

People may seek to create a new roof over their heads by choosing or creating a faith and style that aspires to completeness. This totalitarian drive for a universe made meaningful by a coherent system of belief and sensibility may take the form of a revival of old traditions, or may ostentatiously repudiate the local past in favor of some foreign faith and style of life. Revival, of course, requires revision, often very radical; and borrowed doctrines always change in

163

important ways when transplanted from one society to another. Recent examples of these phenomena are easy to detect. Gandhi and his followers, for example, set out to return to a better past, and in trying to do so actually generated new cultural currents in India which may, or may not, endure. Chinese Communists, on the other hand, disdained the Confucianism and Buddhism of China's past, borrowed their doctrines from the West, and then set out to make a new kind of human being who would act, think, and feel according to the scientific dictates of the party. Even more rigorously than in Russia, the Chinese regime believed that all art and thought should simply help the party to make new men and women.

On the other hand, when confronted by a real or threatened breakdown of familiar cultural patterns, people may just grin and bear it, permitting, or indeed encouraging, individual thinkers and artists to depart from convention, even at the risk of becoming incomprehensible to their contemporaries. Throughout our time, this sort of uninhibited, individualistic, innovative pluralism has predominated in western Europe, and in the countries closely tied to Europe. Whether coherence will emerge from all the wild artistic and literary experimentation of the twentieth century remains to be seen. Stylistic pluralism and random striving for private and personal originality may continue for a long time. How long probably depends on how persistently other kinds of social confusion and uncertainty beset people's minds and feed the fires of artistic rebellion.

The Progress of Science: Atoms and Genes. Though it seems impossible to offer a convincing overview of the direction and meaning of recent art and thought, some observations about segments of contemporary cultural achievements deserve attention. First, let us consider the progress of science. In the 1920s and 1930s the reigning branch of science was physics. In those decades, electron accelerators and mathematical theory joined forces to penetrate the atom for the first time. During those two decades, Einstein's strange world of relativity came alive before ordinary imaginations through the theory's demonstrated applicability to the astronomically large and to the very, very small, where velocities approaching the speed of light could be observed. The new physics achieved its most dramatic practical application during World War II, when an international team of scientists, led by Enrico Fermi, and organized under the aegis of the United States Army, assisted a team of engineers and technicians from the DuPont Corporation in manufacturing the first atomic bombs.

The consequences for international relations and the future of mankind were obviously great, as well as incalculable; but no new theoretical insight resulted from the controlled release of atomic energy. After 1939, physicists accumulated much new data, identified a confusing number of new subatomic particles, and widened the spectrum of experimental observation, thanks to new and improved

164

engineering devices that allowed control over both very high and very low temperatures. New observations came in faster than they could be fitted into theory. Considerable confusion and intellectual disarray resulted. So many questions within the proper domain of physics awaited solution that the influence of the science upon other branches of human thought weakened. Hence, beginning with the 1950s, biology—particularly genetics—displaced physics from its earlier role as the natural science whose recent progress seemed to have the greatest importance for other intellectual disciplines.

In genetics the landmark date was 1953, when F. H. C. Crick and J. D. Watson first suggested a physico-chemical model for the molecule that carries genetic information from cell to cell in all living things. Subsequent experiments validated their idea and rapidly filled out details. The double helix of the DNA (deoxyribonucleic acid) molecule, comprised of hundreds of thousands of atoms arranged into a limited number of standard blocks, which are then grouped into triplets, and the triplets in turn into lengthy chains whose overall pattern is almost infinitely variable, is, in its way, as beautiful and compelling as Newton's law of gravitation. The further fact that either half of the helix, when separated from its partner, is capable, in a suitably nutritive environment, of regenerating a new matching chain provides a delightfully ingenious mechanism for the processes of cellular multiplication and biological reproduction.

Speculation as to how such a molecule might have formed initially from chance combinations of its constituent parts became much more specific after the chemical definition of life as known on earth became so much clearer. For many scientists a corollary was that life—or self-replicating systems equivalent to terrestrial life—must exist elsewhere in the universe. Among billions of stars, and presumably even larger numbers of planets, statistical chance seemed to require the repeated occurrence of conditions propitious to the spontaneous generation of living molecules.

Practical applications of the new theoretical understanding of genetic mechanisms have only begun, but in principle it certainly looks as though nothing would prevent scientists from tinkering with the genetic codes as fixed in plants and animals by the long process of evolution. As chemists, beginning only a little more than a century ago, created entirely new materials for human use, it now looks as though biological engineers of the future may be able to manufacture new plants and animals, not by the clumsy method of selection from natural variation as hitherto, but by using physical and chemical forces to alter the arrangement and detailed structure of the DNA molecule. To alter human genetic character by deliberate changes may also prove possible. If such techniques are ever put into effect on a general scale, human society would change more radically than anything our age has yet seen. History as we know it would come to an end; humanity would wither before a post-human population whose qualities we cannot expect to comprehend.

165

MARGARET MEAD AND
SIMONE DE BEAUVOIR

Margaret Mead and Simone de Beauvoir exerted an enormous influence by challenging the middle-class patterns of male-female relationships in which they had been brought up. They did so both by their numerous writings and by the way they lived. Between them, they did much to lay the groundwork for women's liberation movements of the 1960s and 1970s.

Margaret Mead was the daughter of a professor of business and economics. Born in 1901, she went to college just after the end of World War I. This was the "jazz age," when a vast economic boom, rapid urbanization, and exposure to movies, radio, and the automobile were transforming American life at an unprecedented pace. With high intelligence and enormous energy, Margaret Mead responded to another sort of novelty with enthusiasm—the new winds of doctrine filtering into the United States from Europe, particularly the ideas of Sigmund Freud. Bachelor's and master's degrees in psychology were the result.

But as a senior in college, Margaret Mead met anthropology for the first time and decided to get a Ph.D. in that field. As part of her training she undertook a field trip to Samoa, 1925–26. She went with a simple question in mind: Were the problems that often beset adolescents in American society also to be found in Samoa, or was it something in the way Americans treated their children that made growing up so painful in the United States? Careful observation of how Samoans behaved convinced her that adolescents there escaped the sorts of personal problems that had so much bothered her friends and her as they had grown up.

This was the central message of her first book, *Coming of Age in Samoa,* published in 1928. It was a great popular success, and has influenced generations of college students even to the present.

Subsequent field studies of other peoples of the South Seas convinced her that sex and temperament were independent variables, so that what was properly "feminine" in one society might be "unfeminine" in another.

The implications for American society were obvious. Women ought to be able to choose to conform or to reject traditional roles and limitations on their activity. Margaret Mead herself combined a very distinguished professional career with three marriages to men who shared at least some of her intellectual interests. At the age of thirty-eight she became a mother, and in due season a grandmother.

Simone de Beauvoir, born in 1908 into a high-ranking Parisian professional family, arrived at much the same conclusion about the roles of women by way of philosophy and literature. Following a brilliant student career, she began teaching philosophy in secondary schools. After several years of such teaching, she met Jean-Paul Sartre in Paris during World War II and began to live with him without the formality of marriage. The success of her first book, a novel that came out in 1943, encouraged her to give up teaching and earn her living by writing. In the following years, novels, plays, books of travel, philosophical essays, and memoirs poured from her pen, as well as from Sartre's. Between them they popularized the philosophy of existentialism.

A major theme of Simone de Beauvoir's writing was the relation between the sexes. Like Margaret Mead, she argued, often with passion, that women's traditional roles in Western society were artificially imposed and, indeed, degrading. But Simone de Beauvoir was far more pessimistic than Margaret Mead, for she saw no easy cure for the human condition in general, nor for that of womankind in particular. Refusal to bring children into the world was therefore logically consistent with her whole philosophical position.

De Beauvoir: Robert Cohen, AGIP-Pictorial Parade

The Mechanical Brain. Two other zones of scientific activity have been unusually fertile since 1939. The first of these was the invention and then the use of electronic computers to solve both practical and theoretical problems. Pioneer models of these machines were built during World War II, but until relatively short-lived vacuum tubes could be replaced by the more dependable transistors, computers broke down too often to be really useful. Beginning in the 1950s, however, computers came into their own as devices that permitted storage, manipulation, and retrieval of enormous amounts of information in very short periods of time. The implications of this technical advance are enormous, and even experts are only beginning to understand what can be done.

Immediate practical uses are legion. Librarians can know where their books are; tax collectors can check individual returns; corporations can control inventory and the flow of materials throughout the manufacturing and distribution process; and census data can be refined and correlated as never before.

The theoretical importance of the new kinds of tabulation and calculation which entered the range of the practicable with computers is probably no less great. In principle, surely, it should become possible to derive sociological and historical generalizations from statistical records of individual life careers, if enough data gets recorded, as it seems the improvement of public and corporation management will, in due course, bring about anyway. Precision in social management and statistical exactitude in theoretical statements about human society thus seem attainable.

In yet another field, computers may open a path for fundamental breakthroughs. The human brain resembles a computer in some respects, and as computers become more sophisticated, the resemblances between electronic circuits and human brain cells increase. Theoretical comprehension of what goes on inside human brains may advance as computers advance. Insight into the nature of thought and of meanings, the uses and limitations of various ways of organizing information, definition of basic alternative categories and terms of classifications: these, and who knows what else pertaining to human intellectual processes, may attain important new precision from the work being done in the design and programming of computers. But so far, at least to an outsider, much talk and bold extrapolation have yet to produce tangible results.

The Sky Above; The Earth Below. The second zone of conspicuous scientific activity is geophysics, or perhaps we should rather say, the terrestrial and space sciences. Beginning in 1957, rocket explorations of space beyond the limits of the atmosphere provided scientists with brand new information about electrical and other phenomena surrounding Earth. More sensitive devices for analyzing earth tremors have also permitted deductions about the interior of the globe. Simultaneously, new ways of exploring oceanic depths and atmospheric heights have very greatly extended the range and accuracy of data at the disposal of the world's scientific community.

One of the most successful and spectacular demonstrations of the world-girdling character of modern science was the International Geophysical Year, 1957–1958, when special efforts to coordinate observations of all sorts of relevant phenomena were made all around the globe. The participants agreed to a free exchange of observational data, even across hostile political lines, and apparently were able to carry out this plan successfully.

More recently, artificial earth satellites and manned orbital laboratories have produced abundant data about the physical state of the earth, as well as measuring radiation from the stars and outer space across a range impossible from underneath Earth's blanket of air. Men have even visited the moon, beginning in 1969, and have left various sensors behind to record changes in the moon's state, as well as returning with samples of the moon's crust. In addition, rockets have sent sensors to Mars and Venus, Earth's nearest neighbors in the planetary system, and a probe of Jupiter is currently being prepared.

Compared to any previous age, the resources poured into scientific investigation and education since 1939—and particularly since about 1950—have become enormous. More scientists are alive today than in all previous history; and the devices they command for investigation have become enormously complex, sensitive, and ingenious. Whether some grand new theory, comparable in scope and precision to the Newtonian laws of motion, will emerge from the data-gathering of our age, or whether multiplicity and incoherence will prevail indefinitely, remains for the future to discover. But whichever direction science may take in time to come, it seems certain that the years since 1939 will be remembered as a time of flood tide—a time when new data of tremendously variegated types were gathered in faster than they could be organized or their interrelationships comprehended.

The Visual Arts and Writing. Generalizations about art and literature are especially risky, since each literary language of the world has its own at least semiautonomous history, and art traditions, while not insulated from one another by language barriers, are nonetheless very numerous and in our age ill-defined. But let us try anyway.

One very widespread characteristic of the literary and artistic history of our time is the decay of peasant cultures—oral literatures, folk art, folk dances, and the like. This is an aspect of the disruption of age-old peasant styles of life discussed above. Efforts to sustain or revive peasant traditions have been made in many lands, and in some cases the result has been to impart a distinctive stamp to a self-consciously nationalistic literary and artistic circle. The revival of Gaelic in Ireland and of Hebrew in Israel, the cultivation of "Negritude" in West Africa, and the harking back to Amerindian motifs in recent Mexican art offer examples of what can be done to preserve local cultural autonomy in the face of the sort of cosmopolitan internationalism which modern communications permit.

On the other hand, the extraordinary spread of the so-called international style of architecture, the wide initial impact of American movies, the remarkable homogeneity of airports in widely scattered parts of the earth, and the global diffusion of new products like nylon all attest to the links that unite the peoples of the world in spite of local efforts to retain or reassert distinctiveness.

Tension between the desire for local uniqueness and the glamor of the latest style emanating from some distant metropolitan cultural center—whether Paris, Moscow, Peking, or New York—seems likely to persist as a major axis of cultural development all around the world. Local capitals—Dublin, Dakar, Jerusalem, Bangkok—have taken on the role once played by villages vis-à-vis some nearby city. Modern communications tend to make everything provincial outside of two or three world centers. On the other hand, the ease with which people can travel, and the instantaneousness with which they can communicate with one another from any part of the globe, act to erase the difference between capital and provinces, and diffuse the geographical loci of cultural leadership. Individual pacesetters may be in Rome one day, in Buenos Aires the next; visit Chicago en route to a holiday in some remote Scandinavian village; or travel toward the sun from Hong Kong to San Francisco, Acapulco, or Marrakesh, and yet remain in contact with one another and with the events that matter in their particular social universe.

Socialist Realism. If we shift attention from these global considerations to the content and character of recent art and literature, one broad and basic distinction between Communist and non-Communist styles becomes quickly apparent. In Russia and China, and in lesser Communist countries as well, official control and censorship of art is taken for granted. Officials encourage wholesome, moral, inspirational work, and oppose any expression of personal alienation or isolation from society as a whole. Officially approved works of art therefore celebrate puritanical self-control extending across the full gamut of human indulgences. Communist artists idealize effort directed to community purposes, and treat a life that is naively dedicated to forwarding party directives as the highest form of human achievement. How effective such works may be in schooling the general public in new patterns of conduct cannot be estimated accurately; nor is it possible to tell how much hypocrisy and toadying enters into "socialist realism," as this sort of officially prescribed art is termed.

New Themes in the West. In the Western world, high art and literature have continued since 1939, as in the decades following World War I, to explore exactly the themes forbidden in Communist countries. Sexuality in all its forms has obsessed many famous writers, and the plight of the isolated human personality in the face of an unfriendly society and an indifferent universe has become a central literary theme. Characteristically, the heroic ideal inherited from the ancient Greeks has been turned inside out, so that instead of portraying an individual striving to impose his will upon things, writers have preferred to demonstrate how things impose themselves upon their

170

antiheroes. Depersonalization of art corresponds to the dethronement of the hero in literature. Instead of painting human figures, the most influential painters have preferred abstract designs or distorted fragmentation of optical experience.

At the bottom of these artistic departures from older conventions lies a widespread doubt, or outright denial, of human rationality. Yet while Western artists and writers have been proclaiming human helplessness and exploring the subconscious, others have tried to control and channel human behavior by use of their powers of reason and observation. Economists, for example, have made advances in analyzing the factors affecting the production and exchange of goods. In particular, knowledge of how to manipulate the business cycle by using monetary devices, first proposed by John Maynard Keynes, has found wide application. Despite all the irrationalities and rigidities of the political process, the new economic ideas have allowed the world's major governments to prevent recurrence of economic setbacks like that which was so disastrous in the 1930s.

Philosophy has largely abdicated its role as synthesizer and interpreter of thought. The most influential thinkers have either retreated into specialized technicalities of the analysis of meaning, or have advertised their despair of reason and mankind in existentialist rhapsodies that dismiss the achievements and methods of the sciences as irrelevant to the real poignancy of the human condition. History and anthropology have in some measure filled the gap philosophy left open. An example is Arnold J. Toynbee's effort to comprehend the scope and structure of human experience in his *Study of History* (published between 1934 and 1954). Other students of mankind have embarked upon interpretive essays which, like the astronomer's cosmological sallies, boldly face ultimate questions. In particular, cultural anthropology, more than other branches of social science, has attained the sort of sweep and speculative range which contemporary philosophers usually deny themselves.

Echoes of Dissent. Once again, in the realm of social thought as in the arts, the contrast between Communist dogmatism and the pluralism of the non-Communist world has been very marked. Marx, Lenin, and (in China) Mao Tse-tung, laid down the truths of dialectical materialism for all time; and nothing has been allowed publicly to contradict revealed doctrine. On the other hand, the Communists have found plenty of room for differences of opinion on how to apply such truths to particular circumstances, as the bitter quarrel between China and Russia after 1960 has amply demonstrated.

The theoretical repercussions of this quarrel have run deep, making forever untenable the old assurance of Stalin's time that there was indeed *one* Marxian truth and *one* way to apply that truth to all matters of society and politics. By implication, this discovery has challenged the theoretical basis of the Communists' totalitarianism, in matters cultural as well as in economics and politics. Signs are not wanting that many sensitive and intelligent people in Russia have indeed drawn these conclusions. Disenchantment with official dogma appears to be widespread. The recent publication of several literary works that had to be smuggled out of the country because they failed to conform to the official line provides hard evidence of the existence of a cultural underground in the Soviet Union, much resembling the revolutionary underground that opposed tsarism so ineffectually during most of the nineteenth century. China, too, harbors dissidents. A brief time in 1957, when the government relaxed censorship and invited a "hundred flowers to bloom," showed that not all Chinese writers and artists felt at ease in the leading strings imposed by the thought of Chairman Mao.

Outward unanimity and apparent conformity, therefore, may hide inward dissent and doubt among the Communists; nor is it fantastic to suggest that the Western world's literary exploration of personal alienation may also mask a relatively effective moral consensus which survives even among artists and writers of the avant garde. After all, their rebellion against the pieties and taboos of the past acquires its meaning and shock value only because so much of what they mock is still alive.

The Ecumenical Spirit. The vitality of traditional religions also attests to the continuity of old attitudes. Among Christians, efforts to reinterpret the traditional doctrines that divided Christendom into numerous rival churches have gained headway throughout the period under consideration. For a long time the Roman Catholic Church stood apart from all such ecumenical aspiration, asserting that truth could easily be found by anyone ready to submit to the papal obedience. Then, with the accession of Pope John XXIII (1958), a new tone came to prevail. Instead of inviting other Christians to repent of their errors and conform to the papal definition of truth, Roman Catholic ecclesiastics became willing to enter into friendly discussions with representatives of other faiths. The changed tone was especially apparent at the Second Vatican Council summoned by Pope John to meet in 1962. A second and final session of the council in 1965 occurred after Pope John's death. Protestant and Orthodox observers were invited to attend the council, and on a number of points the assembled bishops defined doctrine in a conciliatory manner, or brought Roman Catholic practice closer to the patterns accepted in other Christian churches. Thus, for example, the use of languages other than Latin for celebration of the mass was authorized, and the plenitude of papal power was modified by the Pope's voluntary appointment of episcopal advisers.

Nevertheless, despite some mergers among Protestant churches of the English-speaking world, old sectarian demarcations have persisted. Moreover, a number of emotional, separatist sects, like Jehovah's Witnesses and the Latter-Day Saints (or Mormons), have met with substantial missionary successes, especially in places like Africa and Latin America, where more staid and moderate forms of religion have failed to cope with the trauma of modernization. Thus, taking Christianity as a whole, the tendency toward consolidation and rapprochement among the more established churches has been balanced by the continued growth and proliferation of sects, especially along the sociological margins of the modern world.

The Realm of Islam. Christian ecumenism has reached out to embrace the Jews, or at least to soften the harshness of the historical collision between the two faiths. The Moslems, however, for all practical purposes have remained apart, both by their own choice and because most Christians have little knowledge of or interest in Islam. In the Arab lands and in Pakistan, Islam is very closely associated with the reassertion of political independence vis-à-vis the imperial and at least nominally Christian powers of western Europe. Hence the thrust of Moslem preaching has tended rather to renew ancient religious antagonisms than to explore things held in common by the two faiths. This has proved, in fact, a source of strength. In Africa and southeast Asia, for example, when local conditions give them any sort of a choice, peoples emerging from paganism usually prefer the non-Western if not anti-Western faith of Islam to the West's Christianity; and where Christianity does prevail, it is often in heterodox forms.

Efforts to erect a state along Moslem lines in Saudi Arabia, in Pakistan, and in Libya have met with indifferent success, since so much that seems vital for progress contravenes the sacred law of Islam. Revolutionaries in the Moslem community of nations have consequently found it hard to reconcile Islam with effective modernity. Nevertheless, the traditional outward signs of piety continue to command general assent in all Moslem countries except Turkey and in central Asia, where Russian and Chinese rulers have effectively discouraged Islamic worship. But even in Turkey, where in the 1920s and 1930s Mustapha Kemal launched a virulently secular assault upon Islam, a widespread revival of traditional religion has taken place since World War II.

Throughout the realm of Islam, the faith of Mohammed and all the emotions associated with it have made acceptance of the secular Communist faith an unambigious act of apostasy. This barrier to the spread of Communist ideas is more effective than the similar incompatibility between Christianity and Marxism, since in Islamic lands there is no anticlerical tradition such as has long permeated Roman Catholic countries.

Islam, after all, lacks a clergy, and in recent times has reaped advantages as well as disadvantages from that fact. Absence of anticlericalism and of any lively tradition of dissent from revealed truth as interpreted long ago makes Islam a seamless robe compared to the multiplicities and logical complexities of traditional Christianity. The conservative strength of the Moslem faith depends upon this fact. At the same time the absence of an authoritative clergy means that there are no authorized interpreters who might soften the collision between old doctrines and new conditions of life, in the way that Christian clergymen have tried vigorously to do both before and after

173

Gandhi: Photoworld, Div. FPG

Saints as well as scoundrels abound in troubled times. Our age has its share of scoundrels, but is not without its saints, as the careers of Mohandas Karamchand Gandhi (1869–1948)—called "Mahatma," that is, "Great Souled," by his admirers—and of Angelo Giuseppe Roncalli (1881–1963), who became Pope John XXIII, may remind us.

In most respects the lives of these men were polar opposites. Gandhi was born at the top of India's social ladder, the son of the Brahmin prime minister of a small Indian state. Roncalli was born an Italian peasant. Gandhi's fame and power arose from his rejection both of British law and of Hindu custom. Roncalli preferred obedience. Both were moral athletes, but Gandhi cut his own path between right and wrong, whereas Roncalli accepted and came close to embodying the long-standing ideals of Christian faith, hope, and love.

Gandhi studied law in London and then went to Natal, South Africa, to practice. There he led the Indian immigrant community in protests against discriminatory laws. Gandhi organized demonstrations, instructing his followers to break the unjust laws deliberately and submit peacefully to any punishment that might follow. By being right and behaving with quiet courage, he believed that they would eventually win their opponents over. The Indian community of Natal rallied behind the young lawyer, and Gandhi's tactics did finally persuade the whites to repeal the objectionable laws.

During World War I, Gandhi returned to India and set out to use the same nonviolent tactics to win independence from Great Britain. The campaign was long and tortuous. Gandhi was often jailed, and several times he retired from politics because he felt his followers were not yet ready to live up to his ideals. Finally, in 1947, the British granted India independence. Bloody riots between Hindus and Moslems ensued. While trying to quell this violence, Gandhi was killed by a Hindu fanatic. News of his death abruptly stilled the riots. Even in death the Mahatma was victorious.

Angelo Roncalli's career was quiet by comparison. He became a priest in 1904 and served with the Italian army in World War I. In 1921 he became an official of the papal court, and between 1931 and 1933 he held various diplomatic posts for the Vatican. In 1953 Roncalli was named patriarch of Venice and cardinal; and in 1958 his fellow cardinals elected him pope. Taking the name of John XXIII, the new pope discarded many formalities that had previously fenced in the pontiff. He encouraged new ideas and called a general Council to discuss such issues as relations between Catholics and other Christians, relations with Jews, the liturgy, and patterns of church administration. Most major decisions came at the Council's second session, after Pope John's death. Nevertheless, during his short pontificate, Pope John had opened the way for far-reaching changes in the Roman Catholic Church.

By any standard, the practical achievements of Gandhi and Pope John were impressive. But their greatest success lay in the moral example each man gave the world. Gandhi's nonviolence and the pope's unaffected loving-kindness were the product of their scrupulous effort always to act morally, privately as well as publicly.

It is probably as difficult to achieve moral greatness by conformity to tradition and submission to institutional authority, as it is to carve a moral path for oneself in defiance of established tradition and all outside authority. Certainly, moral greatness in either role is rare and hard to attain. But both Pope John XXIII and Mahatma Gandhi endowed their lives with a moral quality that made them models for others—so much so that the force of their saintliness seems likely to outlast their practical achievements.

Pope John: UPI-Compix

175

1914. Hence individual efforts to reconcile Islamic tradition with modern thought can command only the personal authority of their propounder; no general council or ex cathedra pronouncement can authorize a new formulation. Modernism has therefore never come very far in Islam; puritanical reform, seeking return to the severity and simplicity of Mohammed's original community, has had, and continues to have, far greater appeal to Moslem minds.

Eastern Religions. Hindu and Buddhist religious traditions are so multiform that generalization is next to impossible. The most recondite atheism and naive scientism, mystical discipline and crude peasant magic, all fit easily within both the Hindu and the Buddhist fold. Perhaps the most important thing about these two faiths is that in eastern and southern Asia they offer familiar handholds to uprooted and discontented ex-peasants who find themselves adrift in urban situations. Familiar rituals and phrases, sacred postures and moral injunctions, are valid alike in village and in town, in prosperity and in adversity, when with friends and relatives as well as when isolated amid a crowd of strangers. Vital continuities and moral direction amid bewilderingly new circumstances thus may assist young people to make the transition from village to city life. And the fact that these pieties and moral injunctions are not indelibly associated with any particular definition of metaphysical or theological truth makes it possible for persons who have accepted radically new and untried secular social doctrines—whether Communist or nationalist—still to cling to Hindu or Buddhist patterns of piety.

Shinto in Japan and Confucianism in China, on the other hand, appear to be dead or dying. Shinto was discredited by Japan's defeat in World War II. The emperor Hirohito's official renunciation of divinity, not to speak of his son's marriage to a commoner, seems to prohibit any revival of Shinto, at least in anything like the form practiced in Japan during the 1930s.

In China, even before the Communists came to power, the continuity of the Confucian tradition was gravely in question. In 1905 the traditional imperial examinations were abolished. Thereafter, the old reasons for studying the Confucian classics disappeared, and young Chinese flocked instead into Western and Japanese schools. The Communists completed the revolution; and since the Confucian tradition was always very much an upper-class matter, requiring long years of study and leisure appropriate to a gentleman before anyone could fully expect to master the Sage's wisdom, it was easy to destroy.

Yet in the way all successful revolutionaries must, the Chinese Communists have in fact appropriated many traits from their Confucian predecessors. Indeed, Mao Tse-tung's political role since 1949 exactly parallels the traditional religio-political role of the founder of a Chinese dynasty. For just as Mao has applied and interpreted Marxian scripture, and through his pronouncements provided a basis for political legitimacy, so in times past every successful new emperor applied and interpreted the Confucian classics and conferred legitimacy upon his appointees by the virtue and precision of his piety. In this indirect way Confucianism may indeed live on; but in itself it has become more an object for scholarly study than a living faith.

PROSPECTS

It is easy to look upon the haste and confusion of our age with despair. Many wise and sensitive people, especially in their old age, have expressed such a mood. Logical premises, carried to their conclusion, point to all sorts of disaster. If we escape atomic destruction, then the horror of society divided rigidly between the posthuman sheep and their superhuman shepherds seems to loom before us. On the other hand, history never has followed logical paths, and acute and sensitive observers have often predicted disasters which in fact never occurred.

Despair, therefore, seems as silly as naive confidence that the future can only bring betterment to mankind. It is wiser to believe that great changes will come, and at great speed, compared to the pace of past social changes; that possibilities both of disaster and of enormous gain to the quality of human experience lie open before us; and that courage, patience, and wisdom, in matters private and personal, as well as in public affairs, have never been more important than they are now, when the guidelines of a wide-open future are being laid down, whether we like it or not, by each act and thought we and the rest of mankind entertain. Other times may have been more comfortable— though it is easy for us to underrate the anxieties of the past and to forget the omnipresence of hunger, dirt, and disease. But no age has been more exciting than our own, and none ever beckoned heroes more imperiously.

SUGGESTED READING

Recent thinking about population growth, urbanization, and economic development may be sampled through the following books: Fairfield Osborn, *Our Crowded Planet: Essays on the Pressure of Population;* John B. O. Boyd-Orr, *The White Man's Dilemma: Food and the Future*; The Study of Urbanization,* ed. Philip M. Hauser and Leo F. Schnore; Gunnar Myrdal, *Challenge to Affluence*;* Eugene Michel Kulischer, *Europe on the Move: War and Population Changes, 1917–47; Twentieth Century Sociology,* ed. George Gurvitch and Wilbert E. Moore; Robert L. Heilbroner, *The Great Ascent: The Struggle for Economic Development in Our Time*;* Burt F. Hozelitz, *Sociological Aspects of Economic Growth;* and W. W. Rostow, *Stages of Economic Growth.** India's dilemmas in these matters are explored by Ansley J. Coale, *Population Growth and Economic Development in Low Income Countries: A Case Study of India's Prospects.*

Science and technology and their impact on human society are discussed from various points of view in the following: Siegfried Giedion, *Mechanization Takes Command;* John Jewkes, David Sawers, and Richard Stillerman, *The Sources of Invention;* Homer G. Barnett, *Innovation: The Basis of Cultural Change;* S. C. Gilfillan, *The Sociology of Invention;* Norbert Wiener, *Cybernetics, or Control and Communication in the Animal and the Machine*;* John von Neumann, *The Computer and the Brain*;* Robert P. Weeks, *Machines and the Man*;* and the speculative sally by John R. Platt, *The Step to Man.* Two books deal graphically with the American experience of World War II, when the atom bomb project and other programs organized scientific effort in new ways: James Phinney Baxter III, *Scientists Against Time,* and Laura Fermi, *Atoms in the Family.** On recent changes in molecular biology, see John Maddox, *Revolution in Biology: A Decade of Discovery,* James D. Watson, *The Double Helix,** a highly personal account of his role in the discovery of the structure of DNA, and George and Muriel Beadle, *The Language of Life: An Introduction to the Science of Genetics.*

Among numerous efforts to reinterpret human experience in the light of contemporary changes, the following may be suggested as simpler or clearer or more emphatic than the average: H. Stuart Hughes, *Consciousness and Society: The Reorientation of European Social Thought 1890–1930*;* Erich Fromm, *Escape from Freedom*;* Fritz Stern, *The Politics of Cultural Despair*;* C. A. R. Crosland, *The Future of Socialism*;* Daniel Bell, *The End of Ideology;* Franklin L. Baumer, *Religion and the Rise of Scepticism;* F. S. C. Northrup, *The Meeting of East and West*;* Milovan Djilas, *The New Class: An Analysis of the Communist System*;* Arnold J. Toynbee, *Civilization on Trial* and *The World and the West*;* Fred Polack, *The Image of the Future;* David Riesman, *The Lonely Crowd*;* Karl R. Popper, *The Open Society and Its Enemies*;* and C. P. Snow, *The Two Cultures* and *A Second Look,** 2nd ed.

The best way to study art and literature is of course to visit museums and art galleries, read novels or poems, and see plays; but this is only sometimes possible. Thanks to modern photography, histories of art can be very passable substitutes for the more authentic experience. Emile Langui, *Fifty Years of Modern Art,* A. H. Barr, *What Is Modern Painting?,** or Werner Haftmann, *Painting in the Twentieth Century,** 2 vols., are good starting places. Histories of literature are much less satisfactory, but Edmund Wilson, *Axel's Castle,** M. Colum, *From These Roots: The Ideas That Have Made Modern Literature,* and C. Mauriac, *The New Literature* have interesting things to say about the European and American literary scene. Donald Keene, *Japanese Literature,** and C. T. Hsia, *A History of Modern Chinese Fiction, 1917–1957* may introduce a foreigner to these Far Eastern literatures.

Like the time that preceded it, the period from World War II to the present has been full of intellectual ferment. The following list is a selection of some of the most representative works of the period.

Africa. Chinau Achebe, *Things Fall Apart*;* James Ngugi, *Weep Not Child*;* Alan Paton, *Cry, the Beloved Country,** *Too Late the Phalarope*;* Amos Tutuola, *The Palm-Wine Drunkard.**

Asia. Osamu Dazai, *No Longer Human*;* Yasunari Kawabata, *Snow Country,** *A Thousand Cranes*;* Yukio Mishima, *Spring Snow.*

Europe. Samuel Beckett, *Waiting for Godot,** *Krapp's Last Tape,** *Endgame*;* Heinrich Böll, *The Clown,** *Billiards at Half-Past Nine*;* Hermann Broch, *The*

Sleepwalkers: A Trilogy*; Albert Camus, *The Myth of Sisyphus,* The Fall,* The Rebel*;* Joyce Cary, *Mister Johnson*;* Simone de Beauvoir, *The Second Sex,* The Coming of Age*;* Ilya Ehrenburg, *War,* Change of Season;* Jean Genêt, *The Blacks*;* André Gide, *The Immoralist,* Lafcadio's Adventure*;* Jean Giraudoux, *Electre*;* Günter Grass, *The Tin Drum,* Dog Years*;* Graham Greene, *The Power and the Glory,* A Burnt-Out Case,* The Honorary Counsel;* Dag Hammarskjöld, *Markings;* Hermann Hesse, *Magister Ludi*;* Rolf Hochhuth, *The Deputy*;* Nikos Kazantzakis, *Zorba the Greek*;* Arthur Koestler, *Darkness at Noon*;* André Malraux, *Man's Fate*;* Alberto Moravia, *The Time of Indifference*;* Vladimir Nabokov, *Lolita,* Pale Fire*;* John Osborne, *Look Back in Anger*;* Harold Pinter, *The Homecoming*;* Bertrand Russell, *Autobiography;* Jean-Paul Sartre, *Nausea,* No Exit,* Being and Nothingness*;* Mikhail Sholokov, *And Quiet Flows the Don*;* Ignazio Silone, *Bread and Wine*;* Aleksandr Solzhenitsyn, *One Day in the Life of Ivan Denisovich,* First Circle,* The Cancer Ward,* August 1914*;* Dylan Thomas, *Collected Poems*;* Peter Weiss, *The Investigation*;* Yevgeny Yevtushenko, *Selected Poems.**

North America. Edward Albee, *American Dream,* Who's Afraid of Virginia Woolf?*;* Mariano Azuela, *The Flies,* The Bosses,* Underdogs*;* John Barth, *The Sot-Weed Factor,* Giles Goat-Boy*;* Saul Bellow, *The Adventures of Augie March,* Herzog*;* Ruth Benedict, *Patterns of Culture*;* Rachel Carson, *Silent Spring*;* John Dos Passos, *Midcentury*;* Ralph Ellison, *Invisible Man*;* Joseph Heller, *Catch-22*;* Oscar Lewis, *Children of Sanchez,* La Vida*;* Malcolm Lowry, *Under the Volcano*;* Norman Mailer, *The Naked and the Dead,* An American Dream,* Miami and the Siege of Chicago*;* Margaret Mead, *Male and Female*;* Eugene O'Neill, *Selected Plays;* Eudora Welty, *The Optimist's Daughter.**

South America. Jorge Luis Borges, *Ficciónes,* A Personal Anthology*;* Pablo Neruda, *Selected Poems,* Pablo Neruda: A New Decade.*

INDEX

New Zealand, 81, 101, 102, 155
Nguyen Van Thieu, 134
Nicholas II, Tsar, 14, 67
Nigeria, 135, 156
Nixon, Richard M., 133, 137, 138
Nkrumah, Kwame, 122, 135
North Atlantic Treaty Organization. *See* NATO
Norway, 79, 106, 109
Nuclear weapons. *See* Atomic Weapons

Okinawa, 90, 114

Pacific area, World War II, 82, 83, 87, 90
Pakistan, 100–1, 135, 173
Palestine, 28, 103
Paris, 54–55; peace conferences, 23–25, 94; World War I, 5, 20
Pearl Harbor, 81
Peasants' revolt, 151–53ff.
Pétain, Henri Philippe, 80, 92–93, 98
Philippines, 81–82, 90, 98, 99
Philosophy, 167, 171
Physics, 58–61, 64, 164–65; geophysics, 168–70
Picasso, Pablo, 54–57
Planned invention (technology), 13, 88–89
Planning. *See* Economic and social planning
Poetry, 56–57
Poland, 27, 43, 47, 75, 79, 91, 94, 96, 105, 108, 127, 132, 133; World War I, 5, 7, 17, 25–26; World War II, 75, 79, 89
Population increases, 138, 158–61, 178
Portugal, 1, 109
Potsdam Conference, 85, 94
Princep, Gavrilo, 2, 3
Protestants, 173, 174
Psychoanalysis, 62ff. (*see also* Freud, Sigmund)

Radio, 55, 57, 152, 161
Relativity theory, 58, 60–61, 164
Religion, 49, 53, 123, 156, 172–77
Reparations: World War I, 24–25, 43–46; World War II, 94
Rhodesia, 123
Rockets, 86, 107, 118, 120, 137, 138, 168–69; Cuban crisis, 129
Roman Catholic Church, 53, 123, 157, 172–76
Roosevelt, Franklin D., 61, 66, 70–71, 81, 84, 87, 90–93, 95
Ruhr crisis, 44–45
Rumania, 94, 96, 105–6, 108, 132; and World War I, 8, 22, 26; and World War II, 80, 82
Russia (Soviet Union; U.S.S.R.), 1ff., 13–19, 24–29, 42–44, 50–53, 66, 68, 71,

74–76, 91, 94ff., 99, 103ff., 134, 157, 161, 176; art, socialist realism, 170–72; and China, 94–97, 105, 111–13, 115, 130–31; and Cold War, 116–18, 120–30, 139; and Cuba, 116, 128–30; and Eastern European satellites, 91, 94, 96–97, 105, 107, 108, 126–27, 132; and Egypt, 127, 128, 132; Five Year Plans, 52–53, 63, 66, 107; and Germany, 3ff., 94, 96, 108; and Khrushchev, 127, 129–31, 162; and Korea, 114, 124–26; compared with non-Communist nations, 161–63; purges, 63, 66, 105, 108, 126; revolution, 8, 13–16ff., 40; and rockets, 107, 118, 120, 129, 137; and U.S., 84, 91, 94–97, 104–7ff., 114, 116–18, 120–21, 124–30, 137–38; and World War II, 79–85, 87, 90

San Francisco Conference, 90–91
Saudi Arabia, 7, 49, 173
Science, scientific research, 58–64, 86–87, 163–70, 178
Serbia and World War I, 2ff., 7, 22
Ships, shipping (submarines), 8, 19–20, 83, 86
Singapore, 98, 132
Social planning. *See* Economic and social planning
Social sciences, 62–64, 171–72
Socialism, socialists, 14, 18–19, 27, 29, 43, 47, 64, 72–73, 105, 109, 117, 161
"Socialist realism," 170–72
Society (*see also* Economic and social planning; specific countries, events), future trends, 150–63
Soviet Union. *See* Russia
Space program, 118, 120, 138, 168–70
Spanish Civil War, 56–57, 74, 76
Speer, Albert, 88–89
Stalin, Josef Djugashvili, 51–53, 66, 74; and China, 94–96, 105, 130; de-Stalinization, 127, 162; post-World War II, 94–97 *passim*, 104–10, 124 *passim*; purges, 63, 66, 105, 107, 126; and satellites, 94, 96–97, 105, 107–8; and Tito, 107, 109; and World War II, 79–81, 84, 91, 94
Stein, Gertrude, 54
Stravinsky, Igor, 54
Submarine warfare, 8, 19–20, 83, 120
Suez Canal crisis, 127–28
Sweden, 79, 106
Switzerland, 8, 106
Syria, 22, 28, 49, 98; and Egypt, 132

Taiwan, 111, 113, 127
Technology, 88–89, 178; post-World War II, 152–53, 157–59
Tito, Josip Broz, and Titoism, 107, 109, 126, 127, 131

Totalitarianism, 64, 163, 172
Triple Alliance, 3, 5
Trotsky, Leon, 51
Truman, Harry S., 91, 94, 106, 117, 124, 125
Tunisia, 83
Turkey, 1, 27–29, 49, 96, 133, 176; and U.S., 104, 106, 124; and World War I, 7, 8, 10, 12, 24

Ukraine, 17, 22, 26, 67, 83
Underdeveloped *vs.* developed lands, 155–61, 178
Union of South Africa, 101, 123, 136–37, 174
Union of Soviet Socialist Republics. *See* Russia
United Nations, 82, 90–91, 97–98, 103, 123, 128; and Israel, 103; and Korea, 124, 125
United States and Americans, 1, 14–15, 29, 42–43, 45–46, 76–77, 90–91, 98–99, 103–4ff., 108, 128, 132–34, 137–38, 151, 157, 180; and China, 95–97, 103, 104, 110–11, 125, 137; and Cold War, 116–18, 120–30, 139 *passim;* compared with Communist countries, 161–63; and Cuba, 116, 128–30; émigrés in Paris, 54; European aid programs, 105–7; and Far East, 28, 94–96, 104, 111 (*see also* specific countries); future trends, 161–63; and Germany (*see* Germany); Great Depression, 54, 63–66, 92; and Japan, 28, 82, 83, 87, 90, 94, 95, 98, 104, 111; and Korea, 114, 124–25; Lend-Lease, 80, 83–84, 91; mass entertainment, 57; mass production, 59, 83; Roosevelt and New Deal, 66, 70, 92–93; and Russia, 84, 91, 94–97, 104–7ff., 114, 116–18, 120–21, 129–30, 137–38; and Vietnam, 126,

133–34, 137; and World War I, 8–9, 12, 15–16, 18–21, 25; and World War II, 80–90, 102

Values, 62–63; changing of, 150ff.
Versailles, Treaty of, 25, 27, 42–48 *passim,* 70, 71
Vietnam, 114, 123, 126, 133–34, 137

War on poverty, 162
Washington Conferences, 28, 48, 84
Watergate burglary, 133, 137
Weapons. *See* Arms, armaments
Weber, Max, 62
Weimar Republic, 27, 45
West Germany, 106–9, 126, 133, 136; Common Market, 133
Wilhelm II, Kaiser, 3, 27
Wilson, Thomas Woodrow, 15–16, 18–19, 22, 42 (*see also* Wilsonianism); Fourteen Points, 15, 17; and peace treaties, 22, 24, 25
Wilsonianism, 18, 116, 134, 138; post-World War I, 22, 24, 25, 29, 42, 43, 46–48, 71, 74
Women, place of, 166–67
Work, changing meaning of, 153, 155
World War I, 1–29, 65, 66, 69, 72; armistice and negotiations, 21–29, 41; mobilization and controls, 4–5, 10–13; revolution, 13–19
World War II, 78–115, 152 (*see also* specific participants); background of, 65–75
Writers, writing, 54, 56–57, 163–64, 166–67, 169–73, 179–80

Yalta Conference, 85, 91, 95
Yugoslavia, 22, 97; and Titoism, 107, 110

1 2 3 4 5 6 7 8 9 10 –CP– 80 79 78 77 76 75 74